Contents at a Glance

Home
Wireless
Networking

Joe Habraken

Teach
Yourself

Sams Publishing, 800 East 96th Street, Indianapolis, Indiana 46240 USA

Home Wireless Networking in a Snap

International Standard Book Number: 0-672-32702-3

Library of Congress Catalog Card Number: 2004092816

Printed in the United States of America

First Printing: March 2006

09   08   07   06   4   3   2   1

Trademarks

Warning and Disclaimer

Bulk Sales

Sams Publishing offers excellent discounts on this book when ordered in quantity for bulk purchases or special sales. For more information, please contact

    U.S. Corporate and Government Sales

    1-800-382-3419

    corpsales@pearsontechgroup.com

For sales outside of the U.S., please contact

    International Sales

    1-317-428-3341

    international@pearsontechgroup.com

Acquisitions Editor
Betsy Brown

Development Editor
Alice Martina Smith

Managing Editor
Charlotte Clapp

Project Editor
George Nedeff

Production Editor
Benjamin Berg

Indexer
Ken Johnson

Technical Editor
Dallas G. Releford

Publishing Coordinator
Vanessa Evans

Interior Designer
Gary Adair

Cover Designer
Gary Adair

Page Layout
Patricia Ratcliff
Michelle Mitchell

About the Author

Joe Habraken is a best-selling author and information technology and new media professional who has written more than 25 books on networking, desktop operating systems, and computer software applications such as Microsoft Office and OpenOffice.org. Joe serves as an assistant professor at the University of New England, where he teaches a variety of information technology and communication courses. His recent book titles include the *Absolute Beginner's Guide to Networking* (Fourth Edition), *Skinning Microsoft Windows XP*, and *Novell Linux Desktop 9 User's Handbook*.

Dedication

To my wonderful wife Kim, my brother Pete, my sister Sue, and of course my mom and dad.

Acknowledgments

It definitely takes a team to create a book and I have a number of people to thank. I would like to thank all the folks at Sams who had a hand in creating this book. A big thanks to my acquisitions editor, Betsy Brown, who pulled the editorial team together for this book and managed the book-creation process from initial idea to published manuscript. I would also like to thank Dallas Releford, the technical editor on the project, and Alice Martina Smith, the development editor. Also a big thanks goes out to Vanessa Evans and Ben Berg. Last but not least, I would like to thank the project editor, George Nedeff. And if I've forgotten anyone else: Thank you!

We Want to Hear from You!

As the reader of this book, *you* are our most important critic and commentator. We value your opinion and want to know what we're doing right, what we could do better, what areas you'd like to see us publish in, and any other words of wisdom you're willing to pass our way.

You can email or write me directly to let me know what you did or didn't like about this book—as well as what we can do to make our books stronger.

Please note that I cannot help you with technical problems related to the topic of this book, and that due to the high volume of mail I receive, I might not be able to reply to every message.

When you write, please be sure to include this book's title and author as well as your name and phone or email address. I will carefully review your comments and share them with the author and editors who worked on the book.

Email: **networking@samspublishing.com**

Mail: Mark Taber
           Associate Publisher
           Sams Publishing
           800 East 96th Street
           Indianapolis, IN 46240 USA

Reader Services

Visit our website and register this book at www.samspublishing.com/register for convenient access to any updates, downloads, or errata that might be available for this book.

PART I

Networking and Windows Fundamentals

IN THIS PART

1

Start Here

It is certainly not uncommon to have multiple computers in a home or small office. And most home and small office users have dealt with the problems of connecting these computers so that they can share files and other resources such as printers and a single high-speed Internet connection.

Evidence of these forays into computer connectivity is often quite apparent in the form of network wires underfoot and overhead. A better solution is the creation of a wireless network or WLAN (wireless local area network). Not only do you do away with most network cabling, you also place an "intelligent" device, a wireless router, to act as the intermediary between your wireless network and your broadband Internet connection.

In this chapter, we take a look at how computers communicate and how wireless networking actually works. We also discuss wireless networking components and how you can get the most out of your home or small office wireless network.

Why Create a Wireless Home Network?

Unless your home or small office has been hard-wired for a local area network (meaning network wiring in the walls, wall network ports, and a central switch or other connectivity device in a closet), the reason to create a wireless home network is fairly self evident. And while many homes and small offices may have started out with one shared computer that had a dial-up Internet connection, lower-cost computers and the availability of extremely fast broadband Internet connections make the creation of a home network highly desirable and affordable.

Wireless networking provides an excellent alternative to wired networks and provides enough bandwidth (up to 54Mbps) for sharing printers and files, and even gaming on the network. Because the **WLAN** requires an **access point** for the various wireless-enabled computers to communicate, the access point can consist of a wireless **router** that can also serve as an intermediary between the WLAN and a broadband Internet connection. The router allows all the computers on the wireless network to share the same high-speed Internet connection.

▶ KEY TERMS

WLAN (wireless local area network)—A network that is limited to one localized site (thus the "local" in the name).

Access point—A hardware device that acts as the central connecting point for wireless-enabled devices. Access points can also provide LAN ports so that computers on the network can be connected to the access point using traditional network cabling. WiFi routers contain access points so that the WiFi-enabled computers can access the network and take advantage of a high-speed Internet connection where the WiFi router serves as the intermediary between the home network and your Internet connection.

WLANs also provide your users with mobility, which is in sharp contrast to a wired LAN. Users with a notebook computer that is wireless-enabled can roam anywhere inside and outside of the home or small office, just as long as they stay in range of the wireless access point (distances of more than 150 feet—and in some cases 300 feet—can be achieved).

The costs related to creating a WLAN are actually quite reasonable, especially where only a few computers will be connected. And most new notebook computers come with a wireless network adapter as part of the base price.

▶ NOTE

Even if you have already networked your home or small office computers using network cabling, you might want to clear away the "spaghetti mess" of cables. And if you have older network connectivity devices such as hubs and network adapters, replacing these devices with newer WLAN devices will actually increase the data rate on the network.

It definitely makes sense to go wireless if you already have multiple computers in a home or small office that are not networked. As already mentioned, networking allows you to share files, printers, and the Internet connection. When adding computers to your home or office, you certainly should consider buying a new computer with a wireless network adapter.

Even if you already have a "wired" home network, you can still go WiFi and add new computers to the network by outfitting them with WiFi network adapters. Because most WiFi routers also provide switch ports, you can connect wired computers directly to the WiFi router. The WiFi-enabled computers on the network connect using radio waves. So, whether a computer is connected by network cabling or radio waves doesn't really matter in terms of the computer taking advantage of the high-speed Internet connection provided on the network and the ability of all the computers to share resources such as files and printers.

One last word about taking advantage of WiFi networking: Although WiFi networking is easy to take advantage of, the fact that your data travels on WiFi radio frequencies means that security can be an issue for your network. Other people can "listen in" on your wireless communications unless you take steps to secure your network. It makes sense to use the security features provided by WiFi-enabled devices such as wireless routers. For more information on WiFi security, **see** **70** **About Basic Network Security**.

How Computers Communicate

Before we take a look at how wireless networking actually works, let's take a quick look at how computers communicate on a network. For computers to communicate on a network, there must be a network architecture in place that dictates how the data moves from one computer and then over the wire (on a cabled LAN) or wireless signal (on a WLAN).

The most widely embraced network architecture is Ethernet. The Ethernet standards define how an Ethernet network adapter, Ethernet switch, Ethernet access point, and other Ethernet devices transmit data on the network. Data transmission speed is measured in bits per second (bps). A *bit* is one binary digit, either a 1 or a 0 (it is the smallest unit of data; 8 bits make up a byte). Ethernet provides data transmission speeds in excess of a million bits per second (Mbps). In terms of networking, bandwidth is considered the number of bits that can be sent across the network medium (such as the wired or wireless network) at a given time. So, the terms data transmission speed and bandwidth are often used interchangeably.

▶ NOTE

Ethernet got its start in 1972 at the Xerox Palo Alto Research Center (PARC). Xerox released a commercial version of Ethernet in 1975 that provided a transmission speed of 3Mbps. Ethernet has matured to the point where today we have gigabit Ethernet that provides a huge amount of bandwidth. Wireless Ethernet networks can provide up to 54Mbps of bandwidth, which is greater than what some hard-wired LANs can deliver.

Ethernet is a passive, wait-and-listen network architecture. Computers must con-
tend for transmission time on the network medium. To receive data, computers
just sit and wait, listening to the network. When they sense that a particular
transmission is meant for them, they receive it on their network adapter.

Ethernet takes care of the movement of data at the hardware level. But users like
us deal with software. Software that provides our method of communication with
the computer's hardware. For our various computer software applications to talk
over the network, there must be some software standards. These standards are
communication protocols. A *protocol* is really software code that provides the
rules for how computers communicate over the Ethernet hardware.

▶ KEY TERM

Protocol—A set of software rules that dictate how computers and other devices communicate over a network architecture such as Ethernet.

The only network protocol we really need to discuss is the *TCP/IP* network protocol stack (it's a stack because it contains a number of protocols that have different
jobs). A protocol stack such as TCP/IP must provide an address system and also
take care of converting data we create in our software applications to a form that
can be moved by Ethernet hardware as a bit stream.

▶ KEY TERM

TCP/IP (Transmission Control Protocol/Internet Protocol)—The common language for
the networking world. TCP/IP is the protocol suite (or stack) that serves as the founda-
tion for the mega-network known as the Internet. Nearly all computer operating systems
embrace TCP/IP as their default networking protocol.

To make a long story short, TCP/IP takes care of the data conversion process and
also provides the addressing system for computers and other devices on the network. The addressing system consists of IP addresses. A unique IP address is
assigned to each device on the network. Each piece of data sent over the network
is labeled with the IP addresses of the sending device and the receiving device,
allowing for the movement of data from point A to point B.

Computers and devices on a TCP/IP network can have their IP addresses configured manually or dynamically. To manually configure a computer with a static IP
address (meaning an address that never changes), you configure the computer
with a unique IP address and an accompanying *subnet mask* (the subnet mask
helps other computers determine which part of the address is network information and which part is specific device information).

The alternative to manually configuring devices with an IP address and subnet
mask is to use a DHCP (Dynamic Host Configuration Protocol) server on the

network. The DHCP server leases IP addresses to computers and other devices on the network. Wireless routers (discussed in several chapters in this book) can act as DHCP servers, so you won't have to assign IP addresses to all the computers on your wireless network—the router does that automatically and behind the scenes.

In Windows XP (both the Home and Professional versions), the IP address is configured in the **Internet Protocol (TCP/IP) Properties** dialog box. You can either configure a Windows XP computer with a static address or configure it to accept an IP address from a DHCP server on the network (such as your wireless router).

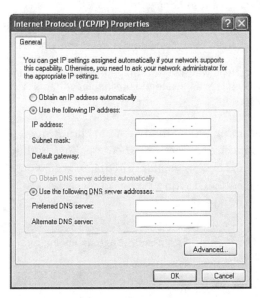

Computers running Windows XP can be configured with static IP addresses or configured to accept an IP address from a DHCP server.

▶ NOTE

We discuss IP configuration and other network settings in **42** **Configure TCP/IP Settings**.

TCP/IP takes care of network communication at the software level, and Ethernet takes care of communication at the hardware level. The wireless standards used for WLANs are actually Ethernet standards. We discuss wireless Ethernet in "Understanding Wireless Networking Standards," later in this chapter.

How Wireless Networking Works

Now that you have a feel for how computers and other devices talk on a network, we can take a look at how wireless networking actually works. Wireless network connections take advantage of radio signals and infrared light (these connections are limited in range). WiFi connections between WiFi-enabled computers and other WiFi devices such as wireless routers have a maximum range of around 300 feet.

▶ **NOTE**

Other wireless and longer-distance communication strategies (such as those used by cell phones that take place through cellular telephone technology) can provide greater range. This is because a cell phone can connect to a cellular antenna that is miles away from the phone. Some Internet service providers (that also happen to be cellular phone companies) such as Verizon and even Google are looking at technology that offers a high-speed wireless network (which is being called WiFi but differs from the home WiFi we are discussing here). This cellular technology can be accessed from nearly anywhere in a geographic location (such as a city) and can also be used to access the Internet. So, the physically wired high-speed Internet connections we take advantage of through DSL and cable modems might be slowly replaced by this WiFi-on-steroids technology that is beginning to roll out in major metropolitan areas.

In terms of home and small office networking, the Ethernet WLAN hardware available takes advantage of radio connectivity. The equipment operates in the part of the frequency range that the FCC has reserved for unregulated use; you will find that wireless LANs operate in the 2.4GHz and higher ranges.

▶ **NOTE**

Wireless networking equipment operates in the same frequency range as analog and digital home telephones and other devices.

The only difference between a (wired) Ethernet LAN and an Ethernet WLAN is that the WLAN sends data over radio waves rather than through network cables. A WLAN is still an Ethernet network, plain and simple. However, wireless Ethernet has its own set of standards that have been developed by the IEEE (the Institute of Electrical and Electronics Engineers, a worldwide standards organization). Let's take a look at the wireless Ethernet standards.

Understanding Wireless Networking Standards

The IEEE has created a set of standards for networking that fall under the IEEE 802 specifications (a series of engineering specifications for devices). The standard for wireless Ethernet is designated as 802.11. Three types of 802.11 standards are currently in use for wireless networking:

▶ **NOTE**

The 802.11 wireless standards are also often referred to as *WiFi*. You will often see 802.11 hardware labeled as "WiFi devices." It's not a different wireless standard, just a nickname.

- **802.11a**—This 802.11 specification can provide up to 54Mbps of bandwidth and operates in the 5GHz band of the usable (public) radio spectrum. 802.11a is just starting to make its way into the home networking marketplace, and wireless equipment vendors such as Linksys have begun to roll out products using this specification. Oddly enough, WiFi 802.11b and 802.11g were available WiFi standards before 802.11a was implemented.

- **802.11b**—This specification provides up to 11Mbps of throughput and operates in the 2.4GHz band. 802.11b was the first wireless Ethernet specification available (in 1999). The speed of a computer connected to a 802.11b access point decreases the further the computer is from the access point. The 802.11b standard does not provide the type of range you get from 802.11g. A distance of 100 feet or more between the access point and the WiFi-enabled computer typically does not provide an adequate signal strength.

- **802.11g**—This specification provides bandwidth between 20 and 54Mbps in the 2.4GHz band. It is currently the fastest growing implementation of wireless networking for home networks and small LANs. This specification can provide good connections between access points and WiFi-enabled computers that are up to 300 feet apart.

▶ **NOTE**

You probably wonder what the 802.11 numbering is all about in terms of the wireless Ethernet standards. The IEEE provides the specifications for all types of networking standards. For example, 802.3 is the specification for Ethernet LANs (meaning wired LANs).

In terms of cost, 802.11a devices are the most expensive and only a few vendors currently have 802.11a products available for home and small office networking. 802.11g products are certainly the most common and provide the most bandwidth in relation to cost. You really can't go wrong building your network with 802.11g devices.

802.11b products are starting to disappear from stores and you will find that most 802.11b hardware is on sale. If you can deal with the slower data rate that 802.11b provides, you can put together a wireless home network for practically a song. However, you certainly won't get the performance or range you can get from 802.11g devices.

▶ **NOTE**

The 802.11 wireless standards aren't the only wireless standards out there. Another wireless standard is called Bluetooth. Bluetooth is gaining momentum in the cellular phone industry and is used for a variety of peripheral devices such as hands-free devices for cell phones. Toyota has even built Bluetooth into some of its vehicles such as the Prius, which allows you to sync your cell phone to your car's hands-free phone system. Bluetooth does not yet support TCP/IP data transfer, so for now, Bluetooth does not compete with the 802.11 standards.

Selecting Wireless Network Components

A number of vendors market WiFi hardware including *WiFi routers*, *access points*, and wireless *network adapters*. I certainly don't want to alienate any companies that make wireless networking devices, but I would have to say that in terms of availability (and probably marketing) the big three in terms of WiFi home and small office products are Linksys, Netgear, and D-Link (in no order related to the significance of the company or their products).

▶ KEY TERMS

WiFi router—A device that provides a connection for a home network to a high-speed Internet connection (which is, in turn, provided by a device such as a cable modem). The WiFi router also provides an access point through which WiFi-enabled computers can connect to the network. Computers with traditional wired network adapters can also be connected to the WiFi router through to the network switch built in to most WiFi routers. The WiFi router is an intelligent device in that it can be configured to make decisions about the type of access that can be made to the high-speed Internet connection and what type of data traffic can be allowed through the router onto the local area network.

Network adapter—A device that allows a computer to participate in the network. The network adapter takes the data from the computer and prepares it for transmission over a network medium such as network cabling or WiFi radio signals.

Because the wireless devices made by these companies embrace the same 802.11 standards, in theory all the devices should be compatible even if you have devices on your wireless network from different vendors. I use WiFi products from different vendors on my wireless network, and I have not experienced any problems in terms of compatibility.

If you are starting from scratch in terms of purchasing your WiFi hardware, you might want to purchase a wireless router and WiFi network adapters from the same manufacturer. The only reason I say this (and I don't totally believe the complaints) is because you can find some chatter on the Web related to incompatibility problems when using devices from different WiFi vendors. Just do a search on the Web for "WiFi hardware incompatibility" and make your own judgment about the posted complaints.

When you purchase your WiFi hardware, cost might or might not be an issue. However, we all certainly like to get a bargain, so you should take advantage of sales (jump on those back-to-school specials) or "package" discounts. It's not uncommon for a manufacturer to package a wireless router and at least one WiFi network adapter together and discount the price so that it is lower than the cost of buying the items separately. Whether you like to shop on the Web or like to read the hardware box, you will find that there are a huge number of web stores and brick-and-mortar stores in your town that stock consumer electronic products such as WiFi devices.

In terms of sorting out the best WiFi devices for your wireless network, you need to do a little research. Each of the WiFi vendors has put its own spin on the 802.11 standards.

For example, Netgear has developed MIMO, a wireless strategy that makes use of multiple antennas. MIMO devices are completely compatible with the WiFi standards 802.11g and 802.11b but are advertised as providing greater coverage, range, and speed than standard WiFi (meaning 802.11g). The cost for a MIMO wireless router is more than that of a standard 802.11g wireless router (from 60 to 80 dollars more). So, you must decide whether the cost differential is worth the advertised performance boost. Remember that MIMO is still an implementation of 802.11g; it's the multiple antennas (the MIMO) that provide better connectivity between WiFi computers and the router.

Linksys has 802.11g compatible devices that take advantage of Linksys's proprietary SpeedBooster technology. SpeedBooster provides increased network performance. Again, as with Netgear MIMO devices, Linksys SpeedBooster-enabled routers are more expensive than vanilla-flavored 802.11g WiFi wireless routers (which are also sold by Linksys). We are talking about a $20 differential (at most retail stores) between a regular Linksys 802.11g router and a SpeedBooster 802.11g router, so you must determine whether the potential speed boost is worth the price differential.

▶ WEB RESOURCE

http://www.linksys.com

http://www.netgear.com

http://www.dlink.com

Start at these sites to do your own research before you purchase WiFi products. Also search for WiFi product reviews and see what the WiFi gurus have to say about the various products.

The bottom line is that there are a lot of different WiFi products on the market. You will have to do a little reading, a little comparison shopping, and then some decision-making to assemble your WiFi network. Let's take a look at the WiFi devices and other items you will need to create your home or small office WLAN.

Wireless Router

I am assuming that you are creating a WLAN that will share a high-speed Internet connection and have both wireless and wired computers participating on the network. You only need a single device, a wireless *router*, to realize all these different types of connections.

The wireless router typically contains the following features and functionality:

- **Wireless access point**—The access point is the connection point to the WLAN for wireless computers and other devices. Most wireless routers now available support both 802.11g and 802.11b wireless clients.

- **Ethernet switch**—The switch allows you to connect your wired network computers to the wireless router. Most wireless routers for home and small office use provide four Ethernet LAN ports. In most cases, you can also connect a dedicated switch to the router if you need more LAN ports.

- **Broadband connector**—The router also serves as the network's connection to your broadband device such as a cable modem or DSL router. This means the whole network has access to the Internet. Most wireless routers also help protect the network from intrusion from the Internet by providing a firewall.

As I have said before, a number of manufacturers sell wireless routers. Read the specifications for the available routers, and also take into account additional features provided by the router. This should help you select the correct router for your home network (and there is certainly more than one that will work, so take price into account).

The Linksys WRT54G Wireless-G Broadband Router is one example of a wireless router (photo courtesy of Linksys).

▶ TIP

Although 802.11b wireless routers and WiFi adapters are dirt cheap right now, I suggest that you go with 802.11g devices for your network. You will appreciate the additional bandwidth provided by these upgraded devices.

WiFi Network Adapters

You will also need WiFi *network adapters* for the computers that will take advantage of a wireless connection to the network. Most new notebook computers come outfitted with a WiFi adapter (in almost all cases a 802.11g adapter) that also provides a port for a wired LAN connection.

If you need to upgrade existing computers to WiFi, you have two options: You can install a WiFi adapter in an expansion slot on the computer (both desktop and notebook computers have expansion slots, although they differ greatly) or you can buy a WiFi USB adapter and plug it into an open USB port on the computer (either a desktop or notebook computer).

▶ NOTE

It has been my experience that the performance provided by a WiFi (802.11g) USB adapter is equal to the performance provided by a WiFi adapter installed in a computer's expansion slot. However, don't take my word for it; it's your network. You can search and find any number of articles on the Web that provide product information and comparisons.

If you are purchasing a WiFi adapter for installation in an expansion slot on a desktop computer, make sure that you have an open PCI slot in your computer and then purchase a PCI Wireless G adapter.

To upgrade a notebook computer for WiFi, you need an open PC card type II slot (or you can replace an existing wired LAN card if necessary). PC card adapters are very easy to install because it's really just a matter of sliding them into the open slot on the notebook computer.

Network Cabling

You will also need some network cables so that you can attach your broadband Internet device to the wireless router and connect any wired computers to the wireless router's LAN ports. Ethernet network cables are UTP (Unshielded Twisted Pair) Category 5 (CAT 5) cables with four pairs of twisted wires inside the plastic cable covering. These cables are terminated by RJ-45 plugs. You might hear these types of cables referred to as *Ethernet cables* or as *CAT 5 cables*.

Although CAT 5 cables might look like regular telephone wire, they certainly aren't the same thing; just compare the RJ-45 plug on a CAT 5 cable with the RJ-11 plug on a telephone cable. The RJ-45 is bigger.

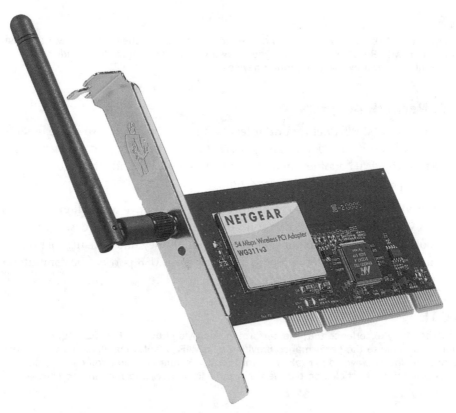

You can upgrade a desktop computer for WiFi by installing a PCI adapter such as the Netgear WG311 54 Mbps PCI adapter (photo courtesy of Netgear).

You will need a CAT 5 cable to connect your wireless router to your broadband device. This cable is often included with the wireless router. You will also need CAT 5 cables to connect any "wired" PCs to the router's LAN ports.

▶ **NOTE**

A "newer" Ethernet cable type called CAT 6 is used on high-speed corporate networks such as Gigabit Ethernet (which requires expensive network cards and network devices such as switches). You don't need CAT 6 cables for your WiFi network. CAT 5 cables will work just fine.

Any store or website that sells WiFi hardware will also typically sell CAT 5 cables. Make sure that you buy the correct lengths for your wiring needs. Pace off or measure the distance between the computer and the router so that you buy a cable that is a correct length. In some cases, you might only be able to find longer cables than you need, but there isn't any down-side to using a 50-foot cable when a 10-foot cable would have sufficed (other than the excess wire laying around). The limit for CAT 5 cable (because of impedance on the wire) is 328 feet.

Getting the Most Out of a Home Network

Just to give you some perspective on the use of wireless networking hardware in the home, almost 7 million WiFi devices were sold to home computer users in 2004. So while you certainly aren't on the cutting edge in terms of adopting wireless technology, you can rest assured that the standards have been tested and used successfully by a huge number of home and small office computer users just like yourself.

After you have set up your wireless network (as detailed in this book), you will want to share printers, files, and other network resources, particularly that high-speed Internet connection. **20 Install the Router** and **22 Access Router Configuration** provide you with the necessary steps for connecting the wireless router to your Internet connection. **45 About Sharing Network Resources** provides details on how to share printers and files on the network.

To get the most out of your home WiFi network, you will want to make sure that you create a secure network that negates the possibility of security breaches from outside the network. Because WiFi uses radio signals for data transfer, unscrupulous folks can eavesdrop on your network and actually view data. And we have all read about the different types of attacks that can be launched over the Internet. **70 About Basic Network Security** is a must read. You won't get the most out of your WiFi hardware if you are constantly experiencing intrusions on the network.

Outfitting your home or small business with a WiFi network is definitely a smart move. It not only makes it easier for users on the network to collaborate, but the network can also be used for multiplayer gaming and other recreational pursuits.

Sorting Out Broadband Internet Connections

If you haven't taken the plunge and already signed up for a broadband Internet connection, this section provides some basic information regarding broadband and broadband ISPs (Internet service providers). Depending on your location, you might have more than one option for a broadband Internet connection.

The two most common types of broadband connections used in homes and small offices are DSL (Digital Subscriber Line) and cable broadband. DSL offers simultaneous voice and data communication over regular phone lines. With DSL, you can talk on the phone and access the Internet at the same time—from a single phone line.

To sign up for DSL, talk to your local telephone provider (typically one of the Baby Bells). In many cases, the phone company provides the DSL router, which connects to the phone line coming into your home. You then connect your WiFi router to the DSL router using a traditional network cable to make the connection to the Internet.

A DSL router such as the Cisco 675 ADSL router is used as the Internet connectivity device for a home-based DSL connection.

DSL connection speeds and the cost of the service vary from provider to provider. Downstream speeds (the speed of data being pulled from the Internet by computers on your network) average around 1.54Mbps and upstream speeds (the speed of data being pushed from your network to the Internet) range from 256Kbps–512Kbps. For you to take advantage of DSL, your local phone company must offer the service.

Another common high-speed Internet service is cable broadband. Cable broadband is provided by your cable television company. Data is moved on the same cabling as your television signal. Because cable broadband has different channels, one channel can be used for upstream data communication and a separate channel can be used for downstream data communication. As with DSL, the connection speeds and cost vary from cable company to cable company. Speeds for home cable broadband implementations can be range from 500–700Kbps downstream and 128–256Kbps upstream (faster data rates can be attained, but in most cases you might have to pay more for the faster data rate).

When you sign up for cable broadband, your service provider will typically provide you with a cable modem (at no cost). The device isn't really a modem but is designed to connect to the Internet (through your television cable). You attach your wireless router to the cable modem to share the Internet connection with the WiFi network.

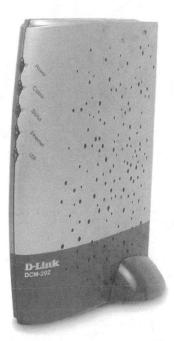

A cable modem is used to connect a home network to the Internet (photo courtesy of D-Link).

DSL and cable broadband are certainly not the only possibilities for a broadband connection in your home. Satellite television services also offer options for broadband Internet connections, and there are also dedicated Internet broadband services such as satellite Internet access, which connects your home or small business computers to the Internet using a small dish to relay data signals via a satellite in the earth's orbit. Speeds of up to 500Kbps can be attained with this type of Internet connection.

It makes sense to take advantage of the broadband service that provides you with the most bang for your buck in terms of bandwidth speed for a monthly fee. Some broadband services also charge you for the broadband device that is installed in your home, and there might also be startup fees. As with all the WiFi equipment discussed in this chapter, you should research the various broadband service providers and select the one that works the best for you.

2

Navigating
Windows XP

IN THIS CHAPTER:

1. About the Windows XP Environment
2. Navigate the Windows Desktop and Start Menu
3. Browse and Search for Files and Folders
4. About My Network Places
5. Use the Control Panel
6. View the Windows Security Center
7. Get Help in Windows
8. About Windows Update
9. Use Windows Update

Wireless networking lets you quickly and easily access network resources and Internet services such as the World Wide Web. To take advantage of all the features wireless networking provides, you need to have a solid understanding of how to navigate the Windows XP operating system's graphical user interface. This chapter provides an overview of navigating the Windows environment, locating files on your computer (and the network), and accessing the Windows Control Panel.

1 About the Windows XP Environment

✔ BEFORE YOU BEGIN	→ SEE ALSO
Just jump right in!	**45** About Sharing Network Resources
	46 Share a Printer
	47 Share a Folder

Windows XP embraces a minimalist approach in terms of the working environment it provides to its users. The Windows desktop (labeled by Microsoft as the "user experience" desktop) is basically uncluttered with icons, initially providing only a **Recycle Bin** icon. Access to installed programs and Windows tools (such as **My Computer**, **My Network Places**, and **My Documents**) is provided by the **Start** menu.

▶ **NOTE**

Desktop icons are optional; you can add icons to the desktop if you want on an as-needed basis. Any icon present on the **Start** menu can be copied and pasted onto the desktop.

The **Start** menu appears in a double-column format; recently used applications are listed in the left column (two icons are permanently pinned to the left column by default) and icons for quickly accessing files and other tools such as the Help system are located in the right column. Accessing icons for all the applications you have installed on your computer is just a matter of selecting **All Programs**, which opens the **All Programs** list. After you have programs open on the desktop, you can switch between multiple application windows by clicking its application button on the taskbar.

▶ **TIP**

You can pin applications to the **Start** menu as needed. Right-click any application icon shown on the **All Programs** list and select **Pin to Start Menu** from the context menu.

*The **Start** menu provides access to all your applications and Windows tools.*

▶ **TIP**

To add an icon for **My Documents** or **My Computer** to your desktop, right-click the **My Documents** or **My Computer** icon on the **Start** menu and select **Show on Desktop** from the context menu.

Although icons can easily be added to the desktop, the desktop really serves as the workspace for your running applications and other software tools. So rather than adding icons to the desktop, you may want to add the **Quick Launch** toolbar to the taskbar. The **Quick Launch** toolbar can be the home for icons that are typically on the desktop, and you can add other icons to the **Quick Launch** toolbar as needed. Right-click an empty space on the taskbar, point at the **Toolbars** option in the context menu, and then select **Quick Launch** to place the **Quick Launch** toolbar on the taskbar. You can drag any icon from the desktop onto the **Quick Launch** toolbar to add a copy of the icon.

▶ **TIP**

If the taskbar is locked, the **Quick Launch** toolbar only shows the icons that were placed on it before the toolbar was locked (because it was sized to accommodate those original icons). Right-click the taskbar and select **Lock the Taskbar** to remove the check mark and unlock the taskbar. You can now drag the **Quick Launch** toolbar handle to increase its size and show all the added icons. You can then lock the taskbar again if you choose.

One other area of the desktop that should be mentioned is the notification area. This portion of the taskbar is on the far right and provides information on running programs and important alerts. For example, when updates have been downloaded for your Windows XP installation, a notification box opens in the notification area to let you know that an update is ready to be installed. The notification area is also of interest to us because you can choose to show LAN and WiFi connection icons in the notification area. These icons allow you to quickly check the speed of a connection and whether the connection is active (particularly useful in the case of WiFi connections).

2 | Navigate the Windows Desktop and Start Menu

✔ **BEFORE YOU BEGIN**

1 About the Windows XP Environment

Navigating the Windows desktop and Start menu is really just a matter of becoming familiar with the Windows user environment. Easy access to applications, tools, and settings is typically just a couple of mouse clicks from the desktop.

1 Open an Application

Select the **Start** menu, point at **All Programs**, point at **Accessories**, and then select a program icon from the list of programs installed on your computer (for example, **Microsoft Paint**). The application opens on the Windows desktop.

2 Minimize the Application

You can maximize, minimize, and close application windows using the appropriate buttons on the top right of the application window. To minimize the application and show the desktop, select the **Minimize** button.

▶ TIP

To quickly minimize all the applications running on the desktop (so that you can see the desktop), click the **Show Desktop** icon on the Quick Launch toolbar.

3 Open an Application from the Quick Launch Toolbar

Applications can also be launched from the **Quick Launch** toolbar. To do so, click an application icon in the **Quick Launch** toolbar, such as **Internet Explorer**, to start the web browser on the desktop.

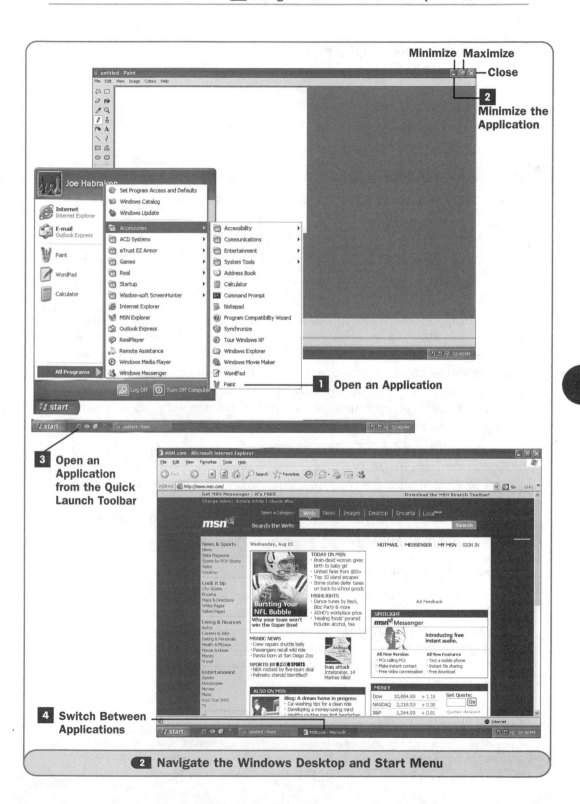

Minimize Maximize

— Close

2

Minimize the Application

1 Open an Application

3 Open an Application from the Quick Launch Toolbar

4 Switch Between Applications

2

2 Navigate the Windows Desktop and Start Menu

4 Switch Between Applications

If you have multiple applications running on the desktop, you might want to switch between the application windows. In the taskbar, click the button for the application you want to place "on top." Switch between applications as needed using the taskbar buttons for the applications.

---

3 Browse and Search for Files and Folders

✔ BEFORE YOU BEGIN	→ SEE ALSO
1 About the Windows XP Environment	**48** About Accessing Network Resources
	49 Access Shared Folders and Open Shared Files

The **My Computer** and **My Documents** icons on the **Start** menu (or on your desktop, if you placed them there) provide easy access to the folders and files on your computer. **My Computer** allows you to quickly browse your hard drive or other removable media drives such as CD or DVD drives (and other removable media such as USB drives). The **My Computer** window also provides you with links you can use to access your local area network and the shared folders and printers provided by other computers on the network.

The **My Documents** folder is the folder used by the applications installed on your computer as the default location to save files. So when you save a file—say when you are working in Microsoft Word and don't change the folder in the **Save As** dialog box—you will find it in **My Documents**. If you can't find a particular folder or file by browsing your computer using **My Computer** or **My Documents**, you can use the Windows **Search** tool to find a file or files.

1 Open My Computer

Open the **My Computer** window from the **Start** menu (select **Start**, then choose **My Computer**) or by double-clicking the **My Computer** icon on the desktop. The **My Computer** window shows the computer's hard drive and any removable drives. To open the hard drive and view the folders stored on the hard drive, or to open a CD or DVD in a removable drive, double-click the appropriate drive icon.

▶ **TIP**

If you have placed the **My Computer** icon on the desktop (right-click **My Computer** on the **Start** menu and select **Show on Desktop** to put it there), double-click the desktop icon to open the **My Computer** window.

2 Open My Documents

The **My Computer** window also provides a series of links along the left side of the window. To open the **My Documents** folder, select the **My Documents** link in the **Other Places** pane.

3 View My Documents and Change View

In the **My Documents** window, you can view files that you have saved to the folder. Any folders you have created or copied to the **My Documents** folder are also listed.

▶ **TIP**

You can quickly create a new subfolder inside the currently open folder, such as the **My Documents** folder (or any other folder): Choose **File**, **New**, **Folder**. In the **New Folder** dialog box that opens, type a new name for the folder and click **OK**.

The default view for **My Documents** is **Tiles**, which shows the contents of the folder as large icons (which are arranged horizontally in the window). You can quickly change the view of the contents of the **My Documents** folder (or any folder or drive); choose **View** and then select a new view such as **Icons**, **List**, or **Details**. These views are described below:

- **Icons view**—Large icons are shown in the **My Document** window and are sorted alphabetically by default and arranged in horizontal rows.

- **List view**—This view shows a list using small icons where the files are arranged in columns (again, they are listed alphabetically by default).

- **Details view**—This view provides a list where additional information about each file is shown in a columnar fashion. The detail information includes the file size, the file type (which is also shown by the small icon), and the date on which the file was last modified.

▶ **TIP**

You can also arrange the files in a folder using the **View** menu; select **Arrange Icons by** and then select **Name**, **Size**, **Type**, or **Modified**.

4 Open the Search Window

When browsing for a particular file proves futile, you can open the **Search** window and set criteria that help locate the file. To open the **Search** window, select **Start** and then choose **Search**.

3

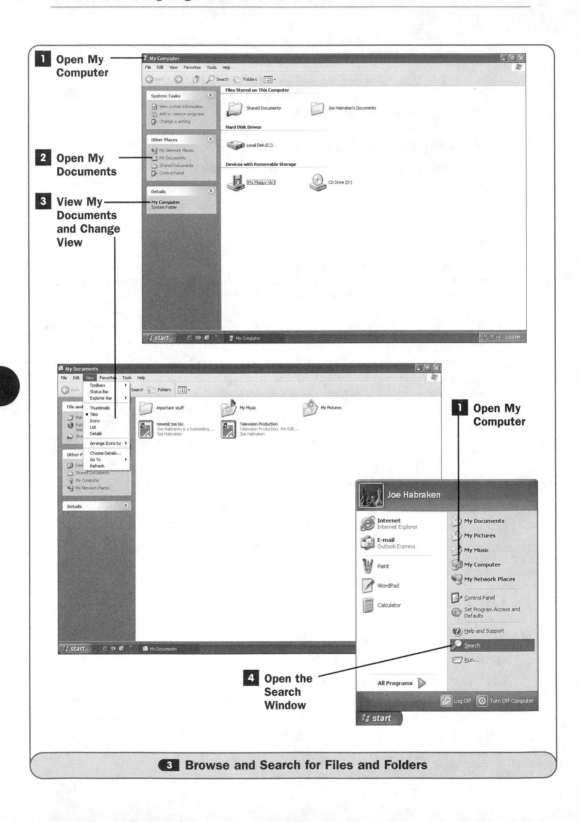

1 Open My Computer

2 Open My Documents

3 View My Documents and Change View

1 Open My Computer

4 Open the Search Window

3 Browse and Search for Files and Folders

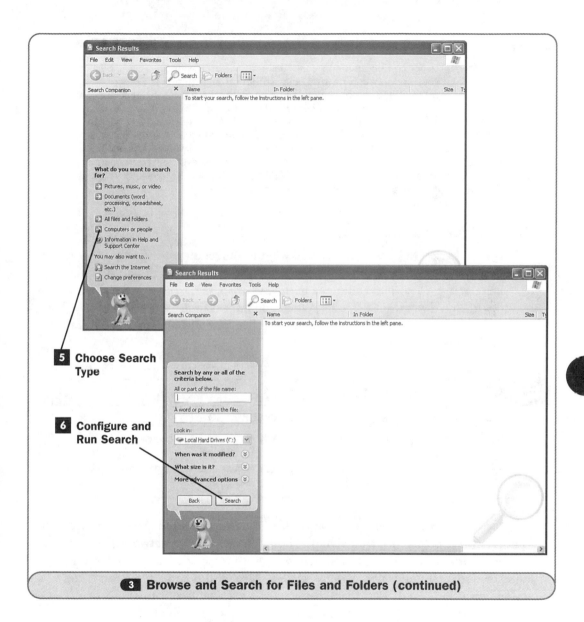

5 **Choose Search Type**

6 **Configure and Run Search**

3 Browse and Search for Files and Folders (continued)

5 Choose Search Type

In the **Search** window, select the type of search you want to conduct in the left pane of the window. If you are looking for pictures or other media files, select **Pictures, music or video**. If you are looking for application documents such as those you create with Microsoft Office, select **Documents (word processing, spreadsheet, etc.)**. To do a more general search for files and folders, select the **All files and folders** link.

▶ TIP

You can also search for computers and people using the Search window. This is particularly useful when you are looking for a particular computer on a network. Select **Computers or people** in the **Search** window and then enter the name of the computer you are looking for. You can connect to a computer listed in the search results by double-clicking the computer's icon. If the computer is providing shared resources such as files or printers, you can then access these items over your network. If a computer is not sharing resources, connecting to the computer doesn't really provide you access to anything on that computer. For more about how computers on a network share resources and what it takes to actually access them see **43** **About Sharing Network Resources** and **48** **About Accessing Network Resources**.

6 Configure and Run Search

After you select the type of search you want to run, enter your search criteria. For example, when searching all files and folders, you can enter part of a file name or enter keywords contained in the file. You can also specify the location in which you want to search. When you have completed entering the search criteria, click the **Search** button. The search results appear in the right pane of the **Search** window.

4

4 About My Network Places	
✔ **BEFORE YOU BEGIN**	→ **SEE ALSO**
2 Navigate the Windows Desktop and Start Menu	**48** About Accessing Network Resources
	49 Access Shared Folders and Open Shared Files

My Network Places is a network browsing tool that allows you to view connected computers and access their shared folders and printers. Use **My Network Places** if you are connected to a network and need a resource (such as a file or printer) on another computer that is part of your network. Because this book is about setting up and configuring a wireless home network, you will find that being familiar with the **My Network Places** window makes it easy for you to both share resources with other computers and access their shared resources.

You can open the **My Network Places** window (which isn't really a place as much as it is a listing of connected computers and their shared resources) from the **Start** menu: Select **Start** and then choose **My Network Places**. Computers on your network that share resources such as folders are listed in the **My Network Places** window (they are typically not listed unless you have accessed them at least once).

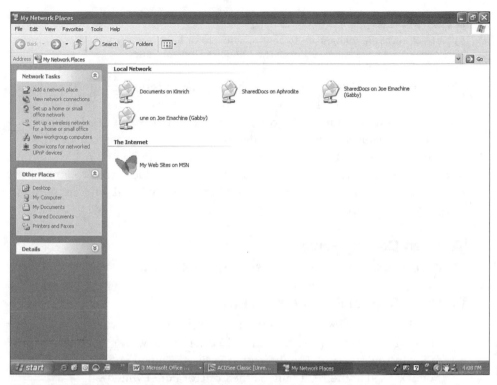

My Network Places provides you with a powerful tool for browsing your local network.

The **My Network Places** window provides links that allow you to add a network place (connect to a particular computer and shared resource), view network connections, and view *workgroup computers* (computers that are part of the same home or small office network). More importantly, **My Network Places** makes it easy for you to create a workgroup network after you have your various computers connected to your wireless network.

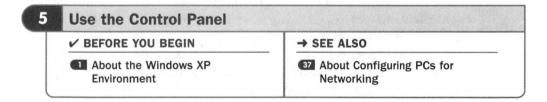

5 Use the Control Panel

✔ BEFORE YOU BEGIN	→ SEE ALSO
1 About the Windows XP Environment	**37** About Configuring PCs for Networking

The **Control Panel** provides access to many of your Windows hardware and software settings. *Applets* (small utility applications) are accessed from categories such as **Appearance and Themes**, **Network and Internet Connections**, **Add or Remove Programs**, **Printers and Other Hardware**, and **User Accounts**.

▶ KEY TERM

Applet—A software utility used to control software or hardware settings. Most of the Windows applets are accessed from the Windows **Control Panel**.

The number of applets available in a category depends on the particular category you select. For example, the **Add or Remove Programs** category provides one applet, the **Add or Remove Programs** applet, that allows you to add or remove software from your computer and add or remove Windows components. The **Network and Internet Connections** category, on the other hand (which is important in terms of networking a Windows computer), provides access to a number of applets such as **Internet Options**, the **Network Setup Wizard**, and the **Wireless Network Setup Wizard**.

1 Open Control Panel

Select the **Start** menu and then select **Control Panel**.

2 View Control Panel Categories

The default view for the **Control Panel** is the **Categories** view. Categories are listed in the right pane of the **Control Panel** window. Shortcut links are provided in the left pane. The shortcut links listed depend on the category you have opened in the right pane of the **Control Panel** window.

3 Open the Network and Internet Connection Category

The category that provides access to applets for configuring your Internet connection and home network settings is the **Network and Internet Connection** category. Click the **Network and Internet Connection** link in the right pane of the **Control Panel**.

4 View Network and Internet Connection Tasks and Icons

Most of the **Control Panel** categories provide you with two ways to deal with a particular setting or issue: You can select from a list of tasks or select an icon that starts a particular applet. For example, in the **Network and Internet Connections** category, you can select a task such as **Set up or change your Internet connection** or you can start an applet such as the **Network Setup Wizard** by clicking its icon.

When you have finished viewing the **Network and Internet Connections** window, return to the **Control Panel** by clicking the **Back** button on the toolbar.

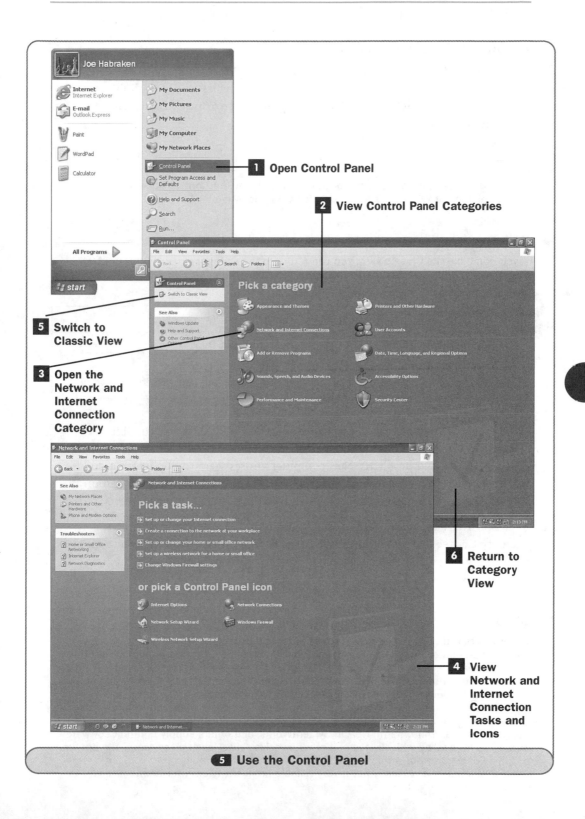

1 Open Control Panel

2 View Control Panel Categories

5 Switch to Classic View

3 Open the Network and Internet Connection Category

6 Return to Category View

4 View Network and Internet Connection Tasks and Icons

5 Switch to Classic View

If you don't like accessing the various **Control Panel** applets by categories, you can switch to the **Classic** view. This view provides icons for all the important **Control Panel** applets. In the left pane of the **Control Panel**, click the **Switch to Classic View** link.

▶ **NOTE**

The **Classic** view is called "classic" because it is the way the **Control Panel** looked in earlier versions of Windows, such as Windows 98 and Windows 95.

▶ **TIP**

If you don't like the **Classic** view, you can return to the **Category** view. In the **Control Panel** window, click the **Switch to Category View** link in the left panel.

---

6 View the Windows Security Center

✔ BEFORE YOU BEGIN	→ SEE ALSO
5 Use the Control Panel	71 About Firewalls
	83 Install and Use Antivirus Software

With incredible advances in computer connectivity and computer capabilities (such as Internet connectivity and wireless networking) have also come a number of security risks and problems. New computer viruses seem to pop up on a daily basis and *crackers* (bad hackers) find new way to exploit computers faster than software companies such as Microsoft can block the attacks.

Microsoft's Service Pack 2 (SP2) update to Windows XP added the Windows **Security Center** to the operating system, providing an easy way for you to monitor security essentials such as Windows updates, virus protection software, and the Windows Firewall.

▶ **NOTE**

It is important that you take advantage of at least basic protection for your computer, such as up-to-date virus-scanning software and the Windows Firewall. A number of other security measures are possible, such as the use of wireless router firewalls and WiFi network security strategies (see 72 **Configure Router Firewall Settings** for firewall information and 76 **About 802.11 Security Strategies** for information on securing WiFi networks). You can also take advantage of software that block spyware and web browser pop-ups and that also protects your email software from virus infection. For example, products such as Zone Alarm, Norton SystemWorks, and others supply different software strategies for dealing with viruses and other invasive "bugs" such as spyware. The amount and type of security software you install on your computer is really up to you, but a virus-infected computer is certainly not a very reliable productivity or entertainment tool.

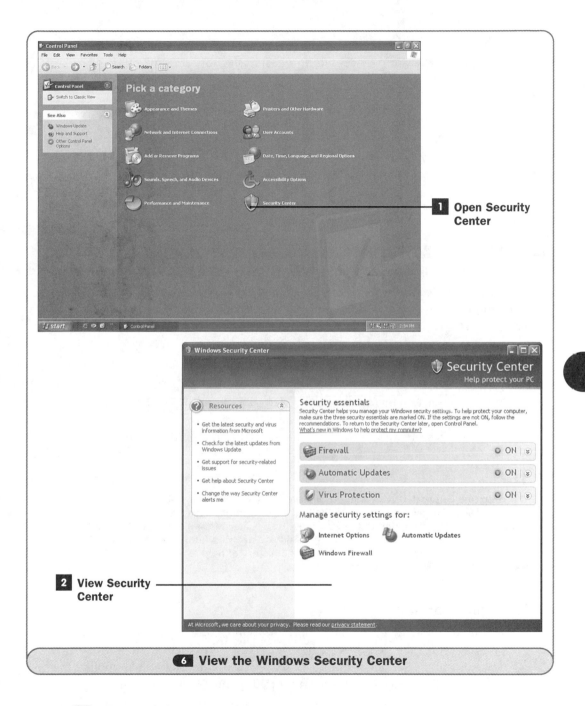

6 View the Windows Security Center

1 Open Security Center

From the **Control Panel**, select the **Security Center** link (or in the **Classic** view, double-click the **Security Center** icon).

2 View Security Center

The **Security Center** provides the current status of your firewall, automatic updates, and virus protection. You can view more information about the status of an item by clicking the toggle button on the far right of the item.

The **Security Center** also provides links in the left pane to security and virus news from Microsoft and to Windows automatic updates. Icons at the bottom of the **Security Center** window provide access to *applets* such as the **Internet Options** and **Windows Firewall**. When you have finished viewing the **Security Center**, close the window.

7   Get Help in Windows

No matter how proficient you become working in the Windows environment, something always crops up that's a puzzler and requires some help. Use the **Windows Help and Support** window to pick from a selection of help topics and tasks and to search the Help system for information about any topic.

1 Open Help and Support Center

Select the **Start** menu and then select **Help and Support**. The **Help and Support Center** window opens. You can select any of the topics or tasks listed in the **Help and Support Center** to read help on that particular subject area.

▶ TIP

The **Help and Support Center** window operates very much like a web browser window. You can use the arrow buttons in the toolbar to go back and forward. You can view Help topics that have been added to the **Favorites** list by clicking the **Favorites** button on the toolbar. (To add a topic to the list, click the **Add to Favorites** button when you are viewing that particular topic.) If you want to see the history of help topics you have already visited, click the **History** button on the toolbar.

2 Search for Help

If you don't see any help topics or tasks that are pertinent to your problem, you can search the Help system. Type your search criteria (a word, words, or sentence) in the **Search** box at the top-left corner of the **Help and Support Center** window. Then click the **Start searching** button (the white and green arrow).

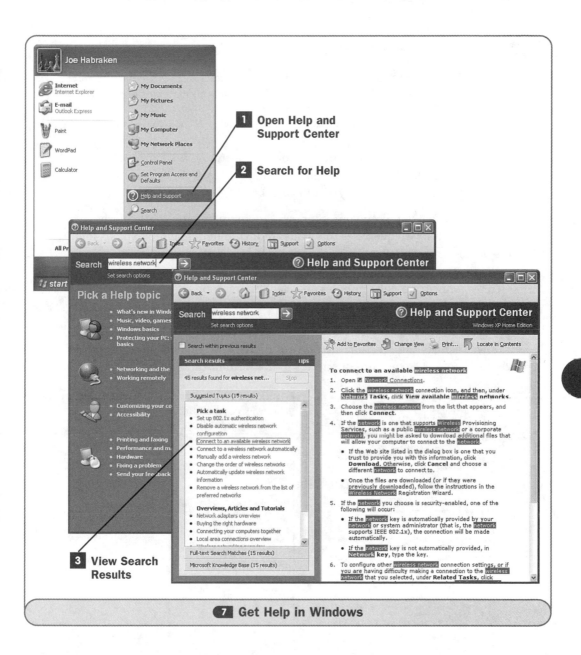

1 Open Help and Support Center

2 Search for Help

3 View Search Results

7 Get Help in Windows

3 View Search Results

The results of your search are listed in the **Search Results** pane. To view a particular subject listed in the results, click the topic. The topic information appears in the right pane of the **Help and Support Center** window. You can search again at any time by typing new search criteria in the **Search** box and then running the search.

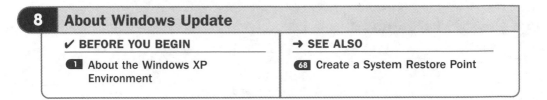

8   About Windows Update

✔ BEFORE YOU BEGIN	→ SEE ALSO
1 About the Windows XP Environment	**68** Create a System Restore Point

Microsoft is constantly updating the Windows XP operating system. Small bugs in the software and security fixes are identified, and Microsoft makes a patch or update available to fix the newly identified issue.

It is important that you keep your Windows system up to date—particularly because of the fairly frequent security issues that crop up related to exploits found in the Windows system. You don't want to leave your system open to viruses or other software attacks, and you certainly don't want to make it easy for someone to secretly connect to your computer and steal information or use your computer to attack another computer such as a web server on the Internet.

How automatic updates are run on your PC is really up to you. If you access the **Windows Security Center** from the **Control Panel**, you can click the **Automatic Updates** icon to view the current settings in the **Automatic Updates** dialog box.

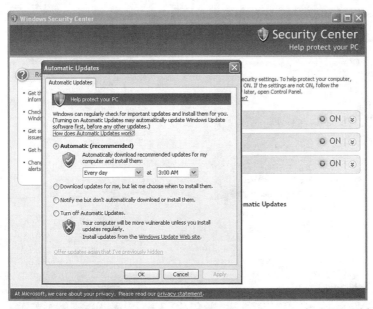

The **Automatic Updates** dialog box allows you to control when and how automatic updates are installed on your computer.

In the **Automatic Updates** dialog box, you can choose the time (and day of the week) when updates are downloaded and installed on your computer. You can also select to have updates downloaded and installed by you (when you want to install them). Turning off automatic updates is an option, but doing so can leave your system open to attack. Windows typically runs better after you install updates anyway.

It's up to you whether you use automatic updates or not, but it is probably a good "best practice" to allow the updates to happen automatically. When a new update is downloaded, you will find an **Update** icon in the Windows notification area (in the right corner of the taskbar). Clicking the **Update** icon allows the update to be installed to your computer.

---

9 Use Windows Update

✔ **BEFORE YOU BEGIN**

8 About Windows Update

If you have configured updates so that they happen automatically, you are all set. However, it's not a bad idea to visit the Windows Update website on occasion and allow your system to be scanned for updates. This can be useful in terms of non-critical updates such as new drivers for your various hardware items or updates of Windows software such as the Windows Media Player.

9

1 Open Windows Update Website

Select the **Start** menu, point at **All Programs**, and then select **Windows Update**. Your web browser window (typically Internet Explorer) opens and loads the Windows Update website. If you want to have only high-priority updates shown, click the **Express** button. If you want to view all updates (including low-priority updates related to drivers and software), select the **Custom** button.

▶ **TIP**

If your system needs to have the Windows Update software updated, a window appears, requiring a scan of your computer. A new page appears, letting you know that updates are available for the Update software; click the **Download and Install Now** button. After the software is installed, click **Close** (to close the installation window) and then click **Continue.** Your system should then be scanned for Windows updates. After the updates are installed, you must often reboot your system.

Your system is scanned for available updates; those updates are listed for you (the updates listed depend on whether you selected **Express** or **Custom** in step 1).

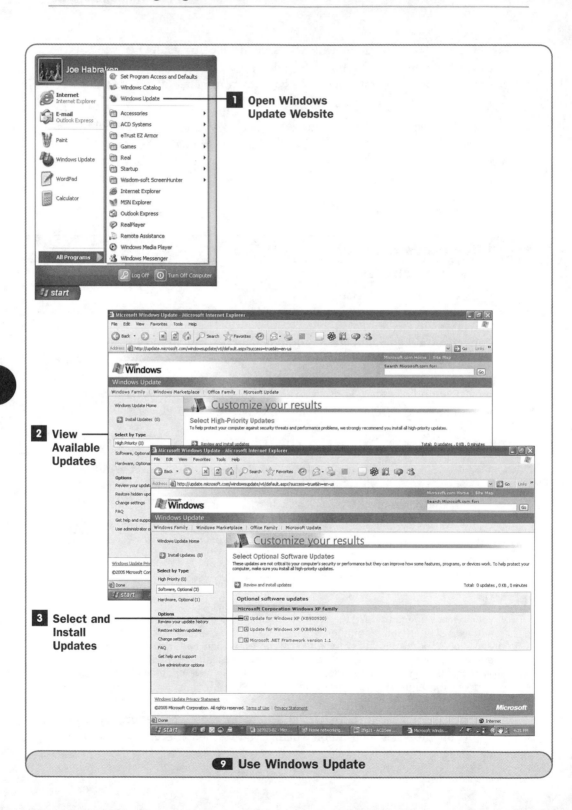

1 Open Windows
Update Website

2 View Available Updates

3 Select and Install Updates

9 Use Windows Update

2 View Available Updates

If you selected **Custom** in step 1, all the high-priority updates (if any are available) and lower-priority updates (software and hardware) are listed by type in the left pane of the browser window. To view updates in a particular category, select the category.

3 Select and Install Updates

The updates in a particular category are listed. To install an update or updates, select the update's check box. Then click **Review and install updates**. The updates you have selected are listed for installation. Click **Install Updates**.

An **Installing Updates** dialog box appears, showing the progress of the installation. When the updates have been completed, you have the option of restarting the system (which is required by most updates) or closing the installation dialog box and restarting the system at a later time. For the update to actually take effect, you will want to restart your system at some point.

9

3

Sharing a Home Computer

IN THIS CHAPTER:

Even in households and home offices that have multiple computers (the reason you are setting up your wireless network), it's not uncommon to share a computer with another user or users. This chapter takes a look at sharing a computer with another person and focuses on creating and managing Windows user accounts. We also take a look at the process of logging on and off your Windows system and switching users.

10	**About Sharing a Windows XP Computer**

✔ **BEFORE YOU BEGIN**

5 Use the Control Panel

When you install Windows XP on a computer (or start a new computer for the first time, with Windows XP pre-installed), you are walked through the process of creating a user account. This first user account is the **Computer Administrator** account for the computer. The initial account has administrative abilities such as the ability to create new users (or delete users) and maintain the Windows operating system, including making changes to the system settings and adding and removing software and hardware.

10

▶ **NOTE**

Because the subject of this book is creating a home wireless network, the steps and figures shown have been created for users of Windows XP Home edition. In almost all cases, however, the material is also appropriate for Windows XP Professional edition users.

When only one account exists on a Windows XP computer (the initial account created immediately after the installation of the Windows operating system), you are taken directly to the Windows desktop after the boot process. This behavior is also attributed to the fact that the initial account is created without a password. So, your system isn't really secure because it boots automatically to your one and only user account, which happens to have administrative capabilities. You specify the name for the account the first time you use Windows and walk through the process of adding at least one user account and activating Windows over the Internet. This means that the administrative account (the one you named) isn't protected by a password. It makes sense to create a password for your administrative user account to provide some basic security for the computer in terms of who can log on to your system. If other users need access, you should create user accounts for them.

▶ TIP

If you go to the trouble of creating a password for your computer's administrator account, don't give your password to other users of the computer. Create an account for each user (which I suggest should be a limited account, which "limits" the user in terms of installing software and changing settings for other users). Each user can then decide if she wants to password protect her own account. Even limited accounts can create and change their own passwords.

Because the initial user account on the Windows system is created with administrative abilities, it falls to this user (you) to create any additional user accounts. If more than one person is using a computer, it makes sense for each user to have his own account. There are benefits to each user having his own account, without even factoring in security. For example, each user can personalize the Windows desktop including fonts, desktop background, and desktop icons.

▶ NOTE

A **Guest** account is also created when you install Windows XP on your computer. The **Guest** account is turned off by default. It is designed to give a user temporary access to a computer as a "guest" user. The **Guest** account can be turned on and off by a user who has a **Computer Administrator** user account. When the **Guest** account is turned on, the **Guest** icon appears on the Windows **Welcome** screen, and a guest can log on to the system without a password.

There are two types of user accounts you can create. You can create user accounts that are designated *computer administrator* (as your initial account is) or you can create accounts that are limited. *Limited user* accounts cannot add, delete, or edit user accounts. A limited user also cannot change systemwide settings or install software and hardware. You determine the type of user account when you create the account, and you do have the ability to change an existing account from computer administrator to limited if required.

▶ KEY TERMS

Computer administrator—A Windows user account that can change system settings, add and remove software and hardware, and create and edit other user accounts.

Limited user—A user account without administrative abilities. This user can change desktop settings and change her password and user account picture.

▶ NOTE

Hopefully, you can see where I am going with this discussion. I suggest that you have only one account on the system with administrative abilities. Additional user accounts can be limited accounts. This arrangement provides the greatest amount of control over the system and also protects the Windows operating system from a user inadvertently changing a system setting or deleting a user account or important software. I'm certainly not advocating that you be a computer control freak, but having one user in "charge" of the system will cut down on potential problems related to user error.

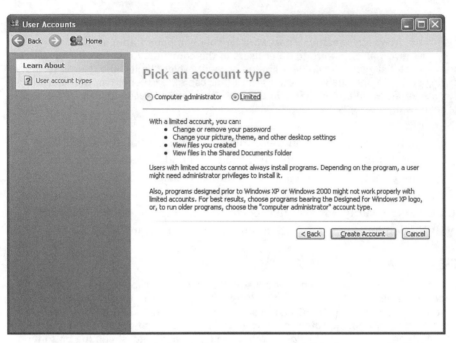

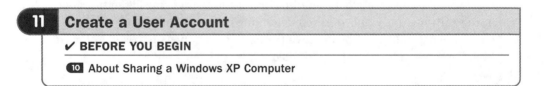

User accounts can be designated as computer administrators or as limited.

If you are using the administrative account and create new user accounts, you must supply the name for those accounts (see **11** **Create a User Account**).

11 Create a User Account

✔ BEFORE YOU BEGIN

10 About Sharing a Windows XP Computer

Windows XP provides the **User Accounts** window (accessed from the **Control Panel**), which allows you to create, edit, and delete user accounts. User accounts are managed using the administrative account created when Windows is initially installed on your system. To work through this task, make sure that you log on to Windows using the account name designated for the first user account on the computer.

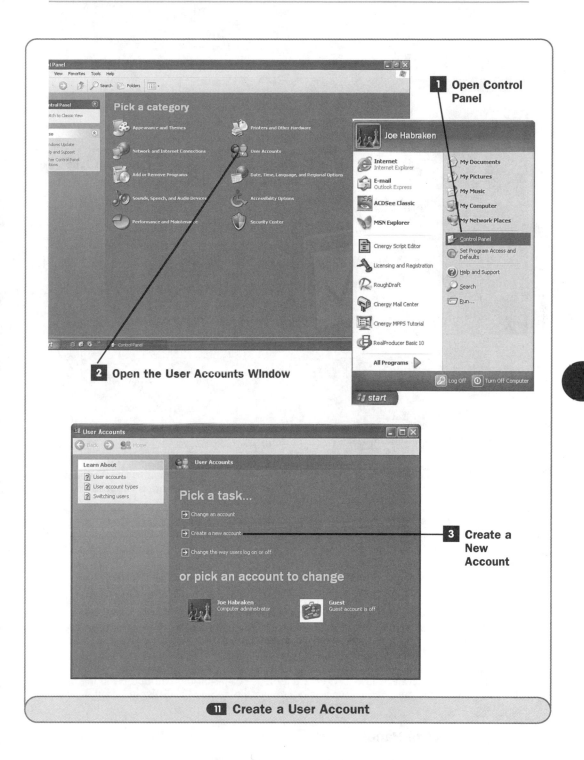

1 Open Control Panel

2 Open the User Accounts Window

3 Create a New Account

11

11 Create a User Account

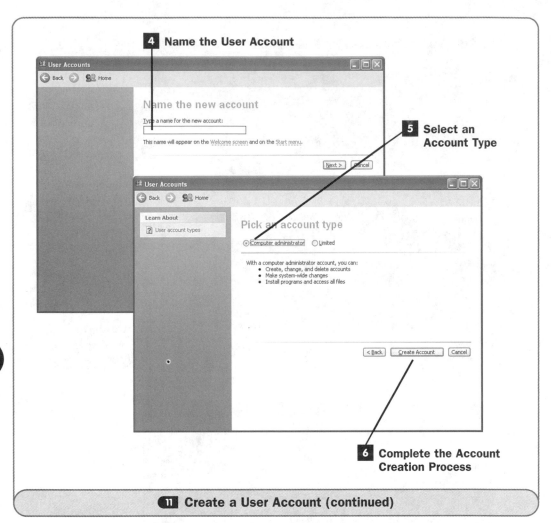

4 Name the User Account

5 Select an Account Type

6 Complete the Account Creation Process

⑪ Create a User Account (continued)

▶ TIP

When you buy a new computer that has Windows XP installed, or when you install Windows XP Home Edition on a computer you already own, you are required to establish at least one user account on the computer the first time Windows XP boots up. You are also required to activate and optionally register Windows with Microsoft. In some rare cases, the process of naming the first user account might be bypassed (for example, if someone turned off the computer when you were working through the steps of naming a user account). A user account called **Owner** is created automatically. This is the administrative account. You can change the name of this account (if you want) in the **User Accounts** window. Because **Owner** is the only account on the computer, you log on as **Owner** until you create other accounts or change the name of the **Owner** account.

❶ Open Control Panel

Click the **Start** menu and then choose **Control Panel**.

2 Open the User Accounts Window

In the **Control Panel**, click the **User Accounts** icon. The **User Accounts** window opens; it provides you with the tools to create, edit, and delete user accounts. You can pick a task to access a particular tool or edit an existing account by clicking the icon for that account.

3 Create a New Account

In the User Accounts window, select the Create a new account task. A series of screens like a wizard will walk you through the process of creating the new accounts.

4 Name the User Account

In the first screen, type a name for the user account. The user account name can consist of 20 characters (uppercase, lowercase, or a combination including spaces). You cannot use these special characters:

" / \ [ ] : ; | = , + * ? < >

After typing the account name click **Next**.

5 Select an Account Type

On the next screen, select an account type: **Computer administrator** or **Limited**. **Computer administrator** accounts have full control over the computer's settings. **Limited** accounts have limited abilities to change settings and install software. Select the account type based on how much structure you believe the user for whom you are creating the account needs.

► **TIP**

If every account you create for Windows XP is a **Computer administrator**, you are setting up a computing environment that will be extremely rich in anarchy and chaos. Consider having only one **Computer administrator** account (your own account) and then create all other accounts as **Limited**.

6 Complete the Account Creation Process

To finish the new account process and create the account, click **Create Account**. You return to the **User Accounts** window. A new icon appears on that screen, representing the newly created account.

12   Change the Account Picture

✔ BEFORE YOU BEGIN

10 About Sharing a Windows XP Computer

11 Create a User Account

After a user account has been created, you can edit its various attributes, such as the account type and the account picture. The *account picture* is the picture used to represent the account on the Windows **Welcome** screen. The picture of the currently logged on user also appears on **Start** menu and in the **User Accounts** window.

A default picture (the chess pieces) is automatically selected when you create a new account. You can change the account picture to any of a number of pictures provided by Windows XP. You can also use your own digital pictures (from a digital camera or scanner) or any pictures you copy or download from the Web.

A user can change his user account picture whether the account is an administrative or limited account. Users with administrative accounts can also change the pictures for other user accounts (another good reason to only have one administrator account).

1   Select a User Account

Assuming that you are using a **Computer administrator**'s account: In the **User Accounts** window (select **User Accounts** in the **Control Panel** to access this window), click the user account for which you want to change the picture. The task list for the selected account opens.

▶ NOTE

Users with **Limited** accounts do not see the other user accounts installed on the computer when they click **User Accounts** in the **Control Panel**. Users with **Limited** accounts are taken directly to a specific user account task screen, which provides the user with the ability to create a password (or change the password) or change the account picture.

2   Select Change the Picture

Select the **Change the picture** task. A picture box opens, showing available pictures.

3   Select a New Picture

Scroll through the pictures in the list box. Click the picture you want to use for the currently selected account.

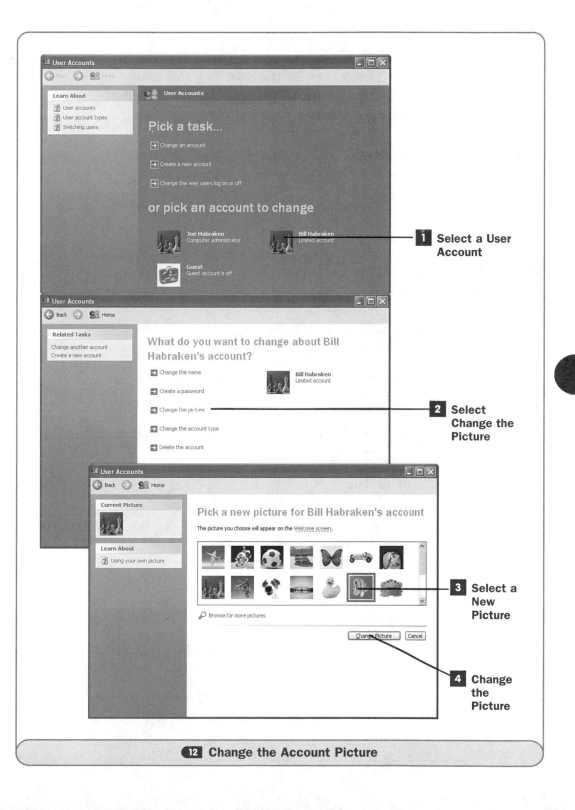

1 Select a User Account

2 Select Change the Picture

12

3 Select a New Picture

4 Change the Picture

12 Change the Account Picture

► **TIP**

To use a digital picture that you have created with a digital camera or scanner or copied from the Web, click the **Browse for more pictures** option below the picture box. The **Open** dialog box appears. Browse to find the picture file on your computer's hard disk. When you have located the picture, select it and click the **Open** button. You are returned to the account's task list, and the new picture is shown as the account's picture.

4 **Change the Picture**

After selecting the picture you want to use, click the **Change Picture** button. You are returned to the account's task list, and the account picture is changed to your selection.

13 | **Password Protect a User Account**

✔ **BEFORE YOU BEGIN**

11 Create a User Account
12 Change the Account Picture

12

Windows XP user accounts can be assigned a password. This means that for a user to log on using an account, she must know the password. A user with an administrative account can assign passwords to other user accounts. Each user (whether she has administrative or limited privileges) can also create and change her account password as needed.

1 **Select a User Account**

In the **User Accounts** window (select **User Accounts** in the **Control Panel** to open this window), select the user account for which you want to create a password (your own account or any account if you are a computer administrator).

2 **Select Create a Password**

Select the **Create a password** task to create a password for the selected user. The **Create a password** window opens. If you are changing an existing password (a password that you set previously), the link appears as **Change the password** instead of **Create a password**.

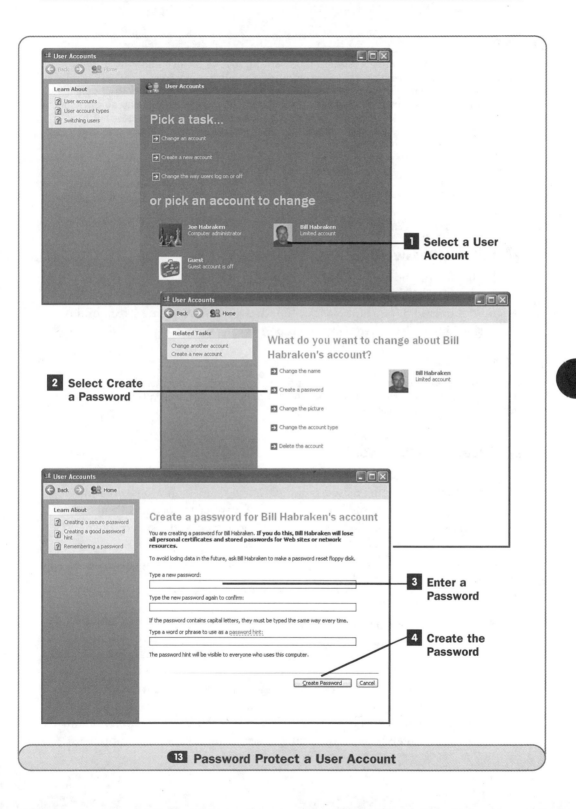

13 Password Protect a User Account

1 **Select a User Account**

2 **Select Create a Password**

3 **Enter a Password**

4 **Create the Password**

▶ **TIP**

It is suggested that you create "strong" passwords if you are serious about using passwords as a protection strategy for your computer (and the various user accounts). Strong passwords use a combination of alphabetic and numeric characters, use both uppercase and lowercase characters, and also use special characters such as @, #, and so on. A password can be up to 127 characters in length; however, Microsoft suggests that the strongest passwords are 7 or 14 characters long. If you are using user accounts merely as a convenience so that different family members can share a computer, you don't need to overdo the passwords. If a user can't remember a password because it is too complex, it really doesn't do anyone any good. If a user does forget his account password, a user with an administrative account can change the password without knowing the original password. The user can then log on using the new password specified by the administrator.

▣ Enter a Password

In the first text box, type a password for the account. Then retype the password as required in the second text box. You can also enter an optional hint for the password. The hint is shown on the Windows **Welcome** screen and is designed to help you remember your password.

▶ **TIP**

If you use a password hint, remember that all the users of the computer can see the hint at the **Welcome** screen. The hint should not be a total giveaway in terms of allowing other users to guess your password.

▣ Create the Password

After you have entered and then re-entered the password (and the optional hint), click the **Create Password** button. The account is now password protected. The password must be provided when you (or the account owner, if you are setting the password for another user) log on to the system.

▣ Change the Account Type

✔ **BEFORE YOU BEGIN**

▣ Change the Account Picture
▣ Password Protect a User Account

A computer administrator account can change the type of account assigned to other accounts on the system. For example, a computer administrator account can be changed to a limited account or vice versa. Because any computer administrator account can change the account type for all other accounts, computer administrator accounts are not protected, meaning that one administrator can demote another administrator to a limited account.

► **NOTE**

It really makes sense and is definitely a best practice (I think you would agree) to have just one computer administrator account on a computer. All the other accounts can then be limited. Allow multiple computer administrator accounts only in an environment where you are sure that the various administrator users aren't going to mess around with the other users' settings, particularly the account type.

1 Select a User Account

In the **User Accounts** window (select **User Accounts** in the **Control Panel** to display this window), select the user account for which you want to modify the account type.

► **NOTE**

When you are changing the settings for *your own* user account, the tasks associated with the account are labeled **Change my name**, **Change my picture**, and so on. When you are changing the settings for another account (which only a computer administrator can do), the tasks are listed as **Change the name**, **Change the picture**, and so on.

14

2 Select Change the Account Type

In the account's task window, select the **Change the account type** task. The account type screen opens.

3 Choose an Account Type

Select the new account type for the account (if the account is currently **Computer administrator**, the only option is **Limited** and vice versa).

4 Set the Account Type

After selecting the account type, click the **Change Account Type** button to confirm the account type change.

► **NOTE**

Windows XP Home is really designed for there to be one administrative account on the computer with all additional accounts existing as **Limited** accounts. This recommendation exists because administrative accounts can change the account type for any existing account, including other administrative accounts. For example, one administrator could demote another administrator to a **Limited** account. So, consider the whole account structure for any computer that is shared by multiple users. If one administrative account demotes another administrative account to a **Limited** account, there are no repercussions on the system other than that the former administrator can no longer change other users' account settings or change administrative settings on the computer.

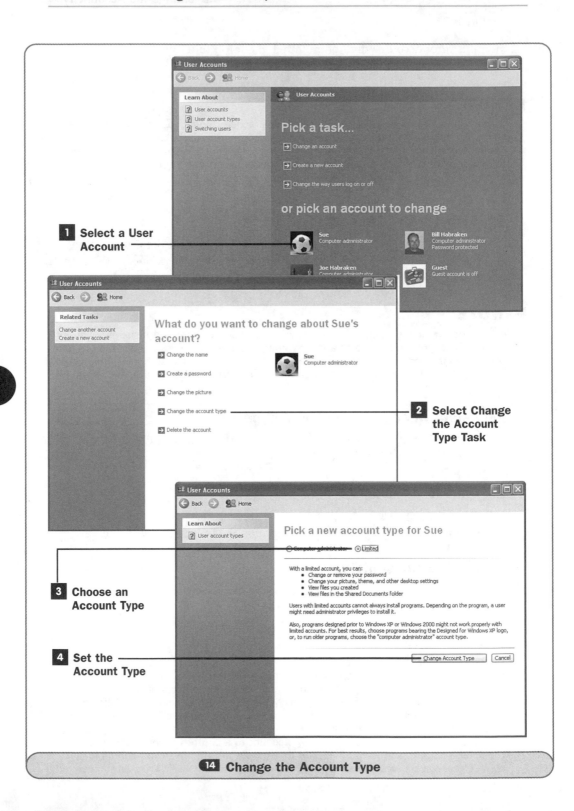

1 Select a User
Account

2 Select Change
the Account
Type Task

3 Choose an
Account Type

4 Set the
Account Type

14

14 Change the Account Type

15   Configure a .NET Passport for a User Account

✔ **BEFORE YOU BEGIN**

11 Create a User Account

Each user account on a computer running Windows XP can be associated with a Microsoft *.NET Passport*. The purpose of the passport is to identify the user when he accesses certain Microsoft content on the Web, including personalized web pages and other tools such as Microsoft's Instant Messaging service. The .NET Passport settings must be configured by each individual user (even an administrator cannot configure the passport for another user). Both **Computer administrator** and **Limited** accounts can be associated with a .NET Passport.

▶ KEY TERM

.NET Passport—A user account that provides access to personalized and special Microsoft web content. The Passport is really just an email account with Microsoft; anyone who signs up for a Microsoft Hotmail account (**www.hotmail.com**) automatically has a .NET Passport (which uses the email address and password established for the Hotmail account).

▶ TIP

You sign up for a .NET Passport by registering for a Microsoft Hotmail email account. Although you can sign up for the account during the process of associating the passport with your Windows user account, you might want to register for the Hotmail account before you begin the process of creating a .NET Passport (it just makes things easier). Go to **http://www.hotmail.com** to sign up. You will establish an email account name and account password during the signup process.

Select Your User Account

In the **User Accounts** window (select **User Accounts** in the **Control Panel** to open this window), select your user account. You must select your own account; you cannot configure a .NET Passport for an account other than your own.

▶ NOTE

When a **Limited** user accesses the **User Accounts** window, the only options available apply to that user. For the user to associate a .NET Passport with his user account, the user selects the **Set up my account to use a .NET Passport** task after opening the **User Accounts** window.

15

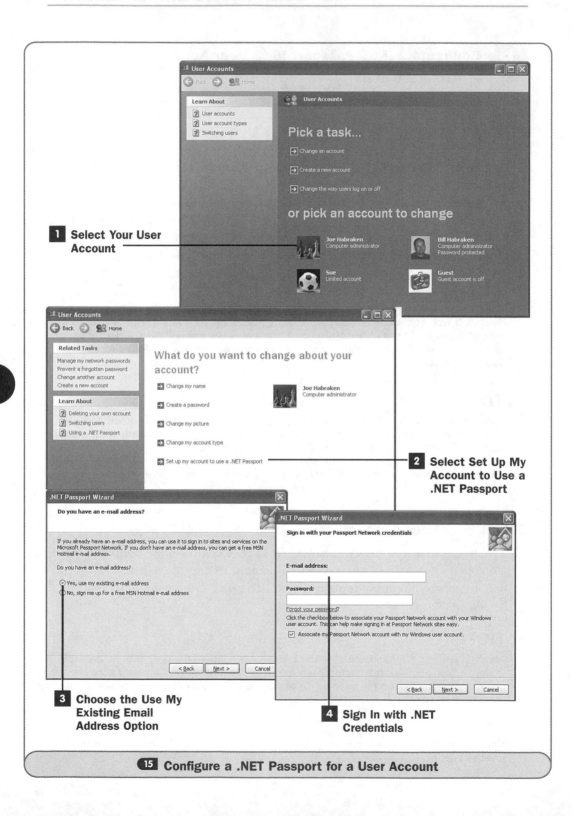

1 Select Your User Account

2 Select Set Up My Account to Use a .NET Passport

3 Choose the Use My Existing Email Address Option

4 Sign In with .NET Credentials

15 Configure a .NET Passport for a User Account

2 Select Set Up My Account to Use a .NET Passport

In the task list for the selected user account (your own account), select the **Set up my account to use a .NET Passport** task. The **.NET Passport Wizard** opens. Click **Next** to bypass the initial wizard screen.

3 Choose the Use My Existing Email Account Option

Assuming that you have already signed up for a Hotmail email account as suggested earlier, on the next wizard screen, make sure that the **Yes, use my existing email address option is selected**. Then click **Next**. The next screen verifies that you will sign in with your .NET credentials. Click **Next** to continue.

4 Sign In with .NET Credentials

Enter your Hotmail email account address and then enter your Hotmail account password. Click **Next** to continue. The final wizard screen appears. Click **Finish**. Now when you log on to the system, your .NET Passport will automatically be activated. As already mentioned, a .NET Passport allows access to special Microsoft web content such as My MSN (**www.msn.com**). The .NET Passport can also be associated with subscriptions you have purchased from Microsoft, such as the paid subscription for the Microsoft Developers Network (MSDN). To use the MSDN subscription and log on to the MSDN site, you must have a .NET Passport to associate with the subscription.

16

16 Log On to Windows

✔ **BEFORE YOU BEGIN**

11 Create a User Account

When you have multiple user accounts on a Windows system, a **Welcome** screen appears after the system boots. Select a user account picture to log that user on to the system. If the account is password protected, the user must enter the password for that account to complete the logon process.

1 Select a User Account

Boot your system. At the **Welcome** screen, click the picture of the account you want to log on to.

▶ NOTE

When a user logs off the system by selecting **Log Off** on the **Start** menu, the **Welcome** screen appears. A new user can then log on without rebooting the system.

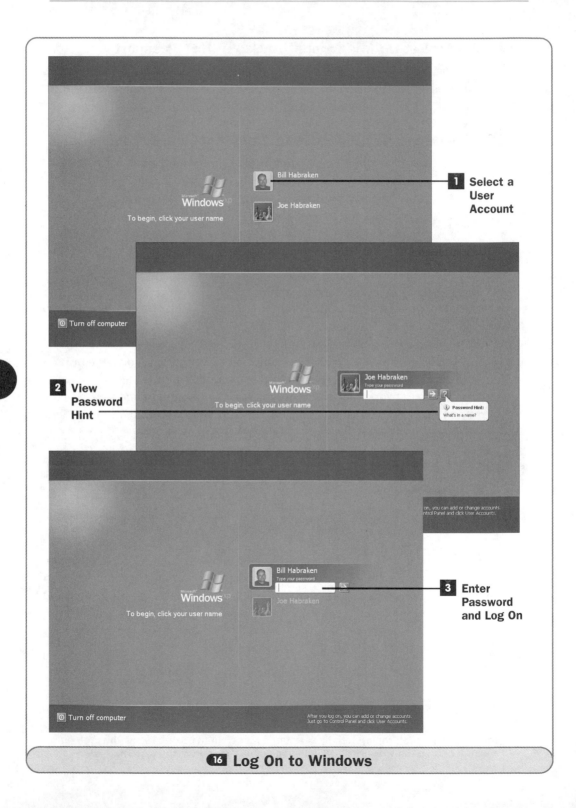

16

1 Select a User Account

2 View Password Hint

3 Enter Password and Log On

16 Log On to Windows

2 View Password Hint

If the selected account has an associated password and you want to view the password hint for the password, click the user account picture. Then click the question-mark icon to the right of the password text box. The hint for your password appears.

3 Enter Password and Log On

Type the password for the user account in the password text box and press **Enter**. Windows verifies the password and then logs you on to the system.

---

17 Switch Users

✔ BEFORE YOU BEGIN

16 Log On to Windows

Logging off the system (using the **Start** menu) makes the system ready for the next user to log on. However, you don't *have* to log off for another user to sign on. In fact, you can leave your applications running (you are, in effect, "parking" your account) and use the **Switch User** feature to allow another user to log on and use the system. This ability to switch users allows multiple users to get on the system without rebooting or shutting down running applications by logging off.

1 Open Log Off Windows Dialog Box

Click the **Start** button and select **Log Off** from the **Start** menu.

2 Select Switch User

In the **Log Off Windows** dialog box that opens, click **Switch User**. The **Logon** screen appears.

▶ **TIP**

Although switching users is a quick way for someone to access the computer without forcing you to close down your applications, having multiple users logged on with multiple applications running does require system resources, meaning that the system will run slower. If you are finished working on the computer and another user wants to use it, log off rather than just switching users.

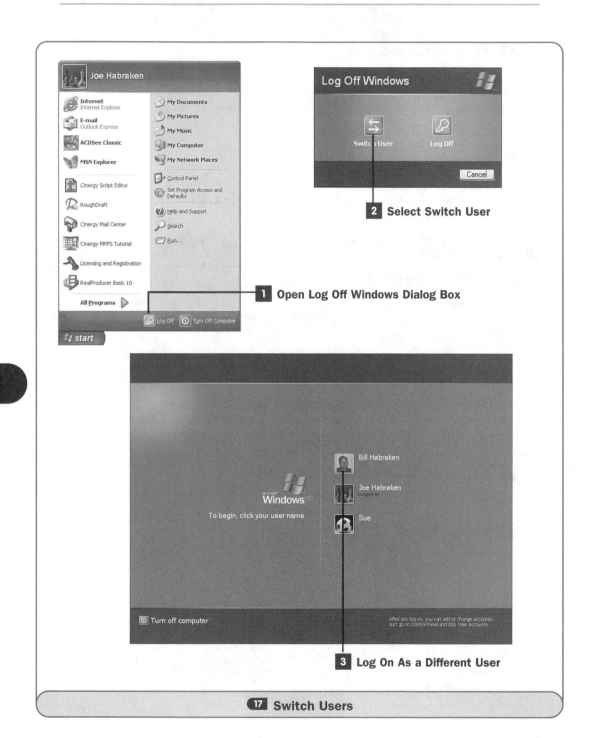

3 Log On As a Different User

The user you are switching to can now log on from the **Logon** screen. He can select an account, enter the appropriate password if necessary, and begin a user session as if he were the only user on the computer. All the applications, files, and settings you left in your account are unaffected by the actions of the second user in the new account.

When you need to switch back to your account, have the second user either log off or choose **Switch User** so that you can log back on to your account and your desktop. Note that, when you do log back on to your account, any applications you left running are still running, any files you left open are still open, and all other aspects of your desktop and system (such as items on the clipboard) are as you left them. In the case of multimedia applications such as Windows Media Player, the application will pause because the control of the computer is switched to the new user.

18 Delete a User Account

✔ BEFORE YOU BEGIN

12 Change the Account Picture
13 Password Protect a User Account

18

You might find it necessary to delete user accounts from the system. Users who have **Computer administrator** accounts can delete any other user account from the computer. Deleting an account removes that user from the system. You can also choose to delete files that were associated with that user account (such as files in the **My Documents** or **My Pictures** folder) or you can choose to have these files remain on the computer (they can be accessed by any of the remaining users on the computer). If you choose to delete the files associated with the user account you are deleting, you cannot recover the files (they are not placed in the **Recycle Bin** as a regular deletion is).

▶ **TIP**

Because administrative accounts can delete other administrative accounts, you might want only one administrative account on the computer in the first place, because then you don't end up with a situation where administrative users start deleting each others' accounts. It really is a "best practice" to have only one administrative account with all other accounts on the computer as limited.

If the computer has only one account (period, no other accounts have been created), there is no option to delete the account. There must be at least one account on the computer (which is why you must set up an account the first time you boot up a Windows XP installation).

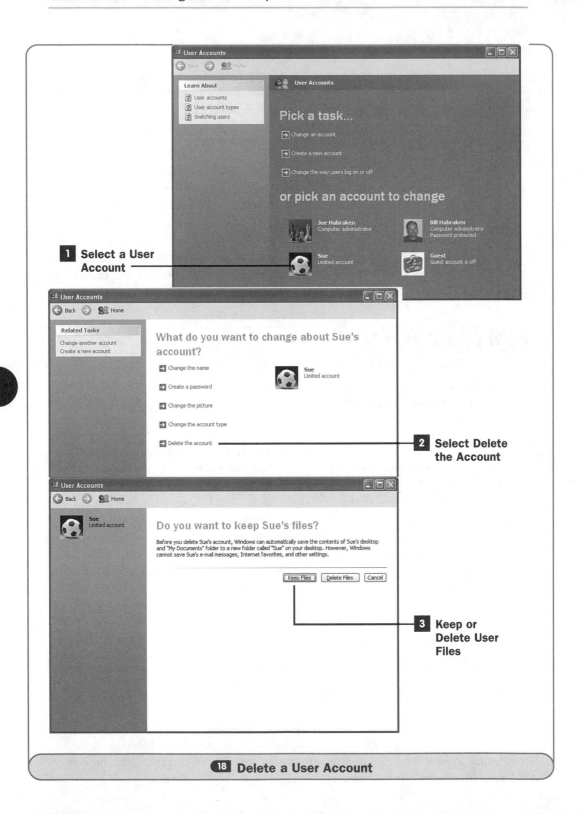

1 Select a User Account

2 Select Delete the Account

3 Keep or Delete User Files

18 Delete a User Account

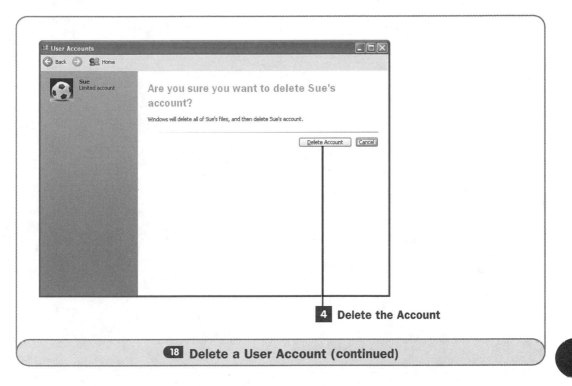

4 Delete the Account

18 Delete a User Account (continued)

18

1 Select a User Account

In the **User Accounts** window (select **User Accounts** in the **Control Panel** to open this window), select the user account you want to delete from the list of accounts at the bottom of the window.

2 Select Delete the Account

From the task list for the selected user account, select the **Delete the account** task.

3 Keep or Delete User Files

When you delete an account, you have the option of either saving the files that are on the user's desktop and in the **My Documents** folder (the files are moved to a folder that is given the same name as the user's account name) or deleting all the account's files when you delete the user account. Click either the **Keep Files** or **Delete Files** button according to your preference.

3 Delete the Account

On the next screen, click **Delete Account**. The selected user account is deleted.

PART II

Creating the Home Network

IN THIS PART

4

Installing and Configuring the Wireless Router

IN THIS CHAPTER:

The first major step in creating a wireless home network that shares a broadband Internet connection is to install and configure the wireless *router*. In this chapter, we look at how to make the various physical connections between the router and the broadband device (such as a cable modem). We will also walk through the basics of configuring the router's wireless and Internet settings.

19   About Installing the Wireless Router

To create a wireless home network that includes a connection to a broadband Internet connection, you need a wireless *router*. The router serves as the intermediary or gateway between the device supplying the broadband Internet connection (such as a DSL router or a cable modem) and your home network, which consists of the computers that want to use the Internet. The wireless router also serves as the WiFi *access point* for the computers on the network that are outfitted with wireless *network adapters*. Computers that have "wired" network cards can also be attached to the *switch* ports on the wireless router, allowing these wired computers to participate on the same network and access the high-speed Internet connection.

19

▶ KEY TERMS

Hub—A connectivity device that provides multiple LAN ports. Computers can be connected to these LAN ports using network cabling. Typically, a hub is considered a "dumb" connectivity device and cannot sense the connection type or switch connection speeds (say between 10 Mbps and 100 Mbps, if that is supported by the network adapters on the computers).

Switch—A more intelligent connectivity device than a hub that allows computers to connect to the network using cables. Ports on the switch autosense the connection speed. Higher-end switches also typically provide capabilities for adjusting the actual throughput (the amount of bandwidth available) on a particular LAN port, allowing certain computers or other devices more network bandwidth.

The switch built into most WiFi routers available today is a high-speed connectivity device that allows a range of connection speeds for computers that are directly connected to the switch by network cables. Most WiFi router switches provide both regular and fast Ethernet connections (10 Mbps and 100 Mbps respectively). The switch is autosensing, so it recognizes when a computer that has a fast Ethernet network card (100 Mbps) is attached to the switch and supplies the appropriate connection speed. Because many of the WiFi routers available for home networking provide only four LAN ports on the switch, you might have to buy an additional switch if you are going to attach more than four computers to the WiFi router using network cables. Make sure that the switch you purchase is autosensing and that it supports both regular and Fast Ethernet connections. Such a switch should accommodate all the computers on your network, regardless of the age of the computer and the speed of the network cards.

▶ **TIP**

Connectivity devices used for connecting wired computers to the network are often confusingly referred to by more than one name. A *hub* is a connectivity device with LAN ports. Hubs are typically inexpensive (when compared to switches) and they typically do not have the ability to switch connection speeds based on the type of network interface card installed in the computer (Ethernet versus Fast Ethernet). A *switch*, on the other hand, is considered a more "intelligent" device because it can autosense and adjust the connection speed. To make things more confusing, companies such as Linksys now sell a device they call an *autosensing hub*, which "autosenses" connection speed and uplinks to other connectivity devices (such as a WiFi router). The bottom line is that you want to purchase a device that can be connected to the WiFi router to expand the number of LAN ports. But you also want the LAN ports to be autosensing so that you can use regular CAT 5 cable for the connection and also take advantage of the maximum speed available through each computer's network adapter. Do a little research on hubs and switches before making your purchase.

In terms of determining the actual placement (location) of your WiFi router, keep in mind some issues such as the fact that the WiFi router needs to connect to the Internet broadband device using a network cable. You must install the router in close-enough proximity to the broadband cable modem or DSL router so that they can be physically cabled together using a CAT 5 networking cable. This cable is typically provided with the wireless router. However, the cable provided is typically less than 5 feet long, so if the wireless router is positioned farther than that from the broadband device, you will have to purchase a longer CAT 5 cable. Although we call the WiFi router a "wireless device," it still must be physically attached to your broadband Internet connection device and any computers that must be wired (physically connected) to the switch on the WiFi router.

▶ **TIP**

The CAT 5 network cabling you use for your home network takes advantage of a *star topology*. Each device (computer) connected by cable to your wireless router's switch is an arm of the star (the router is the center of the star). This topology is particularly efficient because if a cable goes bad between the router and a computer, only the single computer is affected. CAT 5 cable can have a maximum length of 328 feet. This maximum length relates to the degradation of the actual signal over the cable run.

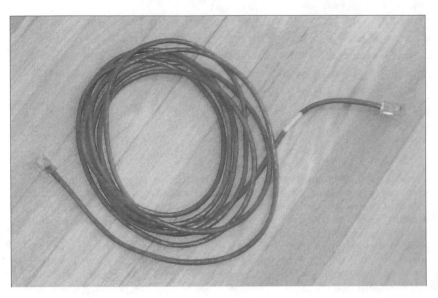

CAT 5 networking cable is used to connect the wireless router and the broadband device.

19

Where you position the wireless router in the home is also very important, because the indoor ranges for the radio transmissions between the router and the wireless-enabled computers is only 150 to 300 feet. This range is also affected by the materials used in the home's construction. A typical wood-frame house should provide decent wireless ranges in all parts of the home and typically onto patios and decks. However, a home with poured concrete floors and other "heavy-duty" construction materials might greatly reduce the range and can even determine whether the computers can access the wireless services. So, the ranges that you experience will depend on the construction materials and layout of your particular home.

In the final analysis, the location of your broadband Internet connection device (such as a cable modem), the location of computers to be directly cabled to the WiFi router, and the overall size and layout of your home will affect where you should place the router. The WiFi router is really an excellent bridge between your wired computers, your WiFi-enabled computers, and your Internet connection.

One other point we should discuss is the need for at least one computer to be physically connected to the router with network cabling. This wired computer is used to configure and monitor the wireless router (although you can enable access to the router over the Web for router configuration and monitoring purposes). To repeat, you must have at least one computer with a traditional network card that is physically connected to the WiFi router. This physical connection to the router actually enhances security in terms of who can access and configure the router (the one computer with the physical connection). It makes the most sense to locate this computer in the same room as the WiFi router (and the Internet connection device such as a DSL router) so that you aren't faced with snaking cables all over the place, which was most likely one of the reasons you wanted to go wireless in the first place.

▶ **NOTE**

You are probably installing a wireless network because cabling is not an option or you have tried to physically connect computers and other devices using network cables and have found it to be a nightmare of tangled cables running in and out of your rooms (not to mention how ugly it can be). Connecting a computer to the wireless router when the devices are in the same room is fairly easy in most cases and doesn't create a "tripping" hazard. For other computers in the home that have traditional network adapters that require CAT 5 cables, you can either replace the network adapter with a wireless adapter or you can buy one of the easy-to-install USB wireless adapters for those computers.

As far as best practices go for connecting all these devices and keeping your home uncluttered by network cabling, I suggest that you designate a room as the home office. This room should be the location where your broadband Internet connection device is located, where the WiFi router is located, and also where the computer that is directly connected to the WiFi router's switch via LAN cables is located. This means that only one room in your home requires network cabling; the other computers in the home can be outfitted with WiFi adapters (eliminating the need for additional LAN cables). If this home office location can also be somewhat centrally located, you have an excellent setup for your new WiFi network. Even if the home office is not centrally located, you should still get good WiFi connectivity in most homes.

19

▶ **TIP**

Although broadband connections from cable providers such as Time Warner and DSL connections from the various "baby Bells" such as Verizon are the most common high-speed Internet connections provided to homes and small offices, satellite broadband connections are also possible (from satellite providers such as Starband). Satellite broadband uses a "satellite modem" as the connection point in the home (it doesn't look that different from other broadband devices such as DSL routers and cable modems), and the satellite modem connects directly to your satellite dish (which is typically on the roof of your home). You will plug your WiFi router into the satellite modem using an Ethernet CAT 5 cable (just like you would do for a DSL router or cable modem). The problem with some satellite services is that they offer different types of modems, so you must make sure that the company installs an Ethernet-compatible satellite modem in your home, which can then be connected to your WiFi router. Also be advised that some two-way satellite broadband connections are actually degraded by the attachment of a WiFi router to the satellite modem. Check with your satellite service provider when planning your home WiFi network and before purchasing your WiFi router and other equipment.

In most cases, one WiFi router can accommodate all the wireless and wired computers on your home network—10 computers or fewer. Because Windows workgroup networking is designed for 10 or fewer computers, 10 is certainly the maximum for this type of home peer-to-peer networking. In cases where you are experiencing WiFi "dead zones" in certain parts of your home, you have a couple of choices: You can purchase a new WiFi router with multiple antennas (hopefully, you can return your current router for a refund) such as the Linksys WAP54GX Wireless-G Access Point, which can extend connection ranges and diminish dead zones. Another fix for a weak WiFi signal is to purchase a range extender such as the Netgear Wireless G Range Extender wall plug. This device plugs into any electrical outlet and extends and strengthens the WiFi signal. In the rarest of cases, you might have to add an additional **access point** to the network. Consider this option if you feel that traffic on the single WiFi router's access point is slowing network access, particularly in high-demand times such as when online gaming is taking place over the network. Again, most homes will not require an additional access point. Understand that the access point does not provide the gateway and router capabilities of the WiFi router, but it does provide another way to extend the range of the network. You will need a second access point in only the rarest of situations. The secondary access points connect wirelessly to the main wireless router so that computers in distant reaches of the home or office can "piggy back" to the main router. You configure the auxiliary access point the same way you configure the access point on the router, meaning that you use the same SSID and other settings.

19

When you have decided where you are going to place the wireless router, you can install it. After the router is installed (meaning physically placed and connected), you can configure the basic settings on the router. Installing the router requires that you shut down your broadband modem (the Internet connection will be unavailable). You should also power down all the computers currently on the network, such as those connected to a switch or a hub that connects to your broadband device. In a nutshell, *shut everything down* to begin the installation process.

You need at least two CAT 5 Ethernet network cables to create the necessary connections for your wireless network: You will connect the wireless router to the cable modem or DSL router. You will also connect one computer to the wireless router (allowing you to access and configure the router). One network cable typically comes with the wireless router. And because you already have a broadband connection to at least one computer, there will be an appropriate cable running from the broadband device to the computer that you can use.

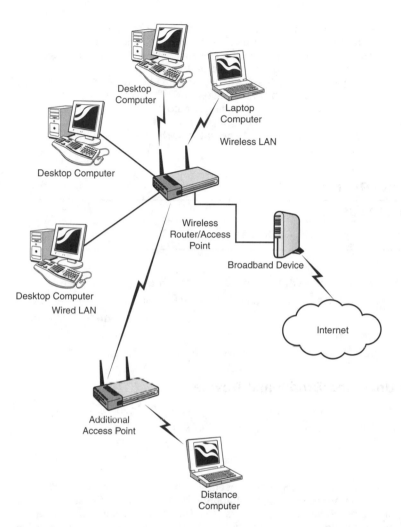

Desktop Computer

Laptop Computer

Wireless LAN

Desktop Computer

Desktop Computer

Wired LAN

Wireless Router/Access Point

Broadband Device

Internet

19

Additional Access Point

Distance Computer

A wireless router allows you to create a home network that includes wired and wireless computers.

▶ TIP

If you are going to connect additional computers or another device such as a hub or switch to the wireless router, you will need additional networking cables. The Ethernet ports on most wireless routers are autosensing, meaning that the port is correctly configured for the device that is connected to the port. You can use "regular" CAT 5 Ethernet cable whether you are connecting a computer or another switch to the wireless router. You should not need to purchase crossover cables to connect the router to switches and hubs (most hubs have an uplink port). However, some older hubs may require a crossover cable to connect from a LAN port on the hub to the WiFi router's switch. A crossover cable looks just like a regular CAT 5 cable (although some companies make their cross-over cables yellow in color so that you know it's a cross-over cable; the cable will also be stamped with the name "patch cord"). A crossover cable is different from a regular LAN cable in that the four pairs of wires in the RJ-45 connectors at the ends of the cable are "crossed over" (rearranged) in the crossover cable; the wires run "straight through" in a regular CAT 5 LAN cable. Make sure that you read the documentation for your existing connectivity devices (such as switches or hubs) before purchasing any additional cables. Because most older hubs are designed for 10Mbps Ethernet, it may make sense to replace them with new switches that supply autosensing ports and 100Mbps throughput, and require no special cables or other considerations. We are talking less than 50 dollars for a four-port switch, so it is probably worth the investment.

20 Install the Router

✔ BEFORE YOU BEGIN

19 About Installing the Wireless Router

After you have unpacked the wireless *router* and taken a quick look at the installation instructions, you are ready to install the router. Installation is really a matter of connecting the router to your broadband device (a cable modem or DSL router) and then powering up the wireless router. You can then access the wireless router by connecting a computer directly to the router.

19

1 Power Down the Broadband Device

Turn off your cable modem or DSL router. This might involve unplugging the broadband device (many do not have on/off switches).

▶ NOTE

Unplugging the broadband device, in effect, resets the device. Because the broadband device keeps track of information such as IP address "leases" (the addresses that have been temporarily assigned) for your computers, it is important to clear this information before setting up the wireless router, which will actually take over the duty of assigning IP addresses to the wireless and wired computers on your network.

2 Connect Wireless Router to Broadband Device

Connect the wireless router to the broadband device using a CAT 5 UTP cable (in most cases included with the router). Plug the cable into the wireless router in the Ethernet port designated for "Internet."

▶ NOTE

No matter what brand of wireless router you are using, a port on the router will be designated for the Internet connection, which is the connection between the broadband device and the wireless router. Other ports on the wireless router are often labeled as "LAN" ports and are used to directly connect computers or other network devices to the router.

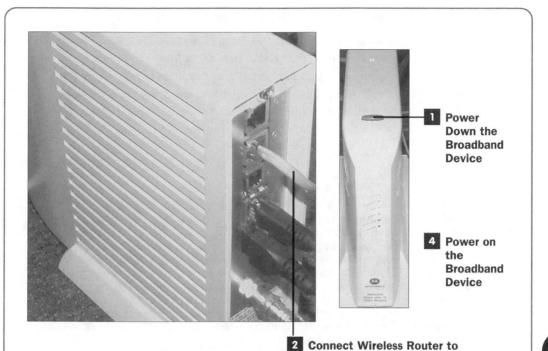

1 Power Down the Broadband Device

4 Power on the Broadband Device

2 Connect Wireless Router to Broadband Device

5 Power on the Router

3 Connect Computer to Wireless Router

3 Connect Computer to Wireless Router

Physically connect a computer (either a laptop or desktop computer) by running a cable from the computer's internal *network adapter* to the wireless router using one of the router's LAN ports. This computer, which is now "hard-wired" to the WiFi router, will serve as the administrator's console for configuring and monitoring the WiFi router. It is also the computer you will use to initially communicate with the router and create the router's configuration using the setup CD or DVD that shipped with your WiFi router.

▶ NOTE

You really should have a computer on the network with a "wired" LAN adapter so that you can initially configure the WiFi router's access point. If you don't have a wired computer on the network, borrow a laptop with a wired LAN adapter. Set up the WiFi router using the setup CD. You can then configure the router so that it can be accessed by any computer on the network using a web browser. However, this approach isn't as secure as having a "hard" cable connection to the router. If you already have a broadband modem in your home (before you decide to go WiFi), it is connected to at least one computer with a "wired" LAN connection. Use this computer to configure the router. For a computer that is not directly connected to the router by a wired connection to configure the router, you must turn on web access to the router, which opens up the router to the possibility of attack from outside the network.

20

4 Power on the Broadband Device

Turn on or reconnect the broadband device to the power source. Wait 2 to 3 minutes to allow the broadband device to communicate with your ISP and connect to the Internet. Make sure that all the ready lights are on the broadband device (particularly the Internet connection light, which is often labeled as "Online").

5 Power on the Router

Plug the wireless router into a power source. Watch the indicator lights on the front of the router. When you see activity on the **Internet** indicator and the **LAN** port connected to your PC, you have completed the installation of the wireless router and are ready to configure the basic settings for the router.

▶ TIP

If you don't get an activity light for your Internet indicator on the WiFi router, check the cable connection between the router and the broadband device (such as a cable modem). If the connection is okay, reverse the cable anyway because sometimes this activity forces you to better connect the cable connectors into the appropriate ports on the devices. Your cable modem (or other connectivity device) will also show an Internet connection light; if this isn't on, shut down the broadband device *and* the WiFi router and repeat the steps in this task. Also check the power connection on the WiFi router. If you have LAN connectivity problems, check the LAN cable between the computer and the WiFi router's switch. For problems other than the obvious, check out **91** **About Network Connection Problems** and **93** **Use Router Diagnostics.**

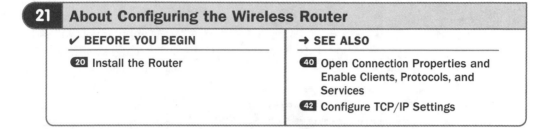

21 **About Configuring the Wireless Router**

✔ BEFORE YOU BEGIN	→ SEE ALSO
20 Install the Router	**40** Open Connection Properties and Enable Clients, Protocols, and Services **42** Configure TCP/IP Settings

When you have powered on the wireless *router* and confirmed that it is "talking" to your broadband device (that is, all the lights are on), you are ready to configure the basic settings of the router. Most wireless routers are configured from the factory with the wireless connectivity turned off. This means that you have to turn on the router's wireless connectivity during the initial configuration. During the initial configuration, you can also change (and should change) the wireless network name or *SSID* (service set identifier), which identifies your wireless network.

▶ **KEY TERM**

SSID (service set identifier)—A unique identifier (32 characters maximum) used to differentiate one WLAN from another. Devices attempting to connect to a particular WLAN must use the SSID configured for that WLAN.

▶ **NOTE**

The default SSID for most wireless routers is the name of the company that makes the router. For example, on a Linksys router, the default SSID is **LINKSYS**. On the Netgear wireless router I used to explain the basic configuration and setup of a router in **20** **Install the Router**, the default SSID was **NETGEAR**.

The two basic sets of configuration options that you will deal with relate to your Internet connection (such as the IP address used by the wireless router) and the wireless network (options such as the SSID name and the network mode). These initial settings can often be configured using a setup wizard that is on a CD or DVD included with the wireless router. In most cases, you have the option of configuring the wireless router without the wizard by connecting to the router using your web browser.

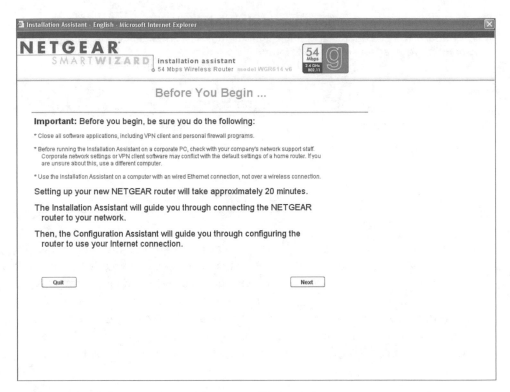

Almost all wireless routers provide a setup CD that helps you to connect to the router.

▶ **TIP**

Make sure that the computer attached to the wireless router is configured to receive its IP address and other TCP/IP settings from the wireless router via DHCP. In the **TCP/IP Properties** dialog box for the computer's network adapter, the **Obtain an IP address automatically** option and the **Obtain DNS server address** option should both be selected.

A URL is provided in your wireless router's documentation that allows you to access the router from the computer connected (via the LAN cable) to the router. For example, the URL for my Netgear router is **http://www.routerlogin.net/ basicsetting.htm**. The documentation for my router also provided a logon name of **admin** and a password of **password**. When you have logged on to the router (either using a wizard provided by the router's setup CD or by using the URL), you can access the various settings using links provided on the various web pages associated with the router's configuration.

22 Access Router Configuration

✔ BEFORE YOU BEGIN

21 About Configuring the Wireless Router

To configure the wireless router, you must access the router. You do this from the computer that is directly connected to the wireless router by a network cable. After the initial configuration, you can later access the router using the computer's web browser, such as Internet Explorer.

After you access the router, it makes sense to turn on WiFi access so that computers on the network can connect to the WiFi router's access point. It also makes sense to allow *SSID* broadcasts (the WiFi network name is broadcast by the router), which makes it easier for you to configure the WiFi-enabled computers that will connect to the router's access point.

▶ **NOTE**

Although network security might not be one of your major worries in relation to your home network, it is definitely a "best practice" to turn off SSID broadcasts after the WiFi network is up and running. See 75 **turn Off Server Set IDs (SSIDs) Broadcasts** for information on how to turn off SSID broadcasts.

1 Enter URL for Wireless Router

In your web browser (such as Internet Explorer), type the URL provided by your wireless router manufacturer (look in the quickstart documentation that came with the router) in the **Address** text box and click **Go**. A security dialog box opens.

2 Enter Username and Password

Enter the username and the password provided in your router documentation (again, you will probably find this information in the quickstart materials shipped with the router). Click **OK**. The router manager window opens in the browser window.

▶ **TIP**

If you want to make it easier to connect to the router in the future, select the **Remember my password** check box in the security dialog box.

22

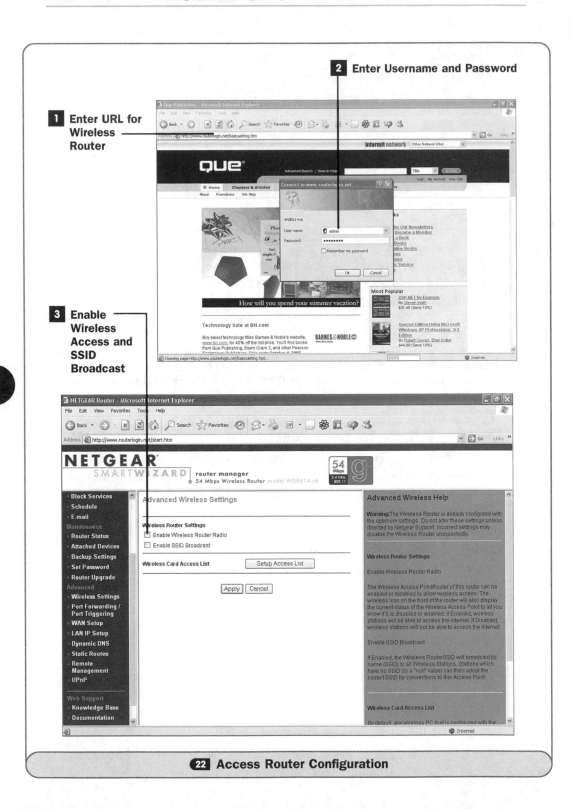

1 Enter URL for Wireless Router

2 Enter Username and Password

3 Enable Wireless Access and SSID Broadcast

22

22 Access Router Configuration

3 Enable Wireless Access and SSID Broadcast

Select the **Wireless Settings** option on your WiFi router's configuration page. For my Netgear WiFi router, I click **Wireless Settings** under the **Advanced** heading on the left side of the browser window. I then click **Enable Wireless Router Radio** and **Enable SSID Broadcast** to turn on WiFi networking and to allow the WiFi router to broadcast the network SSID. The names of the options you choose might vary depending on the configuration software and WiFi router you are using, but you should definitely enable these two settings, whatever they're called, at this point.

▶ **NOTE**

You will find that the web pages used to access the wireless router's configuration are fairly similar regardless of what brand of router you are using. The interface is typically simple and easy to work with as you configure or monitor the router.

---

23 | **About Internet Settings**

✔ **BEFORE YOU BEGIN**

21 About Configuring the Wireless Router
22 Access Router Configuration

23

The wireless *router*'s Internet settings are essential; they must be entered correctly so that the wireless router can connect to the broadband device and ultimately to your ISP that provides your Internet connection. You should have the following information (it was provided to you by your ISP when you signed up with the service) at the ready to configure the router's Internet settings:

- **Login Name and Password**—If your service provider requires you to log in to access the Internet, your ISP should have provided you with a login and password. These settings must be entered into the router configuration to access the Internet. This logon name and password are not the same as the logon name and password you use to access the WiFi router through your web browser. You must get this special logon and password from your Internet service provider.

▶ **NOTE**

Some ISPs might also provide you with a service name to access the Internet. You will also need this information to configure the wireless router. Call your ISP's help desk before configuring the WiFi router so that you can gather the information necessary to configure the router correctly.

- **IP Address and Subnet Mask**—If your ISP has provided you with a static IP address, you will need the address with which you were provided. Otherwise, you will configure the wireless router so that it gets its IP address and other TCP/IP settings dynamically.

- **DNS Server Names**—Some ISPs require you to configure the router so that it knows the IP addresses of your primary and secondary DNS name servers. Otherwise, this information is configured dynamically.

Make sure that you jot all this information down on a piece of paper so that you can configure the router when you access the configuration utility. In situations where you don't need a logon name (and password) and receive your IP address and other TCP/IP settings dynamically through your ISP's DHCP server, you won't need any of this information, which makes the router configuration extremely straightforward.

As with any of the router and wireless network adapter settings that we discuss, the actual settings vary from device to device. However, you will find that the router configuration utilities for various vendors' wireless routers are very similar in terms of how settings are grouped on the configuration screens.

24

24	**Configure Internet Settings**

✔ **BEFORE YOU BEGIN**

22 Access Router Configuration
23 About Internet Settings

In **22** **Access Router Configuration**, you learned how to open the main configuration settings screen for your wireless *router*. Depending on the router you are configuring, you might find the Internet settings located under the **Basic settings** category (as is the case with Netgear routers) because Internet settings are essential to the router providing your network with an Internet connection. However, you might find the Internet settings located in their own category (for example, you might access them using a link named **Internet settings**).

If you are uncomfortable configuring these settings yourself, use the setup CD that came with your WiFi router. It guides you through the basic configuration of the router. The CD should be placed in the computer that is directly connected to the WiFi router by a LAN cable.

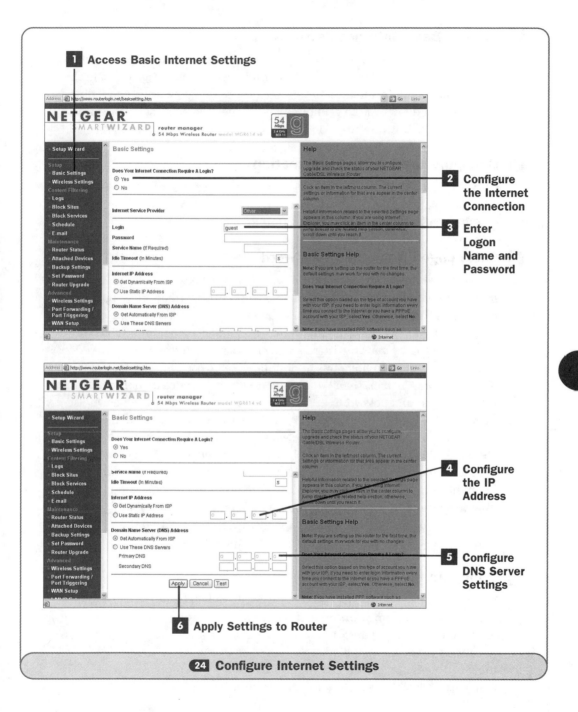

1 **Access Basic Internet Settings**

2 Configure the Internet Connection

3 Enter Logon Name and Password

4 Configure the IP Address

5 Configure DNS Server Settings

6 Apply Settings to Router

24 Configure Internet Settings

1 Access Basic Internet Settings

Connect to the wireless router using your computer's web browser (enter the URL for the router and provide the login and password you were given in the router's quickstart documentation). In the browser window, select the settings category that allows you to configure the Internet-related settings for the router (such as **Basic Settings** on a Netgear router).

2 Configure the Internet Connection

Click the option button that best describes your Internet connection. For example, on a Netgear router, you click either **Yes** or **No** in answer to the question **Does Your Internet Connection Require a Login?**

3 Enter Logon Name and Password

If you selected **No** in step 2, continue with step 4; otherwise, enter your login name and password in the appropriate boxes. This information was provided to you by your ISP when you initially signed up for the service. It is not the same as the router logon and password. Check the documentation that was provided to you by your Internet service provider or call the ISP's support desk to make sure that you have this information. Be advised that most broadband providers such as Time Warner's Road Runner service do not require an Internet logon and password. In the Internet service provider drop-down list, there are three choices: **Other**, **PPTP**, and **Telstra Bigpond**. In the United States, make sure that **Other** is selected, which is the most common type of ISP connection used (it is actually PPPoE, which is the point-to-point protocol used to connect to the Internet service provider). If you are in Austria, you might have to select **PPTP** (another software protocol for connecting to the Internet). If you are in Australia, you might have to select **Telstra Bigpond**. Again, talk to your Internet service provider before configuring the WiFi router to make sure that you have the appropriate information.

4 Configure the IP Address

Whether you get your IP address automatically (it will be the IP address for the WiFi router), from your Internet service provider using DHCP, or are assigned a static IP address depends on your ISP. If you use a static IP address to connect to the Internet (which was supplied to you when you signed up for the ISP's Internet service), enter the IP address in the appropriate boxes. Otherwise, select the **Get Dynamically from ISP** option.

24

▶ **NOTE**

If you are wondering how the computers (wireless and wired) get their IP addresses if the router is using your only static IP address, don't be concerned. The wireless router acts as a DHCP server and provides your network computers with IP addresses and other TCP/IP information. The IP addresses are actually taken from a private range of IP addresses designed to be used with private networks such as the one you are setting up.

5 Configure DNS Server Settings

If you get your IP address automatically through DHCP, the WiFi router also receives the primary and secondary DNS server addresses automatically. However, if you use a static IP address assigned by your ISP, you must also enter the IP addresses of your primary and secondary DNS servers (the ISP's DNS servers) in the appropriate boxes. Otherwise, select the **Get Automatically from ISP** option.

Before you attempt to configure the WiFi router, look through the documentation you received when you signed up for Internet service with your ISP. If you don't have all the information you need, call the ISP's help desk. They will probably tell you that they can set up your WiFi network for a fee. Graciously refuse this offer. Ask them to provide you with the following information:

- Do I need a logon name and password to connect to the Internet? Yes or no? If yes, what is my logon and password?

- Do I get my IP address dynamically? Yes or no? If no, what is my IP address and what are the IP addresses of the primary and secondary DNS servers maintained by the ISP?

6 Apply Settings to Router

After entering the required information, click the **Apply** button (or the button that saves the router confirmation for your particular router). Your wireless router is now set up to access the Internet using your ISP and the broadband connection device to which the router is connected.

24

25 | **About Wireless Settings**

✔ BEFORE YOU BEGIN	→ SEE ALSO
21 About Configuring the Wireless Router	**76** About 802.11 Security Strategies
22 Access Router Configuration	**77** Configure Wired Equivalent Privacy (WEP) Security
	78 Configure WiFi Protected Access (WPA) Security
	40 Open Connection Properties and Enable Clients, Protocols, and Services

In **24** **Configure Internet Settings**, you provided information so that the wireless *router* can access the Internet using the broadband connection device (the cable or DSL modem). The other basic configuration options you should set before you log on to the router for the first time are the router's wireless settings. These settings include the network name (its *SSID*), the region in which the network is located (such as United States), the router's channel (the frequency at which the router will operate), and the type of WLAN modes (802.11g and 802.11b) that the router supports.

25

▶ **NOTE**

If your network includes computers using 802.11b network adapters, they can communicate with the wireless router as long as you configure the router to support this earlier wireless mode.

It is certainly a best practice to change the SSID (service set identifier) on your wireless router. When I am playing around with my wireless notebook computer, you would be surprised at how many wireless networks I can "see" in my neighborhood that have names such as **LINKSYS** or **NETGEAR**. Although having a unique SSID for your router doesn't really provide any security in terms of people accessing your wireless network, it is a good first step in configuring your wireless router so that your network users can easily attach to your WiFi network by name (SSID). The unique name doesn't ensure security; however, you can turn off SSID broadcasts so that your WiFi network name isn't broadcast to "outsiders" scanning for WiFi networks. With no broadcasts, the unique SSID does help secure the network because someone trying to connect to your network from the "outside" can't easily guess the SSID.

Depending on your particular router, the wireless configuration screen might include settings for the router's wireless security settings. **70** **About Basic Network Security** is an introduction to wireless router security. Any security settings you configure on the router must also be configured on each computer that connects to the network with a wireless adapter (otherwise, the computer cannot connect to the network). A simple security measure such as turning off SSID broadcasts actually "hides" your WiFi network from people scanning for available WiFi connections. More complex security measures such as Wired Equivalent Privacy (WEP) or WiFi Protected Access (WPA) use encryption and other strategies for securing your WiFi network.

---

26 Configure Router Wireless Settings

✔ BEFORE YOU BEGIN

22 Access Router Configuration
25 About Wireless Settings

In **22** **Access Router Configuration**, you learned how to open your wireless *router*'s configuration settings screen. In **24** **Configure Internet Settings**, you provided information so that the wireless *router* can access the Internet using the broadband connection device (the cable or DSL modem). In addition to the Internet settings, you should set up the wireless settings for the router the first time you access the configuration settings. You can change these settings as needed in the future. In some cases, you might have to try different channel settings for the router because the wireless router might interfere with any digital telephones you use in the home or office that might be running on the same frequency. (Yes, that's right: The router can interfere with your telephone reception.)

1 Access Wireless Settings

Connect to the wireless router using your computer's web browser (enter the URL for the router and provide the login ID and password for the router's administrative account—my Netgear router uses **Admin** and **password**). In the browser window, select the settings category that allows you to configure the wireless settings for the router (such as **Wireless Settings** on a Netgear router).

▶ NOTE

Some wireless routers such as those made by Netgear provide a **Test** button, located on the various configuration screens. Click the **Test** button to test the settings you've entered to see whether they work before you apply and save them to the router.

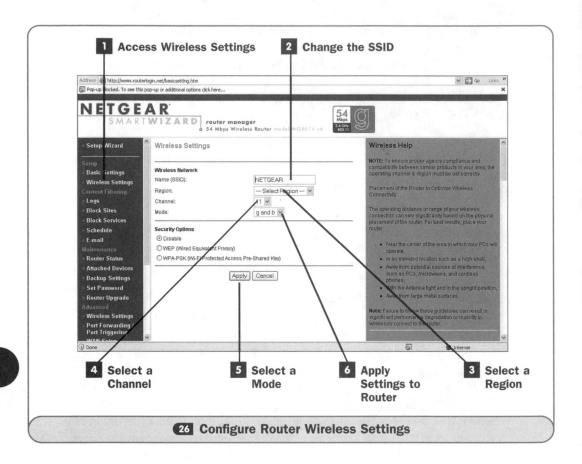

26 Configure Router Wireless Settings

2 Change the SSID

Enter the new name for your wireless network in the *SSID* box. The name can be up to 32 characters. Network names are case sensitive, so keep this in mind when creating the new name. To easily identify the network for your users (and not to be confused by someone in your neighborhood who happens to detect your WiFi network), select a name that is descriptive. For example, for my home WiFi network, I might want to use the SSID **habrakenwifi** or **habraken-family**. If you feel that you need a more "cryptic" name to avoid the possibility of an outsider guessing the SSID and connecting to your network, create an appropriate name as needed.

▶ NOTE

SSID broadcasts from the WiFi router's *access point* can be turned off. The SSID broadcast is nothing more than the router announcing over the configured radio channel that your WiFi network exists. Turning off the broadcast negates other folks, such as nearby neighbors or someone parked on the street, from scanning for your network. See **75** **Configure Turn Off Set IDs (SSIDs) Broadcasts** for information on how to turn off SSID broadcasts.

3 **Select a Region**

You must specify a region for the router. Click the **Region** drop-down list and select the appropriate region (for example, I selected **United States**). Selecting a region does not actually have any functional purpose (the router's access point will work even if you choose the wrong region). However, it is required by law in the United States that you specify your region as **United States**. In the United States, even the "public" spectrum of radio signals is controlled and regulated by the Federal Communication Commission (FCC) and federal law. Outside the United States, laws vary, so selecting the appropriate region such as **Mexico** or **South America** is really just verification by you that you understand that the public radio spectrum may or may not be managed by a governmental agency in your region.

4 **Select a Channel**

The channel is the frequency range that the wireless router uses to communicate with wireless-enabled computers. A default value is typically provided by the router's manufacturer. Change the value as needed using the **Channel** drop-down list, particularly if you are experiencing interference with home telephones or other wireless digital devices. In most cases, you can go with the default. Remember that all WiFi-enabled computers must be configured to use the same radio signal channel that you set on the router. See **33** **Configure Adapter and Connect to the Wireless Router** for more information.

▶ **NOTE**

When you scan for available WiFi networks using a WiFi-enabled computer, the computer cycles through all the available radio channels looking for SSIDs or WiFi network names. When you connect to the WiFi network using the SSID (or name), the channel is set automatically on the WiFi network adapter on the computer. When you turn off SSID broadcasts, you can't connect to the WiFi access point by scanning for the SSID. In that case, WiFi network adapters on network computers must be configured with the same SSID and radio channel that was configured on the WiFi router.

5 **Select a Mode**

Click the **Mode** drop-down list (or a similar option name on your router's configuration screen) to set the modes your router will support. In most cases, the setting of **g and b** is the default and supports both 802.11g and 802.11b devices.

6 **Apply Settings to Router**

After configuring the wireless settings for the router, click the **Apply** button to save the router's configuration.

▶ **TIP**

When you have finished configuring the router, you should log off the router. Select the **Logoff** link on your router's configuration screen (the name of this link varies from router to router). On my Netgear WiFi router configuration screen, I must scroll all the way to the bottom of the browser window and then select **Logoff** on the left side of the screen. Logging off is better than just closing the browser window.

26

5

Installing and Configuring Wireless Adapters

IN THIS CHAPTER:

A WiFi **network adapter** allows a computer to participate on a wireless network. In this chapter, we take a look at wireless network adapters and how to install and configure an adapter so that it communicates with your wireless router.

27 About Wireless Network Adapters

For a computer to communicate on a wired or wireless network, the computer must be outfitted with a **network adapter**. The network adapter provides the connection between the computer and the network's data transfer medium. On a wired network, the medium is typically copper CAT 5 wire. On a wireless network, the medium is a radio signal.

The network adapter, whether it is wired or wireless, is responsible for taking the data from your computer and converting it into a form (a single stream of data) that can be moved over the network medium. Network adapters actually contain a transceiver (transmitter/receiver), which allows for the conversion and sending of data and also for the receiving and conversion of data (the data is converted when it is received so that it can be processed by the computer).

27

▶ **NOTE**

Data travels in parallel on your computer, much like traffic on a multi-lane highway. When data is transmitted onto the network by a network adapter, such as a WiFi network adapter, the data must be converted from parallel to serial by the adapter. Metaphorically speaking, this is like taking traffic on a multi-lane highway and funneling it down to a single-lane road.

Wireless network adapters can be added to a notebook or desktop computer (if an open expansion slot is available). Most new notebook computers come with a WiFi adapter already installed, and most computer manufacturers provide a WiFi adapter option (which often costs you a little more) for the desktop computers they sell. See **28** **Determine Upgradeability of Current Computers** for more information about whether your current computer can support a wireless network adapter.

▶ **NOTE**

PC processor manufacturers such as Intel and AMD have developed computer processors (the brain of the computer) for notebook computers that are tightly integrated with mobile technology features such as WiFi network adapters. For example, Intel offers Centrino Mobile technology and AMD provides AMD Turion 64 Mobile technology. Any notebook computer that you buy displaying the logo of either of these mobile technologies has been specifically designed for WiFi networking.

In terms of choices related to adding a WiFi adapter to your current computer, you can add a WiFi adapter to an expansion slot or you can use an external WiFi adapter that connects to a USB port on your computer. The best and easiest way to go is to add a USB external WiFi adapter to the computer. Even older computers (including those as old as six or eight years) typically have at least one USB port.

In terms of adding a WiFi adapter to an expansion slot on your computer, the add-on WiFi adapter for a notebook computer varies a great deal from the WiFi adapter that you would add to a desktop computer. Notebook computers typically provide at least one PCMCIA (Personal Computer Memory Card International Association) expansion slot that is used to add items such as network adapters (such as a WiFi card). Upgrading a notebook is a matter of sliding a small (PCMCIA) expansion card into the appropriate expansion slot.

▶ TIP

Notebook computers come with one of three types of PCMCIA slots: Type 1, Type 2, or Type 3. Each of these slot types is specific to a card type. Check your notebook documentation to determine the type of slot on your computer. Most WiFi network adapters are Type 2 cards, and most notebook computers provide either a Type 2 slot or a PCMCIA slot that can accommodate multiple card types such as both Type 1 and Type 2. The newest generation of PCMCIA adapter cards for notebooks are typically referred to as CardBus cards.

27

Desktop computers (including towers) typically provide one or more PCI expansion slots. The Peripheral Component Interconnect (PCI) slot is an expansion slot on the motherboard of a desktop or tower computer and is the standard expansion slot type for Intel-compatible motherboards (the main circuit board for the computer). Upgrading a desktop computer requires that you open the case and install the network adapter in an open PCI slot. As already mentioned, most desktop/tower computers provide a minimum of one or two PCI slots. If you haven't added any peripherals such as a new sound card or video adapter to your computer, you probably have a slot for your adapter card. However, you can be sure only by opening the case and examining the motherboard for available slots.

Because both notebook computers and desktop/tower computers have USB ports, either type of computer can be upgraded to WiFi using an external USB WiFi adapter. Newer computers typically have multiple USB ports; new notebooks typically have at least two USB ports and many desktop computers have USB ports both on the back and front of the computer case. If you want to use an external USB WiFi adapter but are out of USB ports, you can purchase a USB hub that expands the number of available USB ports on your computer. The USB hub, which is typically a fairly small device, connects to one of the existing USB ports on your computer. Additional USB devices (such as a WiFi adapter) can then be connected to the hub.

A USB wireless networking adapter can provide a computer that has an available USB port with the capability of communicating on a wireless network. (Photo courtesy of Netgear.)

As far as the actual selection of a WiFi adapter for your notebook or desktop computer, make sure that you select an adapter that can take advantage of the connection speed your wireless *router* provides. If you are using a wireless G router (that is, a router made to the specifications of the 802.11g standards), it makes sense to purchase a wireless G network adapter. Although a wireless 802.11b (wireless B) WiFi adapter can connect to a wireless G router/access point, wireless B (with a connection speed of 11Mbps) isn't going to give you the higher speed connection that is provided by wireless G adapters (up to 54Mbps).

27

▶ **TIP**

Wireless B routers and adapters, which provide a maximum connection speed of only 11Mbps, are really obsolete. You will actually have a tough time finding them. If you do find wireless B devices, you might be tempted to buy them because they are extremely inexpensive. However, wireless G provides connection speeds up to 54Mbps (don't settle for 11Mbps). Wireless G devices (routers, access points, and WiFi adapters) aren't all that expensive and most stores that carry computers stock them.

---

28   **Determine Upgradeability of Current Computers**

✔ **BEFORE YOU BEGIN**

27 About Wireless Network Adapters

Whether or not you can upgrade your current computer with a WiFi *network adapter* depends on the current hardware configuration of your system and the operating system (typically the version of Windows) you are running on the computer.

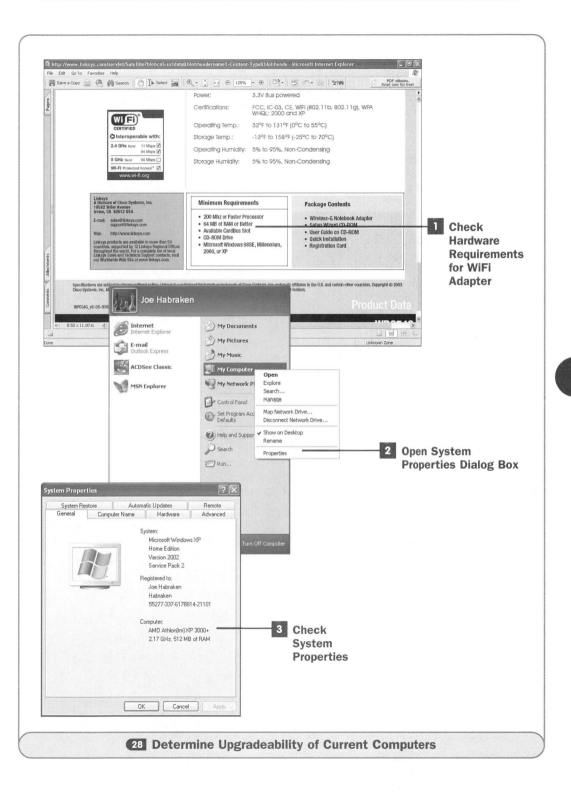

1 Check Hardware Requirements for WiFi Adapter

2 Open System Properties Dialog Box

3 Check System Properties

28

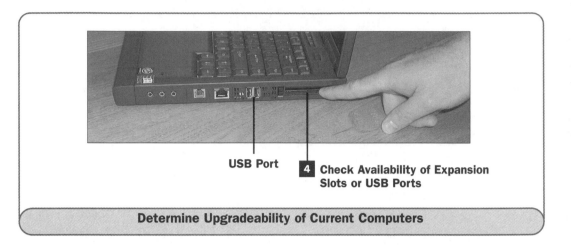

USB Port   **4**   **Check Availability of Expansion Slots or USB Ports**

Determine Upgradeability of Current Computers

28

▶ **TIP**

If your computer is relatively new (one to five years old), you should be able to add a WiFi adapter to the computer with little or no hassle (USB ports have been standard on computers for quite some time). This goes for all the computers in your household, including both notebooks and desktops/towers. If your computer is more than six years old, you may be on the "cusp" of upgradeability in terms of the processor speed and the amount of memory it has. You will have to determine whether it is worth spending additional money to upgrade an older computer so that a WiFi adapter can be added. If you really want to upgrade a computer that is bordering on obsolescence, you must do more research (consider that the cost of a new computer is now so reasonable that your upgrades could cost more). A good place to start your research is the *Absolute Beginner's Guide to Upgrading and Fixing Your PC*, by Michael Miller. Also check out other book titles related to upgrading PCs at **www.samspublishing.com**. With the low cost of computers, buying a new computer on sale might be as cheap as trying to upgrade an old clunker; you have to decide this for yourself.

Don't buy any WiFi upgrades for your computer (notebook or desktop computer) before you determine whether the computer can actually be upgraded. There are also some obvious issues related to adding a WiFi adapter. If your notebook computer does not have an empty or available CardBus slot, you won't be able to add an internal adapter. If your desktop computer (including towers) does not have an available PCI slot, you won't be able to add an internal adapter card. Finally, if you don't have a USB port on the computer (notebook or desktop/tower), you can't add a USB WiFi adapter.

▶ **TIP**

Your computer most likely came with a printout of its hardware specifications. If you can locate this document, it provides the information you need when checking your system's compatibility with a particular WiFi adapter. Don't despair if you find that your system is not compatible, particularly if it is just a matter of upgrading your version of the

Windows operating system (rather than upgrading system memory). Although this update *is* an added expense, Windows has evolved over time, and you will find that the latest version of Windows can actually provide features and functionality you don't get from your current version of Windows.

1 Check Hardware Requirements for WiFi Adapter

Before purchasing, read the hardware requirements for the WiFi adapter you want to use. The information can be found on the WiFi adapter box or online at the WiFi adapter's manufacturer's website. The minimum requirements for a WiFi adapter relate to your computer's processor speed, the amount of RAM (memory on the computer), its available hard drive space (for the software), and your operating system (the version of Windows you are running). If you are buying an internal WiFi card, you must have either an open CardBus slot on a laptop or an open PCI slot on a desktop/tower computer.

2 Open System Properties Dialog Box

You can quickly check the amount of system memory, the processor speed, and the version of Windows your current computer system is running by using the **System Properties** dialog box. To open the dialog box, click **Start**, then right-click the **My Computer** icon on the **Start** menu. From the context menu that opens, select **Properties**. The **System Properties** dialog box opens.

28

3 Check System Properties

Make sure that the **General** tab is selected on the **System Properties** dialog box and make note of the information provided. This tab provides the operating system version that you are running (including service packs installed), the amount of system memory, and the processor speed for your system. Make sure that the information you accumulated about the adapter's requirements in step 1 matches or is exceeded by your computer's system properties. They don't have to match exactly as long as your computer has at least the minimum specifications needed by the WiFi adapter.

▶ **TIP**

No matter how well you plan, there is always the potential for problems when you add new hardware to a computer. Make sure that you have updated your Windows XP installation with the latest service packs. Check the website for the WiFi adapter you plan to purchase and see whether there are any issues with compatibility and Windows XP service packs. If the manufacturer's website provides newer installation software than is available on the CD that comes with the adapter, it makes sense to download it and use it when you install the software for the adapter. A little pre-planning and research will save you a lot of headaches in terms of installing your new WiFi adapter.

4 Check Availability of Expansion Slots or USB Ports

Make a physical examination of your notebook or desktop computer to identify the availability of expansion slots or available USB ports. For example, on a notebook computer, you are looking for an available card slot, which is typically located on the side of the computer. On a desktop/tower computer, look at the back of the computer and see whether the metal slot covers remain on any of the expansion slots; this typically means a slot has not been used. Open the case to make sure that a PCI slot is available. If you're looking for USB ports to which you can connect an external USB adapter, look on the back, front, or side of the computer.

▶ TIP

If you feel you need more information about your system than you were able to glean using the steps provided, use the Windows System Information utility to take a more in-depth look at your computer hardware and software. (Note that this utility can be confusing because it provides way more information than you need.) Click **Start**, point at **All Programs**, and then choose **Accessories**, **System Tools**, **System Information**. Click a particular hardware category such as **Memory** or **USB** to see the specifications for that particular computer hardware item. If you have enough processor speed, memory, and hard drive space for the adapter you're considering purchasing, a physical examination of the PC should be enough to determine its upgradeability. For example, if you have an open USB port (the speed of the port is not important; WiFi adapters can be used on 1.1 and 2.0 USB adapters), you can add a USB adapter. If you have a notebook computer with more than one open expansion slot, check your notebook documentation to determine the type of slots available (or use the Windows System Information utility as mentioned) and then add the appropriate WiFi adapter card type. The bottom line is that the availability of slots and ports is really what determines the type of add-on WiFi adapter you will buy, particularly if your PC is relatively new. I suggest that you go with a USB WiFi adapter in most cases, particularly on a desktop/tower computer (it is not that easy to add a WiFi adapter to a PCI slot). If your notebook/laptop computer has an obvious open slot, it makes sense to fill that slot, since the small PCMCIA cards easily snap into the slot. Knowing your system allows you to consult WiFi adapter manufacturers' websites (such as **www.netgear.com** and **www.linksys.com**) and select the appropriate WiFi adapter upgrade before you go to the store or purchase the adapter online.

28

29 Install a Wireless Adapter

✔ **BEFORE YOU BEGIN**

28 Determine Upgradeability of Current Computers

After you have checked out your system in terms of your system's compatibility with the available WiFi adapters, you can then purchase the appropriate *network adapter* for your computer. If you are adding WiFi adapters to more than one computer and the computer specifications support it, purchase the same adapter for all the computers. Because a laptop PCMCIA slot card won't work in a desktop or tower computer, you should purchase the different types of adapters you need from the same adapter manufacturer. Using equipment from the same manufacturer will make your life a little easier in that you will be using the same or similar software utilities to configure and manage the network adapters.

▶ **TIP**

If you purchased a wireless G WiFi Router (802.11g), it makes sense to purchase wireless G network adapters. You then get the most out of your router and the WiFi adapters in terms of maximum connection speed. I also suggest that you buy the same brand WiFi adapters and WiFi router to negate any possible compatibility issues (although they are very few documented) between hardware from different manufacturers.

The next step is to install the adapter. For notebook computers, this is a matter of sliding the WiFi card into the expansion slot. If you are upgrading a desktop system and want to install an internal WiFi adapter, you might need a screwdriver to open the case and install the card in a slot on the motherboard. As mentioned previously, the easiest way to upgrade either system type (notebook or desktop) is to go with a USB WiFi adapter; there are no tools required for installation. The steps that follow provide you with information on installing a USB, PCI, or PCMCIA WiFi adapter.

29

▶ **TIP**

It is important that you read the installation guide that accompanies any WiFi adapter that you purchase. In many cases, a "quick start" sheet is provided that lists the most important steps in the installation process. New hardware doesn't work on your computer until you install the software and *drivers* (software that allows the device to communicate with the operating system) provided with the hardware device. This software is typically included on a CD. In some cases, you will be advised to install the software before you install the hardware. Depending on the installation steps provided for your WiFi adapter, you might be required to complete **30** Install Adapter Software Utility before completing this current task.

1 Locate USB Port

Locate an open USB port on your computer that you plan to use to attach the new WiFi adapter.

29

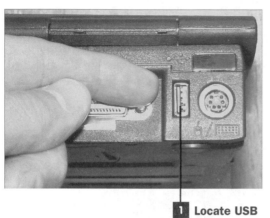

1 Locate USB Port

2 Install USB WiFi Adapter

3 Or Locate Open PCI Slot on Desktop Computer

4 Insert WiFi Adapter in PCI Slot

29 Install a Wireless Adapter

5 Or Locate Open PCMCIA Slot on Notebook Computer

6 Insert PCMCIA WiFi Adapter in Notebook Computer

29 Install a Wireless Adapter (continues)

2 Install USB WiFi Adapter

Insert the USB WiFi adapter directly into the USB port or attach the optional USB cable from the WiFi adapter to a USB port on your computer. Because Windows XP provides Plug and Play technology (that is, it recognizes the addition of hardware to the system), Windows recognizes the new USB WiFi adapter and the **Found New Hardware Wizard** opens. Insert the CD that came with your USB adapter and click **Next** to install the driver for the new USB WiFi adapter. Click **Finish** when the software driver installation process is completed. You do not have to reboot after installing the device driver. You can now proceed to **30** Install Adapter Software Utility.

3 Or Locate Open PCI Slot on Desktop Computer

Open the case on your desktop/tower computer. Locate an available PCI slot on the motherboard. If necessary, remove the metal slot cover by unscrewing the screw that currently holds the slot cover in place.

▶ TIP

If you are going to install a PCI internal WiFi adapter on a desktop PC, *do not use* a magnetic screwdriver and make sure that you open the computer's case in an environment where static electricity is not generated, meaning you should work in a room without carpet. You can purchase an anti-static wrist band that connects to the computer case and acts to ground you while you're working on the system. A static charge can easily damage your system, so you should be careful when opening a computer's case and working around the motherboard. To install any internal WiFi adapter, carefully read the installation instructions that came with the adapter.

4 Insert WiFi Adapter in PCI Slot

Your PCI adapter card has a small notch in the bottom of the card (toward the front of the adapter). Place the short part of the adapter (the part in front of the notch) in the front of the PCI slot. Rock the PCI adapter back toward the rear of the computer to seat the adapter. Press firmly to make sure that the adapter is seated in the slot. Then screw the back of the adapter (the part replacing the metal slot cover) into the back of the computer's case. Replace the computer's case. If your adapter card comes with a detachable antenna, you can screw the antenna into the card where it is exposed at the rear of the computer's case.

When you turn the system on and Windows boots, the **Found New Hardware Wizard** will open. Insert the CD that came with your PCI WiFi adapter and click **Next** to install the driver for the new WiFi adapter. Click **Finish** when the software driver installation process is completed. Proceed to **30 Install Adapter Software Utility**.

5 Or Locate Open PCMCIA Slot on Notebook Computer

Power down your laptop computer. Examine the left and right side of your notebook computer to locate an open PCMCIA slot. Some slots are covered by small plastic hatches that push inward to expose the slot.

6 Insert PCMCIA WiFi Adapter in Notebook Computer

Slide the PCMCIA adapter into the slot. Slide the card all the way in until it clicks into place. Power on your notebook computer; after Windows boots up, the **Found New Hardware Wizard** opens. Insert the CD that came with your PCI WiFi adapter and click **Next** to install the driver for the new WiFi adapter. Click **Finish** when the software driver installation process is completed. Proceed to **30 Install Adapter Software Utility**.

29

30 | Install Adapter Software Utility

✔ **BEFORE YOU BEGIN**

29 Install a Wireless Adapter

Add-on WiFi **network adapters** include software that allows you to configure and monitor the adapter. The software is included with almost all adapters and is typically provided on a CD. Most manufacturers of WiFi adapters also provide you with the ability to download software, **drivers**, and software updates associated with your particular WiFi adapter. Not only does the CD provide a configuration utility, the CD also contains the software **driver** you need when you install the WiFi adapter on your PC (see **29** **Install a Wireless Adapter**).

▶ **TIP**

In most cases, you should install the software utility that the adapter's manufacturer provided for your add-on WiFi adapter (unless otherwise noted by the manufacturer's setup guide). The software is specifically designed to allow you to change the WiFi adapter configuration so that the adapter can connect to the WiFi router's access point and also monitor the adapter's connection. Some manufacturers suggest that you do not need to install the "special" software utility if you are running Windows XP (this exemption varies from manufacturer to manufacturer) because Windows XP provides its own **Wireless Connection** utility. (Earlier versions of Windows such as Windows 98 do not provide this utility.) You can use the Windows XP **Wireless Connection** utility to configure and monitor the WiFi adapter. However, the utility provided on the CD that ships with your WiFi adapter often provides greater ease of use and features not provided by the more "generic" Windows **Wireless Connection** utility. It is your call in terms of how you actually configure and monitor the WiFi adapter, but I suggest that you take advantage of the utility that was provided with the adapter.

30

▶ **KEY TERM**

Driver—Software for a device such as a WiFi network adapter that allows the operating system and the device to communicate correctly.

Each WiFi network adapter provides a different software utility for installing the adapter's software. This task provides a look at the software installation for a Netgear USB adapter. Each adapter's software installation process will be different. Some WiFi adapters require that you install the software (and the driver) before attaching or inserting the WiFi adapter on the PC. Other adapters are installed on the PC first and then the software is loaded. Before installing your WiFi adapter hardware or software, read the installation information provided by the manufacturer so that your WiFi adapter hardware and software is installed correctly.

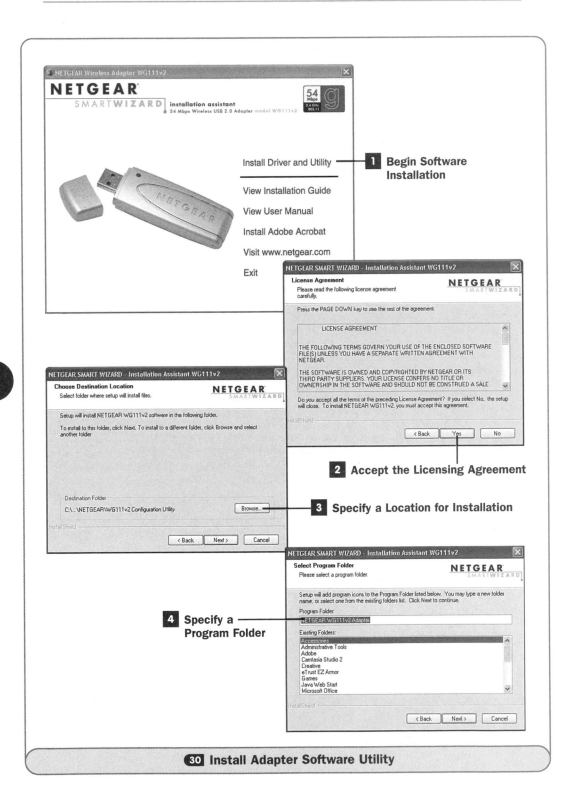

30

1 Begin Software Installation

2 Accept the Licensing Agreement

3 Specify a Location for Installation

4 Specify a Program Folder

30 Install Adapter Software Utility

1 Begin Software Installation

Insert the CD that accompanied your WiFi adapter in your CD-ROM or DVD drive. The software on the CD should automatically open. Select the option for installing the adapter's utility software (in some cases, this option also installs the software driver for the adapter).

2 Accept the Licensing Agreement

In most instances, you must review and then agree to the licensing agreement for the software that will be installed on your system; click **Yes** or otherwise answer in the affirmative and then continue the installation process.

3 Specify a Location for Installation

You will be provided with a default location for the software installation. To change the location, use the **Browse** button and navigate to the location on your hard disk where you want to install the software. When you have identified the hard disk location, proceed to the next step in the installation wizard or instructions.

4 Specify a Program Folder

A default program folder is specified for the installation. This folder will appear on the **Start** menu and provide access to the icons that start the utility associated with the adapter. The utility software you install is used to both configure and monitor the WiFi connection for the adapter (the connection to your WiFi router). In most cases, you will want to go with the default. However, to select another option, select a folder from the list provided. Then click **Next** to complete the installation process. When the installation process is complete, you can remove the CD from your computer's drive.

31

---

31 | Check WiFi Adapter Installation

✔ **BEFORE YOU BEGIN**

29 Install a Wireless Adapter
30 Install Adapter Software Utility

Windows XP provides you with a quick way to check the installation of your new hardware, including the WiFi *network adapter*'s software *driver*. The **Device Manager** not only allows you to check the status of a particular hardware device, it also allows you to update or roll back the software driver for the device. The **Device Manager** also provides easy access to a hardware "troubleshooter" that helps you diagnose problems with a particular hardware device.

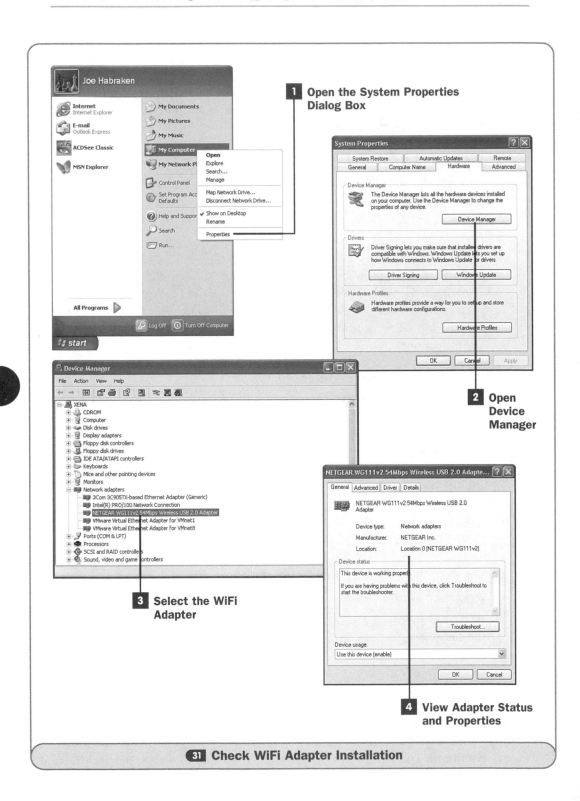

1 Open the System Properties
Dialog Box

2 Open
Device
Manager

3 Select the WiFi
Adapter

4 View Adapter Status
and Properties

31 Check WiFi Adapter Installation

1 Open the System Properties Dialog Box

Click **Start** and then right-click the **My Computer** icon on the **Start** menu. Select **Properties** from the context menu that appears. The **System Properties** dialog box opens.

2 Open Device Manager

On the **Hardware** tab of the **System Properties** dialog box, click the **Device Manager** button. The **Device Manager** window opens.

3 Select the WiFi Adapter

In the **Device Manager** window, expand the **Network Adapters** category and then double-click the listing for your WiFi adapter. The **Properties** dialog box for your adapter opens.

▶ TIP

The **Device Manager** can be hard to deal with in terms of locating a particular hardware item such as your newly installed WiFi adapter because device names can be rather cryptic. However, if your WiFi adapter is the only network adapter installed on the computer, it will be the only adapter that appears in the list when you expand the **Network Adapters** category. If you have multiple adapters (for example, you have a computer with a wired LAN adapter and you have added a WiFi adapter), the WiFi adapter can (in almost all cases) be identified by the fact that its name includes the manufacturer's name. For example, a Netgear WiFi adapter's name will be **NETGEAR** followed by the number designation for that particular adapter. In cases where the adapter name does not include the manufacturer's name (such as some Linksys adapters), the adapter's name will be fairly self explanatory. For example, my Linksys USB adapter appears under the name **Instant Wireless Compact USB Adapter** in the **Device Manager** list.

4 View Adapter Status and Properties

On the **General** tab of the **Properties** dialog box, view the status of the device. For example, a device that is working correctly will have the status of **This device is working properly**.

If the device is not working properly, the status appears as an error message such as **This device cannot start**. Assuming that the device was installed in the computer correctly, most hardware problems are related to the software driver for the device. At this point, you can click **Troubleshoot** on the **General** tab; the **Windows Help and Support Center** opens. The **Windows Help and Support Center** will walk you through different troubleshooting scenarios to help you get the device up and running. In some cases, you might have to remove the WiFi adapter (which is fairly easy to do for USB or PCMCIA adapters but not that easy for PCI adapters because you have to remove the computer's case again) and repeat the installation of the device. Reinstall the software driver and software utility for the device.

▶ **NOTE**

Advice on troubleshooting nonworking devices such as WiFi network adapters could certainly fill an entire book. Here are some general "best practice" tips: Make sure that you install the device correctly in the first place. Make sure that a PCI WiFi adapter is completely inserted in the PCI slot on the motherboard; make sure that a PCMCIA card is snapped all the way into the CardBus slot on your laptop. Also make sure that you have the most up-to-date driver for your device. The CD that ships with your device can, on occasion, actually provide an out-of-date software driver. Consult the website of the adapter's manufacturer for help on downloading the most up-to-date driver for the device or call the Help Desk number provided in the documentation that came with your WiFi adapter. Note, however, that sometimes you just end up with a faulty or "bad" WiFi adapter that isn't going to work no matter how hard you try. Return a bad adapter to the store where you made your purchase. Then try the process again with a new device.

32 | **About Configuring the Wireless Adapter**

✔ **BEFORE YOU BEGIN**

26 Configure Router Wireless Settings

29 Install a Wireless Adapter

30 Install Adapter Software Utility

→ **SEE ALSO**

76 About 802.11 Security Strategies

31

After the WiFi *network adapter* is physically connected to your computer (as a USB, PCMCIA, or PCI device) and you have installed the *driver* and configuration software for the new WiFi adapter, you can connect the WiFi-enabled computer to your wireless network (that is, to the WiFi router's access point). But before we discuss issues related to connecting your WiFi-enabled computer to the WiFi router, we should take a look at what it actually means to "configure the WiFi adapter." There are two things you must configure on a WiFi adapter: the mode and security settings.

The mode relates to the two different ways computers can communicate wirelessly: infrastructure mode or *Ad Hoc mode*. Infrastructure mode is just a computer nerd's way of saying that the computers on the network communicate by connecting to the WiFi router's access point. The WiFi router serves as the central "clearing house" for the network's data as it moves from computer to computer. The alternative connectivity strategy for a home WiFi network is the Ad-Hoc mode, which allows WiFi-enabled computers to connect directly, computer to computer, without an access point. Although Ad-Hoc mode may sound nifty, it has associated problems. First of all, one of the main reasons for creating a home WiFi network is to share a high-speed Internet connection. This is best accomplished using a WiFi router. Second—and here is a really good reason *not* to use Ad-Hoc mode (unless you are sitting in a coffee shop and want to quickly share a file with a colleague by connecting in the Ad-Hoc mode)—the Ad-Hoc mode specifications followed by the manufacturers of WiFi adapters do not require the adapters to operate at their top data transfer speed, which can be as high as 54Mbps for a wireless G network adapter. In fact, wireless G adapters operate at only 11Mbps in the Ad-Hoc mode, and there is no way for you to increase the data throughput speed.

▶ KEY TERM

Ad Hoc mode—A computer-to-computer wireless connection mode that allows WiFi-enabled computers to connect directly without communicating through an intermediary device such as a WiFi access point.

Although we discuss how you can configure a computer for the Ad-Hoc mode in **34 Configure Adapter for Computer-to-Computer Networking** so that you can do it if necessary, you will want to set up each computer with a default configuration that allows it to connect to your WiFi router. This arrangement allows the adapter to operate at its top speed and also allows you to access the Internet through your connection with the WiFi router.

To configure your WiFi adapter for infrastructure mode, you need to configure the adapter with the correct **SSID**, the correct channel for your WiFi network (as configured on the WiFi router), and any security settings required by the security features you enabled on the WiFi router, such as such as WEP (Wired Equivalent Privacy) and WPA (WiFi Protected Access). For more about WEP and WPA, see **77 Configure Wired Equivalent Privacy (WEP) Security** and **78 Configure WiFi Protected Access (WPA) Security**.

Your WiFi network adapter is configured to connect to your home WiFi network using the SSID and optional network security settings.

▶ **NOTE**

The settings you configure for your WiFi adapter to connect to your WiFi router and access point depend on how you configured the router. The SSID and any security configuration settings are determined when you configure the router. You then manually enter the SSID and other configuration settings using the WiFi adapter configuration utility.

Because there is always the possibility that you will want to configure your WiFi-enabled computer so that it can attach to multiple WiFi networks (depending on your location), you will find that most WiFi adapter software utilities provide you with the ability to create *configuration profiles*. A profile contains information such as the SSID and security key (for WEP or WPA security) needed to connect to a particular access point and WiFi network. Obviously, the ability to create multiple configuration profiles is particularly useful when you have a notebook computer that you use at more than one location, such as home and at work. A specific configuration profile can be created for each of these networks (home and work) so that you can quickly access a particular WiFi network. Configuration profiles are explained in ⬛ **35 Create Configuration Profiles**.

You don't necessarily have to configure your WiFi adapter for every WiFi network you access, particularly those wireless *hotspots* that you connect to in coffee shops, hotels, or other establishments that provide easy access to a public, non-secure WiFi access point. You can easily browse for these connections, since they come and go and the SSIDs often change, as explained in ⬛ **60 Use the Web to Locate Hotspots**.

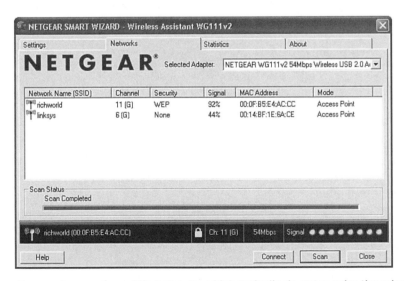

You can browse for public hotspots, which typically do not require the adapter to be pre-configured for access to that WiFi network.

33 Configure Adapter and Connect to the Wireless Router

✔BEFORE YOU BEGIN	→SEE ALSO
32 About Configuring the Wireless Adapter	**35** Create Configuration Profiles

To access the local WiFi network and services such as a broadband Internet connection, you need to connect your computer to your WiFi *router*. Windows supplies a wireless network connection icon in the notification area (also known as the system tray, which is on the far right end of the taskbar). When you open the wireless network icon, you can view the status of your WiFi *network adapter*, scan for an available WiFi network, and connect to it. If you purchased a notebook computer or a desktop computer that was WiFi-ready out of the box (particularly notebooks that use Intel's Centrino technology), you can take advantage of the **Windows Wireless Connection** utility for monitoring your WiFi connection and connecting to available WiFi networks. To use it, right-click the notification area icon (a computer with radio signals).

However, the built-in Windows utility for connecting to wireless networks such as your own WiFi network is disabled when third-party WiFi adapter software is installed on your computer, meaning that you will use the software you installed with your add-on WiFi adapter to configure the adapter and connect to the network. Although you might feel "cheated" that you can't use the **Wireless Connection** utility provided by Windows XP, you will find that the utility software that came with your WiFi adapter typically provides more features and greater ease of use when you're configuring the WiFi adapter, particularly in cases where you are using security features on the WiFi router such as WEP or WPA that must also be configured on the WiFi adapter.

Whether you use the **Windows Wireless Connection** utility or the configuration software that came with your WiFi adapter, you must configure the WiFi adapter to connect to your WiFi network (specifically, to your WiFi router). Because we have not discussed securing the network with WEP or WPA at this point in our discussion of WiFi, the only real configuration items that must be set up on your WiFi network adapter are to select infrastructure mode and to enter the correct SSID for your WiFi network (as configured on the WiFi router). This configuration can be handled automatically by scanning for and then attaching to the WiFi router (since security has not yet been enabled) or by selecting the **Infrastructure** mode and then manually typing the SSID into the WiFi adapter's configuration (as outlined in this task).

33

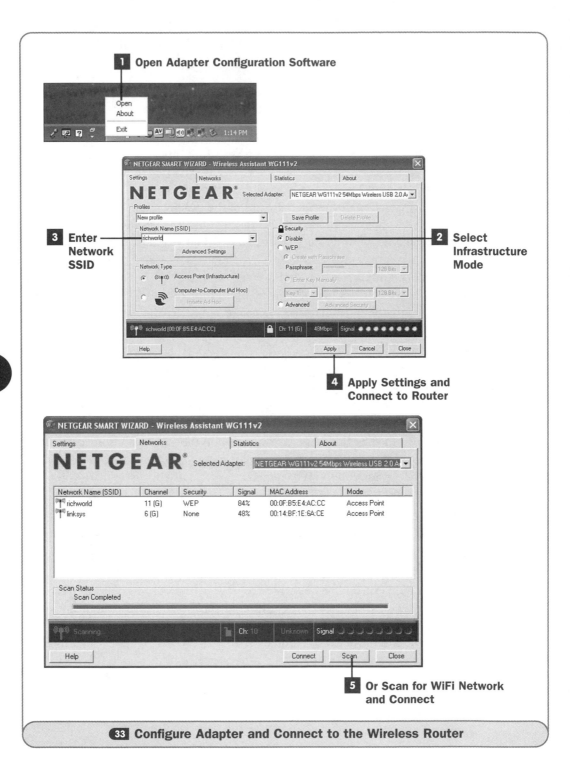

1 Open Adapter Configuration Software

3 Enter Network SSID

2 Select Infrastructure Mode

4 Apply Settings and Connect to Router

5 Or Scan for WiFi Network and Connect

33 Configure Adapter and Connect to the Wireless Router

▶ **NOTE**

The steps for configuring your WiFi adapter depend on the software utility provided by your adapter's manufacturer. Bottom line: You must either scan for or identify your network by its SSID. You also must provide any security pass phrases or encryption keys that you configured on the router if the adapter is going to successfully connect to the WiFi router.

① Open Adapter Configuration Software

Identify the icon for your WiFi adapter software utility in the notification area of the taskbar. Right-click the icon and select **Open** from the context menu. The configuration utility for your WiFi adapter opens.

② Select Infrastructure Mode

Click the appropriate option button or check box (depending on your configuration software) to select **Infrastructure** mode. For example, for my Netgear WiFi adapter configuration utility, I select the **Access Point (Infrastructure)** option under the **Network Type** category.

③ Enter Network SSID

Type the SSID for your network (the SSID you specified when configuring the WiFi router, as explained in **26 Configure Router Wireless Settings**) in the appropriate text box in your configuration utility window.

▶ **TIP**

If you don't remember the SSID, use the software utility's scan feature to scan for WiFi networks within range. You can then select your network from the list provided. If you configured any security settings on the router, you must provide the pass phrase or encryption keys to actually connect to the router. To get started with security on the WiFi router, see **70 About Basic Network Security**.

④ Apply Settings and Connect to Router

Click the **Apply** button to apply the settings to your WiFi adapter and to connect to the WiFi network using your router/access point. If you cannot connect to the network, proceed to step 5.

⑤ Or Scan for WiFi Network and Connect

If you do not want to manually configure the WiFi adapter, you can scan for your WiFi network and connect automatically. After you enable security features on your router (such as WEP or WPA), any attempt to automatically connect requires that you enter the passkey for the security option enabled on

33

the router. After you enable security features on the WiFi router, manually configuring the WiFi adapter and saving the configuration as a profile is your best bet.

Select the **Scan** option for your WiFi adapter's configuration software; for example, the Netgear utility software requires that I click the **Networks** tab on the software window and then select **Scan**. A list of available WiFi networks appears; select your WiFi network (if you see more than one network listed, it means that other WiFi networks are in operation nearby) and then click **Connect**. You should be connected to your WiFi network.

▶ **TIP**

If you don't see your WiFi network when you use the **Scan** feature, you might not have the WiFi router configured correctly. Check your router configuration to make sure that you have SSID broadcasts turned on and that the router is enabled for WiFi networking. If you are still having connectivity problems, check out **91** **About Network Connection Problems**

33

34 Configure Adapter for Computer-to-Computer Networking	
✔ **BEFORE YOU BEGIN**	→ **SEE ALSO**
33 Configure Adapter and Connect to the Wireless Router	**42** Configure TCP/IP Settings
	38 Run the Network Setup Wizard
	45 About Sharing Network Resources

You can configure your WiFi *network adapter* for Ad-Hoc mode (also called *peer-to-peer networking*). This means that you use the WiFi adapter to directly connect to other computers that also have WiFi adapters and have been configured for peer-to-peer or Ad-Hoc networking. Communicating this way allows the computers to share files and other devices such as printers.

▶ **NOTE**

Connecting two computers in Ad-Hoc mode is similar to attaching two computers with a single crossover cable. The two computers can communicate because a network medium attaches them. WiFi networking uses radio signals, which are in effect the same as a LAN cable. So, Ad-Hoc mode is available because the two (or more computers) can be attached invisibly by configuring them for the same WiFi radio channel.

To configure a WiFi-enabled computer for peer-to-peer networking, you configure the computer's WiFi adapter for Ad-Hoc mode. The Ad-Hoc mode doesn't require a WiFi router or access point to connect to another computer that has also been configured for the Ad-Hoc mode. Both computers using the Ad Hoc mode must also be configured to use a particular network name or SSID (even though there isn't an access point involved), and they must be configured for a particular WiFi protocol (80.211b or 802.11g) and a specific channel.

Although Ad-Hoc WiFi networking might seem like a good way to avoid the expense of a WiFi router, be advised that the Ad-Hoc mode doesn't allow you to get the maximum throughput available for a computer's network adapter. Wireless G adapters can connect at up to 54Mbps, but Ad-Hoc mode typically provides only 11Mbps. I suggest that you use Ad-Hoc mode only in situations where you want to quickly attach to another WiFi-enabled computer so that you can swap files or share a printer. In the home network setting, your WiFi router provides both the network infrastructure and the connection to your high-speed Internet connection.

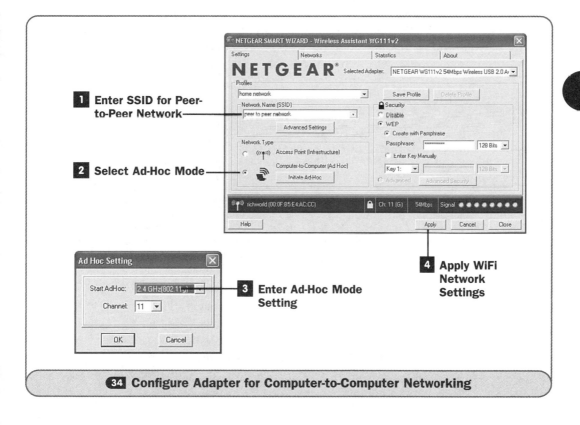

34 Configure Adapter for Computer-to-Computer Networking

▶ **NOTE**

The term *peer-to-peer networking* can be confusing because it is used in two different contexts, both related to home and small office networks. In strict networking terms, a peer-to-peer network is a collection of end-user computers that operate in a network such as a Windows workgroup where computers on the network can share files and other resources such as printers. This type of network does not use a network server, and each resource (including files and printers) is controlled on the computer where the resource resides. Microsoft and other operating system vendors consider a peer-to-peer network to consist of 10 or fewer computers (operating systems such as Windows can only accommodate a limited number of connections—10—to a particular resource such as a shared folder or a printer without deploying a server on the network). In the case of the Ad-Hoc mode, which is also referred to as "peer-to-peer" networking, we are talking about a situation where WiFi-enabled computers can communicate directly without the use of a WiFi access point.

For two computers to share resources when communicating in the Ad Hoc mode, both computers must be configured for Windows file and print sharing and also be members of the same Windows workgroup. The file and print sharing settings are found in the **Properties** dialog box for your WiFi LAN connection. To place Ad-Hoc networked computers in the same workgroup, run the **Network Setup Wizard** from the Windows **Control Panel** (see 🔲37 **About Configuring PCs for Networking**).

34

▶ **TIP**

A range of IP addresses has been specified for use on private networks. There are three different ranges of addresses that you can use for private networking such as configuring computers for WiFi **Ad Hoc** mode. These ranges are 10.0.0.0 to 10.255.255.255 (subnet mask 255.0.0), 172.16.0.0 to 172.31.255.255 (subnet mask 255.255.0), and 192.168.0.0 to 192.168.255.255 (subnet mask 255.255.255.0). Working with IP addresses and subnet masks and understanding some of the nuances associated with IP address classes can be confusing. For more information on IP addressing, see 🔲37 **About Configuring PCs for Networking**. If you want to do some additional reading related to IP addresses and subnet masks, consult a basic guide to networking such as the *Absolute Beginner's Guide to Networking*, Fourth Edition from Que Publishing.

Another important setting required for a WiFi adapter to function in Ad-Hoc mode is a static IP address. This means that an IP address must be assigned to the computer rather than allowing the computer to receive its IP address from the WiFi router, which also acts as a DHCP server (a server that supplies IP addresses dynamically to computers on the network). You specify the IP address (and subnet mask) for a LAN connection such as a WiFi adapter in the **TCP/IP Properties** dialog box for that network adapter.

▶ **NOTE**

The actual steps for configuring the Ad-Hoc mode on a computer vary depending on the software utility provided with your WiFi adapter.

1 Enter SSID for Peer-to-Peer Network

On the configuration screen of your WiFi adapter's software utility (start the utility from the notification area on the right end of the taskbar), type a network name, also called its SSID, for your peer-to–peer/Ad-Hoc network. You can use any name you want for the Ad-Hoc network's SSID. You have 32 alphanumeric characters available (do not use spaces). For example, you could call the Ad-Hoc SSID **joeandkim** to let you know that this is the connection you use to connect between Joe's and Kim's WiFi-enabled computers. If you use this connection often (say, whenever you are away from the home WiFi network), save the Ad-Hoc settings as a configuration profile. Because your infrastructure and Ad-Hoc networks are separate entities, you are not actually dedicating the IP addresses and other settings to the WiFi Ad-Hoc network you are configuring. You can use the same IP addresses and other settings for as many Ad-Hoc networks as you care to configure. Just remember that no two computers on the Ad-Hoc network can have the same IP address.

2 Select Ad-Hoc Mode

Select **Ad-Hoc** mode in the configuration window. For example, in the Netgear configuration utility, click the **Computer to Computer (Ad Hoc)** option button.

34

3 Enter Ad-Hoc Mode Settings

Ad-Hoc mode settings include the WiFi protocol to be used (802.11b or 802.11g) and the channel to be used for the transmission. To specify these settings when using a Netgear adapter, click the **Initiate Ad Hoc** button and use the drop-down boxes on the **Ad Hoc Setting** dialog box to specify the WiFi protocol and channel, then click **OK**.

▶ NOTE

To configure the IP address settings for a computer using the WiFi Ad-Hoc mode, you use the **Internet Protocol (TCP/IP) Properties** dialog box. This dialog box provides the option of configuring fixed IP addresses (such as those needed by the Ad-Hoc mode) and the option of receiving the IP addressing automatically from a device such as your WiFi router. Check out **42** **Configure TCP/IP Settings** for more about configuring IP addresses and subnet masks.

4 Apply WiFi Network Settings

To apply the Ad-Hoc settings and connect to the new peer to peer network, click **Apply**. Repeat these steps on the second WiFi-enabled computer—using the same settings for both computers—so that the two computers can communicate over the new ad hoc network.

To take advantage of the Ad-Hoc network, open the **Network Neighborhood** from the **Start** menu and then browse for the computers currently available in your workgroup. Double-click to open the computer that provides a shared resource such as printer or folder that you want to access. The printer or folder should appear as a shared resource.

35 Create Configuration Profiles

✔ **BEFORE YOU BEGIN**

32 About Configuring the Wireless Adapter

It is quite likely that you will have multiple configurations for your WiFi *network adapter*: a configuration for your home network, perhaps a configuration for a WiFi network at work, and an Ad-Hoc configuration for *peer-to-peer networking*. You can save your various configurations for your WiFi adapter as *profiles*, which allow you to quickly load a particular collection of configuration settings when you want to connect to that WiFi network.

34

▶ KEY TERM

Configuration Profile—A set of configuration options for your WiFi network adapter that have been saved under a profile name. Saving the profile allows you to quickly recall these settings at any time from the WiFi adapter's configuration software.

▶ NOTE

The software configuration utilities for most WiFi adapters provide a feature for saving configurations under a name or as a profile. Check your WiFi adapter's documentation to view the actual steps for saving a configuration or creating a profile. The steps in this task use a Netgear adapter to explain the process of creating and recalling a profile.

1 Configure WiFi Network Settings and Name Profile

In the WiFi adapter's configuration utility window (start the utility from the Notification area at the right end of the Taskbar or from the **Start** menu), set the configuration parameters (the SSID, access point, or **Ad Hoc** mode and so on) for the WiFi network connection. Type a name for the new profile where indicated (in this example using the Netgear utility, type the name of the profile in the **Profiles** text box). In terms of naming conventions, the profile is stored locally, so you do not have to worry about redundantly named profiles on other WiFi-enabled computers on your network. The profile can be as descriptive as necessary and can include spaces in the name.

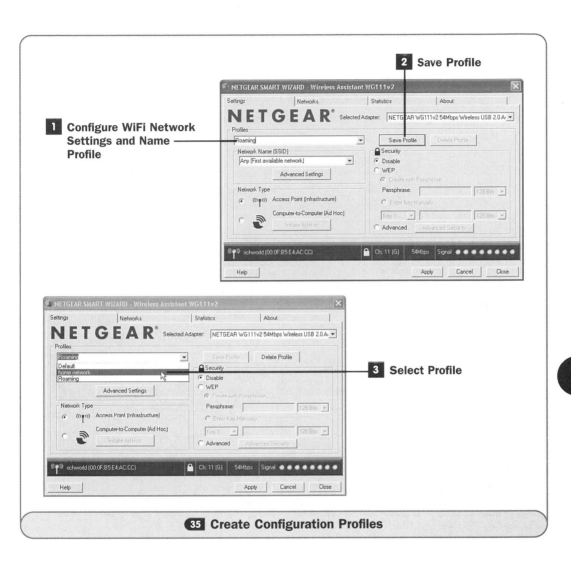

2 Save Profile

1 Configure WiFi Network Settings and Name Profile

3 Select Profile

35

35 Create Configuration Profiles

2 Save Profile

Click **Save Profile** (or another similarly named button) to save the new profile. All the settings you configured for the WiFi network adapter to access the current network are saved in this profile with the designated name. Other Windows settings such as the current workgroup and the TCP/IP settings are not saved as part of this profile. Switching from a WiFi network to another WiFi network (such as from an infrastructure to an Ad-Hoc network) might require that other settings be changed on the computer before you can attach to the specified WiFi network.

3 Select Profile

The next time you want to access a particular network, you can simply select the profile for that network rather than manually configuring all the appropriate settings again. To select a profile (which connects the computer to the WiFi network specified in the profile), open the adapter's software utility (as described in step 1), open the **Profiles** drop-down list, and select the profile for the network to which you want to connect. Then apply the configuration profile. In the case of the Netgear configuration software, I click the **Apply** button. When you connect to the network, a message balloon appears next to the notification area icon for your network adapter.

---

36 About Updating an Adapter Driver

✔**BEFORE YOU BEGIN**

30 Install Adapter Software Utility
31 Check WiFi Adapter Installation

35

For your WiFi *network adapter* to operate correctly, the appropriate software driver must be installed. Most problems with hardware devices are typically related to the software driver.

▶ NOTE

It is not totally uncommon for an adapter's manufacturer to update the software that is available for a particular WiFi adapter. You should definitely check the manufacturer's website every now and then to see whether updates to your network adapter are available. Updated software utilities for a device often provide new features or rework the software to make the device easier to configure and manage.

Your WiFi adapter comes with a CD (or other media) that provides a driver and software utilities for the device. Sometimes, the driver shipped with a device doesn't provide the appropriate functionality for the device. If you are experiencing problems with a WiFi adapter, you should check the manufacturer's website to see whether a new (revised) driver is available for your adapter.

The tasks in this chapter used the Netgear WG111v2 Wireless USB 2.0 Adapter to show how a WiFi adapter is installed and configured. If I go to the Netgear support page for the device, I can see whether updated software and/or drivers are available. Most manufacturer's support pages also include tips on troubleshooting and guides for improving the performance of the adapter.

The manufacturer's support web page for your WiFi adapter can provide links to new drivers and software and provide troubleshooting advice.

If new software is available, it typically includes a new driver. So download the software using your web browser and then run the software on your computer to update the device. If you download an updated driver that does not include a utility for installing the driver, you can install the driver from the **Driver** tab of the device's **Properties** dialog box. Open this dialog box by double-clicking on the device's listing in the Windows **Device Manager**, which in turn is reached through the **Device** tab of the system's **Properties** dialog box.

From the **Driver** tab, you can also roll back a driver if you are experiencing problems with a new driver. I suggest that you update the device's driver only if you are experiencing problems with the device. Before you download updates for utility software associated with the device, read what the update provides in terms of features and functionality and then decide whether or not it is worth downloading and installing the software.

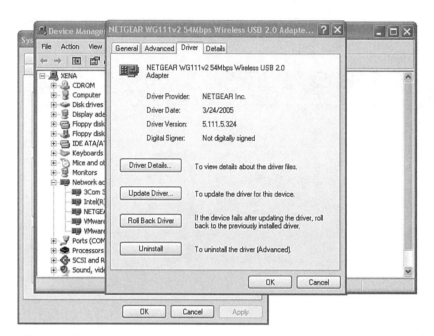

*Click the Update Driver button on the Driver tab of the device's **Properties** dialog box to locate and install the downloaded driver if the driver doesn't come with its own installation utility.*

36

▶ **TIP**

You can also connect to the Windows update website by clicking the **Windows Update** button on the **Hardware** tab of the **System Properties** dialog box. The Windows Update website often provides updated drivers for devices such as WiFi adapters. Using the **Windows Update** feature to update drivers is the easiest way to keep your device drivers up to date because the driver installation process is handled automatically.

6

Configuring the Windows Home Network

IN THIS CHAPTER:

The purpose of networking computers is to share resources such as files, printers, and a high-speed Internet connection. Networking computers also provides you with the ability to game over the network. Whether computers are hardwired for networking or take part in a WiFi network, they must be configured appropriately to participate in the network. In the tasks in this chapter, we take a look at setting LAN properties and configuring computers to participate on your WiFi network.

37	**About Configuring PCs for Networking**

✔ **BEFORE YOU BEGIN**	→ **SEE ALSO**
3 Browse and Search for Files and Folders	**32** About Configuring the Wireless Adapter
4 About My Network Places	**33** Configure Adapter and Connect to the Wireless Router
5 Use the Control Panel	**34** Configure Adapter for Computer-to-Computer Networking

37

For your PCs to correctly operate on your home or small office WiFi network, you must configure some settings. Because Windows networking uses certain conventions to identify computers on the network, and because IP networks such as the Internet require participating computers to use a particular address convention to access the Internet, you must check and configure several settings before a computer will be up and running on the network.

Workgroup Networking

Microsoft networking for home and small office networks (and larger networks that use a network server) is called *peer-to-peer networking* because each computer on the network operates as a peer, meaning that it can both offer services (such as a file or printer) and access services provided by other computers on the network. The network itself is referred to as a *workgroup*.

▶ **KEY TERM**

Workgroup—A Microsoft Windows peer-to-peer network. Each computer in a workgroup can provide and access resources.

▶ **NOTE**

The term *peer-to-peer networking* can cause some confusion. In terms of Microsoft Windows home or small office networking, a peer-to-peer network is a workgroup. The workgroup consists of multiple computers that share resources equally. They are peers. The term *peer-to-peer networking* is also used to describe Ad Hoc WiFi networking, in which two computers are configured to communicate directly using WiFi.

For a computer to participate in the network, it must be a member of the workgroup. Workgroups are limited to 10 computers because a peer computer running an operating system such as Windows XP can accommodate only 10 connections to a particular shared resource such as a folder or printer. You might find that, if several computers print to a printer that is shared by a particular computer in the workgroup, the computer sharing the printer becomes sluggish and runs more slowly because its processing power and memory are being taxed by "serving up" the resource to the other computers in the workgroup. I suggest that you limit your workgroups to 5 or 6 computers, particularly if everyone prints to a single printer that is provided as a shared resource by one of the workgroup computers.

▶ **NOTE**

Although the Windows XP operating system provides the capability to share resources on a network, it is certainly not designed to handle high network traffic or serve multiple resources to a large number of computers. Corporate and institutional networks use powerful servers with network server software to provide printing and file resources. These types of networks can accommodate a large number of users (hundreds and even thousands) because of the dedicated servers that "serve up" the network resources. Windows XP is designed as an end-user desktop environment for running local applications such as your email client, word processor, and web browser. Although Windows XP can also "serve up" resources, it is extremely limited in the number of other computers (the limit is 10 connections) to which it can serve a resource at any one time.

37

Each computer in the workgroup should be identified by a unique name. This name is also referred to as the *NetBIOS name* and can be up to 15 characters in length. The term *NetBIOS* is a holdover from an early Microsoft networking strategy, but unique names are still required to identify the computers in the workgroup.

Computers that participate in the workgroup must be configured for file and print sharing and must also be configured as Microsoft network clients. Both these settings are configured in the **Properties** dialog box for the computer's *network adapter*, which in this case would be your WiFi network adapter. Configuring your WiFi adapter for file and print sharing is described in **41** **Add a Network Client or Service**. Creating the workgroup is very straightforward because Microsoft provides a **Network Setup Wizard** that walks you through the steps of creating the new workgroup. We discuss the Network Setup Wizard in **38** **Run the Network Setup Wizard**.

Let me summarize a couple of important points before we discuss IP addressing and why IP addresses are essential to network communication. In Chapter 5, "Installing and Configuring Wireless Adapters," I discussed how you configure your WiFi network adapter to communicate with the WiFi router on your home network. If we were not using WiFi as our network medium, Chapter 5 would have consisted of one sentence: "Connect a network cable from the computer to the router." Because we *are* using WiFi, the medium (wireless communication through radio signals) must be configured for network communication.

After the network medium (WiFi) is enabled on the computers and the WiFi router, computers must be configured with the appropriate network settings to allow them to share resources and also be a member of a Windows workgroup. Finally, computers on the WiFi network (the same is true for computers on a wired LAN) must be configured with a network addressing system that uniquely identifies each computer. This is where IP addressing comes in.

IP Addressing

The TCP/IP protocol is a set of rules that dictate how computers use *IP addresses* to communicate on a TCP/IP network. We use IP addressing on both large and small networks (workgroups) today because it is necessary for computers to access the Internet, which is itself a huge TCP/IP network.

▶ **NOTE**

The TCP/IP protocol is set up by default on a computer running the Windows XP Home or Professional operating system.

37

Every device (both computers and WiFi routers) on your network must be assigned an IP address. The WiFi router is typically assigned its IP address automatically by your Internet service provider when you connect the WiFi router to your broadband connection device (such as your DSL router or broadband modem).

IP addresses are dotted decimal addresses that are written as four sets of decimal numbers separated by periods. For example, **130.0.1.1** is the correct format for an IP address. IP addresses are also accompanied by a *subnet mask*. The subnet mask helps computers determine what part of the IP address refers to the network and what part of the address refers to the actual computer that has been assigned the address. Subnet masks are also written in the dotted decimal format. For example, **255.255.0.0** would be a subnet mask that could accompany the **130.0.1.1** IP address.

▶ **KEY TERMS**

IP address—A dotted decimal representation of a binary address that is uniquely assigned to each computer and device running on an IP network.

Subnet mask—A dotted decimal representation of a binary mask that is used by computers to determine the portion of an IP address that provides network information and the portion of the IP address that supplies computer address information.

▶ **TIP**

There is no question that IP addressing is confusing for the home network or small office aficionado. A number of websites and many good books can expand your knowledge of the IP addressing scheme and the part that subnet masks play in IP addressing. Most networks currently use the IPv4 standard, which embraces the four-part, dotted decimal numbering system discussed and used in this chapter. A new version of IP, called IPv6, is now available and uses a different numbering system, which will only make it more difficult for home network administrators to understand how to configure IP address settings. I suggest that you allow your WiFi router to dynamically provide the IP addresses and subnet masks for the computers on your WiFi workgroup. The router is typically configured to do this right out of the box. This approach also provides additional security because your network "hides" behind the WiFi router. Only the WiFi router has a "real" IP address, which it gets from the broadband device provided by your Internet service provider.

IP (Internet Protocol) networks require that each computer has a unique IP address. This address is used to identify the computer for both the sending and receiving of data on the IP network. Because the WiFi router automatically provides the IP address for the computers on the WiFi network, you don't have to worry about configuring the computers with the IP address and the subnet mask that are required. The router does this for you using the Dynamic Host Configuration Protocol. When a computer comes online, it asks the router for an IP address and subnet mask. The router answers by providing this information to the computer.

The only time you will have to assign static IP addresses to WiFi-enabled computers is when you want the computers to communicate on an *Ad Hoc network* that does not use a WiFi router (see **34 Configure Adapter for Computer-to-Computer Networking**). Although letting your WiFi router dole out appropriate IP addresses and subnet masks to your workgroup computers keeps you blissfully ignorant of actually working with different IP address classes and static addressing, it certainly doesn't hurt to have a basic understanding of IP addressing and subnet masks.

The IP addressing scheme was actually developed in the 1970s when the Internet was first being created. Today, in the United States (and most of North and South America), IP addresses are "leased" by companies from the American Registry for Internet Numbers (ARIN). The company pays for a range of addresses and then uses them as public IP addresses so that the company can participate on the Internet. Your Internet service provider leases its IP addresses from ARIN and then assigns you an IP address for your high-speed Internet connection using DHCP.

The IP addressing scheme is actually divided into three different classes: Class A, B, and C. These classes were created so that companies and institutions could be assigned IP address ranges based on their size and their need (in terms of the number of addresses required).

37

► **WEB RESOURCE**

http://webopedia.internet.com/TERM/I/IP_address.html

Each of the IP address classes was designed for a particular size of network. For more basic information about IP address classes, check out the Webopedia site.

Each IP address also has a default subnet mask. The mask is used by the computers and other devices on the network to determine which part of an IP address provides network information and which part of the address provides addressing information related to a particular computer.

The class subnets are as follows:

- Class A: 255.0.0.0

- Class B: 255.255.0.0

- Class C: 255.255.255.0

► **NOTE**

If you look at the subnet masks for each class, you can see that for a Class A network, the IP address's first octet is masked by the subnet mask (the 255) and so the network information found in the IP address actually consists of the first octet. In a Class B network, the first two octets are network information; in a Class C network, the first three octets are network information. With fewer octets devoted to actual IP addresses as you move from Class A to Class C, you can see why Class C networks provide fewer individual IP addresses.

Public IP addresses allow computers and other devices to connect directly to the Internet. You don't actually need to worry about public IP addresses and your connection to the Internet. This is all taken care of by your Internet service provider. Your WiFi router is dynamically assigned an IP address to communicate with your Internet service provider and the Internet. Because the WiFi router sits at a gateway between your WiFi network and the Internet (the Internet connection provided by your ISP), the IP addresses used on your local area network (including WiFi and cabled computers on the network) don't have to be actual *public* IP addresses. This is true because your LAN is actually "hiding behind" the WiFi router.

The IP addresses provided dynamically by the WiFi router are private IP addresses. When the IP addressing system was originally designed for the Internet, a group of addresses from the Class A, Class B, and Class C ranges were reserved for private networking. These addresses are used by the computers and other devices on your network to communicate locally. Any communication required with the Internet—such as web browsing or sending email—is forwarded from your local network to the Internet (by your ISP) through the WiFi router.

The ranges of addresses reserved for private use are as follows:

- Class A: 10.0.0.0 to 10.255.255.255 (subnet mask 255.0.0)

- Class B: 172.16.0.0 to 172.31.255.255 (subnet mask 255.255.0)

- Class C: 192.168.0.0 to 192.168.255.255 (subnet mask 255.255.255.0)

You will find that your WiFi router will assign IP addresses to computers on the network using one of the private range of addresses; for example, my Netgear router uses the range of addresses from 192.168.1.2 to 192.168.1.51 (Class C) as the default pool for assigning IP addresses dynamically to computers on the WiFi local area network. Most WiFi routers allow you to extend or change the range if needed. To view the range of addresses, access your router's configuration and then access the screen that provides the LAN IP settings. For example, on my Netgear router, I access the LAN IP setup screen using the router's advanced settings.

▶ **TIP**

It makes sense to let your WiFi router assign the IP addresses for your workgroup computers. That way, there is no chance of having a computer configured with a duplicate IP address. If two computers have the same IP address, they are both "knocked off" the network and cannot communicate. If for some reason you decide to configure static IP address (say in an Ad-Hoc situation), do not use the addresses in the pool that the WiFi router uses to dynamically assign addresses. Use a different range of addresses for your static address assignments (although in most cases you shouldn't have *any* static addresses).

Because the WiFi router takes care of the IP addressing for your computer, you don't need to worry about configuring computers with static addresses unless those computers will be set up in the Ad-Hoc mode. You can use any IP addresses from the private network ranges. Just make sure that you are consistent. If two computers are going to communicate in Ad-Hoc mode, configure each computer with an IP address from the same class, such as the two class A IP addresses 10.0.0.1 and 10.0.0.2.

Successfully configuring a computer to participate on your home or small office WiFi network requires that you configure the computer for workgroup participation (that is, you must give the computer a name and its appropriate workgroup settings). You must also configure the computer so that it receives a valid IP address and subnet mask from your WiFi router or you must configure the computer or computers with static IP addresses when operating the WiFi network in Ad-Hoc mode (meaning that no WiFi router is present to provide the IP addresses). When you have configured all these items correctly, the computer can browse the network for other workgroup members and access network services.

37

38   Run the Network Setup Wizard

✔ BEFORE YOU BEGIN

37 About Configuring PCs for Networking

38

For your computer to actually participate in a Microsoft **workgroup**, you must configure it as a workgroup member. This means that, as already mentioned in the previous section, the computer must be configured with a unique NetBIOS name and must also be made a member of the workgroup (this also means that the workgroup must be created).

When naming your computers, select easily recognized names so that a user on the network knows which computer he or she is actually connecting to (you have a maximum of 15 characters and can use alphanumeric and numeric characters, but you cannot use special characters such as spaces, @, #, $, and so on). You can be as creative as you want in terms of naming your networked computers, but try to adopt a system. For example, you can use names such as **gregPC** or **mrgamester**, or you can adopt a simple designation such as **home1**, **home2**. When you name the computer, you are also provided with the option of including a description for the computer. Use the combination of the name and the description to provide all the information necessary for other users on the home network (the workgroup) to be able to identify a particular computer so they can access resources such as files or printers that are shared by that particular computer.

Your home network or workgroup is also designated by a name. The default name set by Microsoft is **MSHOME**. You will want to create your own network name to identify the workgroup; the workgroup name must be the same on all the computers on the home network (meaning the workgroup). The workgroup name itself should be short and descriptive. It cannot contain spaces or special characters such as @, #, or $. Because the workgroup name is really a "private" network name (you won't have people connecting to the network who are not part of your WiFi home network), you can use any name you want. For example, I call my workgroup **Habraken** (my last name) because it is both descriptive of who owns the network (me) and fairly unique in terms of the number of people who will use this name for their workgroup (there are not that many Habrakens running around).

Finally, for a computer to share resources (such as a printer and folders) in the workgroup, it must be configured with the File and Printer Sharing for Microsoft Networks service. There are two ways you can approach configuring these various settings to make a computer a member of a workgroup. The easiest way to create the workgroup is to run the **Network Setup Wizard**.

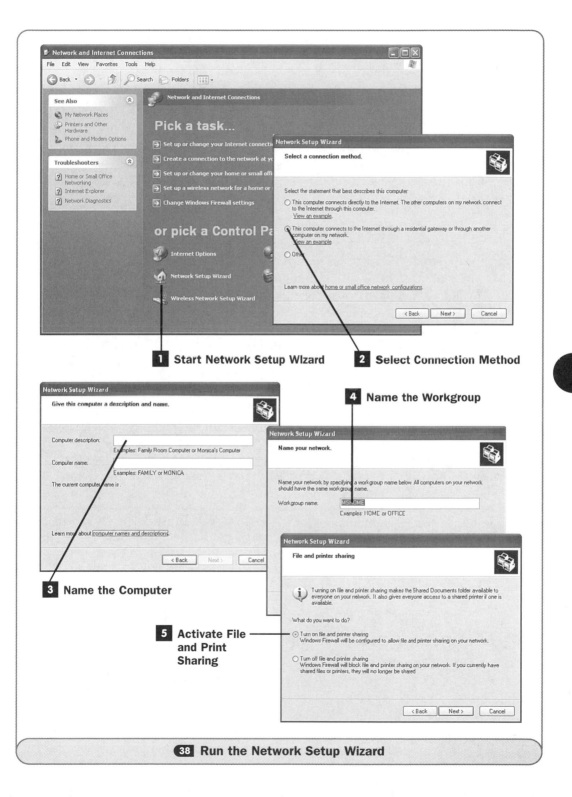

1 Start Network Setup Wizard

2 Select Connection Method

38

4 Name the Workgroup

3 Name the Computer

5 Activate File and Print Sharing

However, to fully understand what the wizard actually does to your computer, you need to have some insight into how system properties are configured for your computer (such as the computer name and its workgroup membership) in the **System Properties** dialog box. You also need to understand how network clients, services, and protocols are used for workgroup communication and the sharing of network resources such as printers and folders.

Run the wizard as explained in this task. Repeat the steps for each computer you want to add to the workgroup. You can then quickly check whether the computers are "on the network" by proceeding to **44 Verify Workgroup Membership and Access Network Neighborhood**.

However, rather than using the wizard as a quick fix and then moving on to using your network, you might want to develop a better understanding of what the **Network Setup Wizard** does in terms of naming the computer and the workgroup and setting up file and print sharing. Refer to **39 Name the Computer and Join a Workgroup**, **40 Open Connection Properties and Enable Clients, Protocols, and Services**, and **41 Add a Network Client or Service**. These tasks show the actual properties dialog boxes that contain your workgroup and networking configurations. So run the wizard and then use the other tasks to better understand (and, if necessary, troubleshoot) the workgroup configuration for your computer.

The **Network Setup Wizard** walks you through the steps of naming the computer and creating the workgroup. It provides the option of creating a network floppy disk you can use to add other computers to the workgroup. You insert the diskette in a computer's disk drive, open **My Computer** from the **Start** menu, access the floppy drive by double-clicking the floppy drive icon in **My Computer**, and then double-click **netsetup.exe** on the floppy disk to run a program that configures the computer for workgroup networking.

You can use the floppy disk or (if you did not create the network floppy disk) run the **Network Setup Wizard** on the other computers participating in your WiFi workgroup network. Remember that every computer that will participate in the workgroup must be configured with the same workgroup name (and a unique name and other network settings) you enter when you run the wizard on the first computer.

38

1 Start Network Setup Wizard

In the **Network and Internet Connections** window (open it from the **Control Panel**), click the **Network Setup Wizard** icon. The first page of the wizard opens; click **Next** to bypass the initial screen. A checklist screen appears, reminding you to install your network adapters and connect the computer to the Internet (meaning that you must make the physical cable connection to the WiFi router or a configured WiFi adapter that attaches to the router by radio signal). Click **Next** to bypass this screen.

2 Select Connection Method

The next wizard screen asks you to select how you are connected to the network and the Internet. Because you are using a WiFi *router* as a *gateway* to your broadband connection, select the **This computer connects to the Internet through a residential gateway or through another computer on my network** option. Then click **Next** to continue.

▶ **TIP**

One of the options on this page of the wizard says **This computer connects directly to the Internet**. A computer connected directly to the Internet is either a computer that connects to the Internet by a modem or a computer that is directly connected to your cable modem or DSL router by a network cable. Because we are using a WiFi router, we don't have any of our computers "connected directly to the Internet."

3 Name the Computer

On the next screen, type a description and name for your computer. If you are happy with the name you previously assigned your computer, type the same name in the text box. The description is optional. Then click **Next** to continue.

4 Name the Workgroup

On the next screen, type a name for the workgroup you are creating. Keep the name simple but also make it descriptive. Do not use the default name (which is **MSHOME**). When determining a workgroup name, do not use spaces or any special characters. After entering a name for the workgroup, click **Next**.

5 Activate File and Print Sharing

On the next screen, make sure that the **Turn on file and print sharing** option is selected and then click **Next**.

The computer is now configured as a member of the workgroup you've just named. The next screen provides you with the option of creating a **Network Setup Disk**; if you decide to create the disk, follow the instructions provided by the wizard. When you have completed the process, click **Finish**.

▶ **TIP**

You can use the floppy disk created by the **Network Setup Wizard** to add other computers to the workgroup. This is a matter of taking the disk to each computer and running the **Network Setup Wizard** with the disk placed in the computer's floppy drive. Because many new computers don't have disk drives, you can also run the wizard on each computer to add it to the workgroup.

39 **Name the Computer and Join a Workgroup**

✔**BEFORE YOU BEGIN**

37 About Configuring PCs for Networking
38 Run the Network Setup Wizard

If you have run the **Network Setup Wizard** as described in **38** **Run the Network Setup Wizard** and can view and access other computers in your *workgroup* (as outlined in **44** **Verify Workgroup Membership and Access Network Neighborhood**), you don't need to make any changes to the **System Properties** dialog box as outlined in this task. This task shows you how to change a computer's name and its workgroup affiliation without re-running the **Network Setup Wizard**. If you want to change a computer's name or the workgroup's name, using the **System Properties** dialog box is a straightforward way to accomplish these tasks.

The **System Properties** dialog box provides you with access to your computer's name and the name of the workgroup to which your computer currently belongs. As you know, each computer on the network must be configured with a unique name that is a maximum of 15 characters. You can use alphanumeric and numeric characters, but you cannot use spaces or special characters such as @, #, $, and so on in the name.

39

1 **Open System Properties Dialog Box**

Click the **Start** menu and then right-click the **My Computer** icon. Select **Properties** from the context menu that appears. The **System Properties** dialog box opens.

▶ **TIP**

If the **My Computer** icon is on your Windows desktop, you can right-click it to access the **System Properties** dialog box.

2 **Open Computer Name Changes Dialog Box**

On the **Computer Name** tab of the **System Properties** dialog box, click the **Change** button. The **Name Changes** dialog box opens.

3 **Enter the Computer Name**

Type a new name for your computer in the **Computer name** text box.

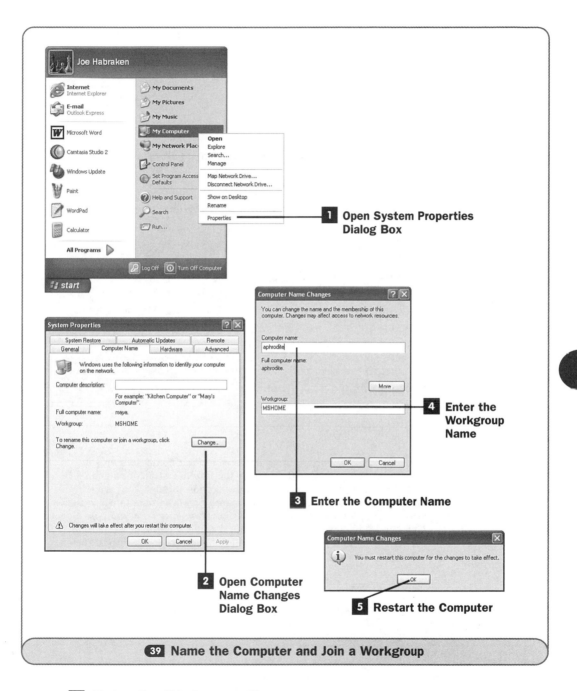

39 Name the Computer and Join a Workgroup

4 Enter the Workgroup Name

Type a new name for the workgroup in the **Workgroup** text box. Even if this is the first computer that will be a member of the workgroup, type the workgroup name; this action, in essence, creates the new workgroup. Then click

OK. A message box appears welcoming you to the workgroup you just created. Click **OK** to close the message box. Another message box opens telling you that you must restart your computer, meaning that the system needs to reboot for the settings to take effect. Click OK, and the system will reboot to Windows. You can now browse the workgroup using My Network Places.

▶ **NOTE**

The **Name Changes** dialog box has a **More** button, which opens a dialog box where you can enter the DNS suffix for your computer's name. Because you are using a workgroup as your network structure, DNS (Domain Name System) information such as the suffix (such as **.com**, **.net**, **.biz**) isn't required; we are not creating a corporate network that requires a DNS hierarchy. In short, you don't need to click the **More** button.

5 **Restart the Computer**

Click **OK** in the **Computer Name Changes** message box. Then click **OK** to close the **Properties** dialog box. A **System Settings** message box opens; click **OK** to restart the computer. Your computer will reboot. After Windows loads, the computer is ready to share resources with other computers in your workgroup.

To add other computers to the network (workgroup), repeat steps 1–5. Each computer must have a unique name and be made a member of your workgroup (by entering the workgroup name).

39

▶ **NOTE**

The workgroup is created so that you can communicate with other computers on your home network. When you go on the road and attach to the Internet at a coffee shop, hotel, or restaurant that provides you with an Internet connection through your WiFi adapter, you don't have to change either the computer name or workgroup name. In this situation, you are *connecting to the Internet* and not *participating in a workgroup*. So when hooking up to wireless hotspots, don't change your computer name or workgroup name because it isn't necessary and you will only have to change the settings back when you return home and want to connect to other computers in your home workgroup.

40 **Open Connection Properties and Enable Clients, Protocols, and Services**

✔ **BEFORE YOU BEGIN**

37 About Configuring PCs for Networking

The **Control Panel** provides you with access to your local area connections. You can view the connections and display the properties for a particular ***network adapter*** such as a WiFi adapter. The properties for an adapter consist of the Windows network settings for the WiFi adapter and are accessed from the **Local Area Connection Properties** dialog box. This dialog box is where you configure services such as file and print sharing and network ***protocols*** such as ***TCP/IP*** (which provides the ***IP address*** for the adapter).

For a computer to participate on a network (such as a Windows workgroup), the WiFi network adapter must be configured with the following:

- **Client**—The client is software that allows you to actually log on to and participate in a particular type of network. In a workgroup, the client software on one computer can talk to the client software on another computer. Because we are creating a Windows workgroup, you need only one client— the **Microsoft Networks** client.

▶ **NOTE**

There are network clients other than the **Microsoft Networks** client. For example, computers that participate on a Novell network (using Novell networking software) use the **Novell** client.

- **Service**—A service is an additional network feature that can be configured for your local area connection. A common service used in workgroup networking is the **File and Printer Sharing for Microsoft Networks** service. This service allows the computers in the workgroup to share files and printers with other members of the workgroup.

- **Network Protocol**—The network protocol provides the addressing system to be used by the computers communicating on the network. At least one network protocol must be enabled and configured for your network adapter. TCP/IP is the only protocol we need to get our workgroup network up and running, and also to allow the computers on the WiFi network to access the Internet through the WiFi router.

To have your WiFi-enabled computer configured so that it can participate in your Windows workgroup, it must be configured with the **Client for Microsoft Networks** (a client), **File and Printer Sharing for Microsoft Networks** (a service), and the TCP/IP **Network Protocol**. *Configured* means not only installed on the computer, but also enabled in the **Properties** dialog box. So, you will find that a client such as **Client for Microsoft Networks** can be listed in the **Properties** dialog box but might not be enabled (the check box for the client has not been selected).

40

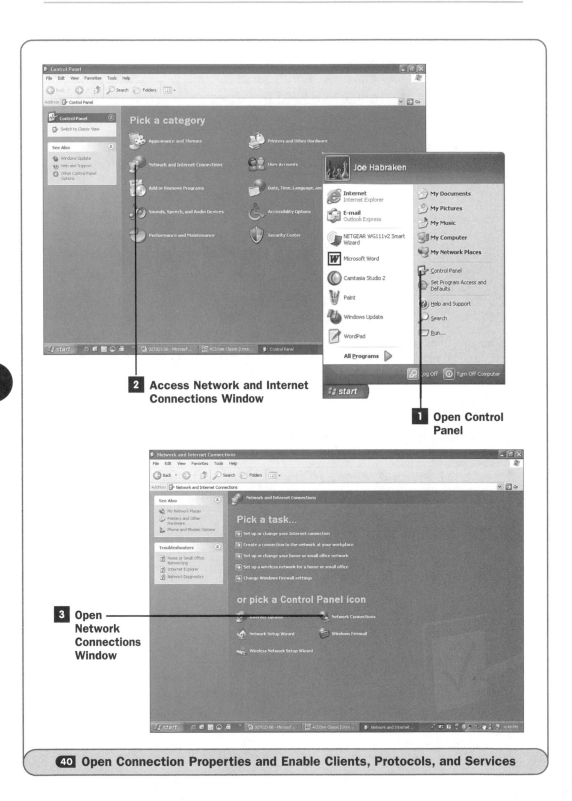

40

2 **Access Network and Internet Connections Window**

1 **Open Control Panel**

3 **Open Network Connections Window**

40 **Open Connection Properties and Enable Clients, Protocols, and Services**

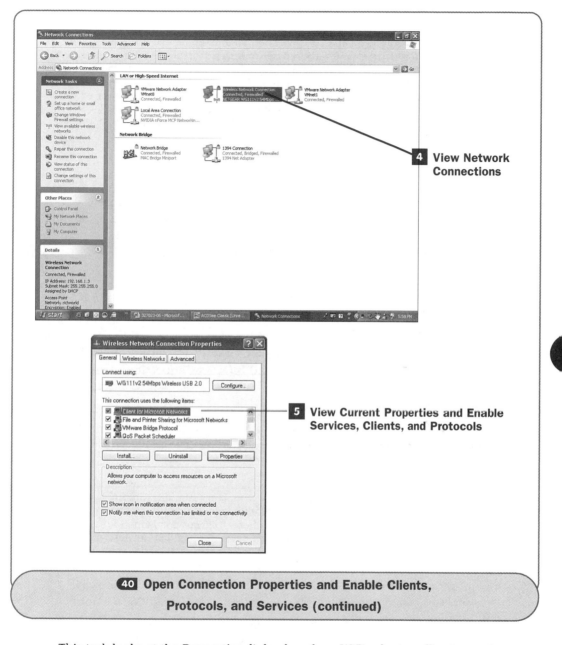

4 View Network Connections

5 View Current Properties and Enable Services, Clients, and Protocols

40 Open Connection Properties and Enable Clients, Protocols, and Services (continued)

This task looks at the **Properties** dialog box for a WiFi adapter, allowing us to access whatever client or service we might need to add and also to enable any service, client, or protocol that is installed but not currently enabled.

► **NOTE**

You can have more than one local area connection on a computer. For example, a computer that has a network adapter for a wired network can also have a WiFi adapter for a wireless network. You can disable any network adapter you are not using in the **Device Manager**, which is reached by way of the **System Properties** dialog box. However, you don't save any system power and you don't increase system resource availability all that dramatically by disabling an unused device, so it is up to you in terms of disabling an unused device. If the device, such as a USB WiFi adapter, is removed from the computer, you don't need to also disable the device in the **Device Manager**.

1 **Open Control Panel**

Click **Start** and then click the **Control Panel** icon on the **Start** menu. The **Control Panel** opens.

2 **Access Network and Internet Connections Window**

In the **Control Panel**, click the **Network and Internet Connections** link. The **Network and Internet Connections** window opens.

3 **Open Network Connections Window**

To open the **Network Connections** window, click the **Network Connection** icon (near the bottom of the **Network and Internet Connections** window) .

4 **View Network Connections**

All the local area network and other connections appear in the **Network Connections** window. Your WiFi adapter should be listed in this window.

► **NOTE**

If you have more than one network adapter on a computer (even if a wired network adapter is not connected), you might see a network bridge listed in the **Network Connection** window. A bridge is created to link different networks together. So computers that have more than one network adapter can have a bridge that provides a connection between the two different local area connections created by the two adapters.

Right-click your WiFi adapter's local area connection icon in the **Network Connections** window and select **Properties**. The **Local Area Connection Properties** dialog box opens for your WiFi adapter.

5 **View Properties and Enable Installed Items**

It is important that you take an inventory (you can write it down or just remember the settings) of the clients, services, and protocols installed for the currently selected LAN connection (your WiFi adapter). Use the scrollbar to

40

scroll through the items in the dialog box to view the items in the properties list. Make sure that the following items appear in the properties list:

- **Client for Microsoft Networks**—This client is necessary for your computer to access a Microsoft network such as a workgroup (which we are using for the home network). If this item is listed but not enabled, click the client's check box. If this item is not listed, you must add the client.

- **File and Printer Sharing for Microsoft Networks**—This service allows you to share folders on your computer with other computers connected to your workgroup. The service also allows you to share a printer attached to your computer with the workgroup. If this item is not listed, you must add it.

- **Internet Protocol (TCP/IP)**—This item appears in the **Properties** dialog box list because it is the default protocol for the Windows XP operating system. You can't communicate in the workgroup or over the Internet without this protocol. Although it cannot be removed from the list, it can be disabled. Click the check box for the Internet Protocol (TCP/IP) to enable the protocol if necessary.

If a listed item such as the **Client for Microsoft Networks** is installed but not enabled (meaning that the check box to the left of the client does not contain a check mark), click the item's check box to enable it. If any of the listed items are missing (the client or the service), you must add the network client or service as detailed in **41** **Add a Network Client or Service.**

41 Add a Network Client or Service

✔ **BEFORE YOU BEGIN**

40 Open Connection Properties and Enable Clients, Protocols, and Services

As discussed in **40** **Open Connection Properties and Enable Clients, Protocols, and Services**, you must have your WiFi *network adapter* configured so that your computer can participate in a Microsoft *workgroup*. This means that the Local Area Connection (this term is synonymous with your WiFi *adapter*) must be configured with the **Client for Microsoft Networks** (the client provides access to the workgroup) and the **File and Printer Sharing for Microsoft Networks** service (which allows file and print sharing on your computer). Finally, the computer must be configured with a network protocol; we'll use the TCP/IP protocol to provide the computer with the ability to communicate in the workgroup and over the Internet (which *requires* TCP/IP). The bottom line is that you must have these three items listed in the WiFi adapter's **Local Area Connection Properties** dialog box. No substitutions are allowed if you want the computer to actually participate on the network.

In some cases, depending on who configured your computer's network settings (and whether or not those settings have been changed since you bought your computer), these three items might already be configured in your **Wireless Network Connection Properties** dialog box. Because TCP/IP is the default protocol for Windows XP, it is already installed on your system; in fact Windows XP does not allow you to remove TCP/IP from the **Wireless Network Connection Properties** dialog box. However, you can disable the protocol by clearing the check box next to the **Internet Protocol (TCP/IP)** item in the properties list.

Because TCP/IP will appear in the properties list by default (because we are talking about Windows XP), you only have to ensure that it is enabled—that is, that there is a check in the **Internet Protocol (TCP/IP)** check box. You can then concentrate on adding the **Client for Microsoft Networks** (the client) and the **File and Printer Sharing for Microsoft Networks** service.

▶ **TIP**

41

You need to run through this task only if one of these required items is missing from the WiFi adapter's configuration. Look back at the configuration inventory you did in the previous task to see whether you are missing any of these required components for workgroup networking or whether TCP/IP has been disabled for the connection. If so, use this task to add that particular component or enable the TCP/IP protocol.

Every computer participating in the workgroup must be configured for Microsoft workgroup networking. This means that all the configuration items detailed in this task must be configured on each computer that will be a member of the workgroup.

▌**1** Enable TCP/IP Protocol

Open the **Wireless Network Connection Properties** dialog box for your WiFi adapter by right-clicking your WiFi adapter's local area connection icon in the **Network Connections** window and selecting **Properties**. If TCP/IP is disabled, enable it. In the **Wireless Network Connection Properties** dialog box, select the **Internet Protocol (TCP/IP)** check box to permit the use of TCP/IP on the system.

▌**2** Open Select Network Component Type Dialog Box

Now you can concentrate on adding required items such as the **Client for Microsoft Networks** (the client) and the **File and Printer Sharing for Microsoft Networks** service. Click the **Install** button. The **Select Network Component Type** dialog box opens.

2 Open Select Network
Component Type Dialog Box

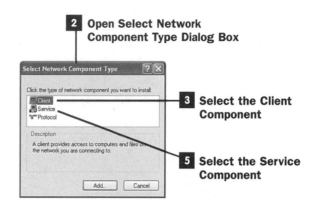

3 Select the Client
Component

5 Select the Service
Component

1 Enable TCP/IP Protocol

4 Add Client for Microsoft
Networks

6 Add File and Printer Sharing for
Microsoft Networks

7 Close Wireless Network Connection
Properties dialog box

41 Add a Network Client or Service

41

▌3▐ Select the Client Component

In the **Select Network Component Type** dialog box, choose the component type to be added. Because we need to add the Microsoft workgroup client, select **Client** from the dialog box and click **Add**. The **Select Network Client** dialog box opens.

▌4▐ Add Client for Microsoft Networks

In the **Select Network Client** dialog box, choose **Client for Microsoft Networks** from the **Network Client** list and click **OK**. It may take a moment, but you will be returned to the **Properties** dialog box, and the client will be added to the list.

▌5▐ Select the Service Component.

Open the **Select Network Component Type** dialog box again by clicking **Install** in the **Wireless Network Connection Properties** dialog box. Select the **Service** component and then click **Add**. The **Select Network Service** dialog box opens.

▌6▐ Add File and Printer Sharing for Microsoft Networks

In the **Select Network Service** dialog box, click **File and Printer Sharing for Microsoft Networks** and then click **OK**. This service is added to the configuration list in the **Wireless Network Connection Properties** dialog box.

▶ TIP

You might see other clients and services available for your system such as the **Service Advertising Protocol** or the **NWLink** protocol. These items are used on networks that deploy a Novell NetWare server. You don't need to add or really do anything with any of the clients or services available other than the **Client for Microsoft Networks** client and the **File and Printer Sharing for Microsoft Networks** service that are required for workgroup networking.

▌7▐ Close Wireless Network Connection Properties Dialog Box

After TCP/IP is enabled and you have the **Client for Microsoft Networks** client and the **File and Printer Sharing for Microsoft Networks** service enabled, you can close the dialog box by clicking **Close**.

▶ TIP

In some cases, the **Client for Microsoft Networks** client or the **File and Printer Sharing for Microsoft Networks** service will be installed in the WiFi adapter's properties list but have been disabled (who knows how, things happen). If either of these items is listed but disabled, click the check box to the left of the item to enable the client or service.

▶ **TIP**

You might not be sure whether some items listed in the **Wireless Network Connection Properties** dialog box are necessary. You can select an item from the list and click the **Uninstall** button to remove unwanted clients, services, or protocols. However, if you aren't sure what an item does or whether it is necessary, don't uninstall it. Removing needed services or protocols can affect the computer's ability to communicate on the network.

42 | **Configure TCP/IP Settings**

✔ **BEFORE YOU BEGIN**

40 Open Connection Properties and Enable Clients, Protocols, and Services
41 Add a Network Client or Service

Your local area connection (the WiFi *network adapter*) must be configured with the appropriate *TCP/IP* settings to communicate on your network and take advantage of your high-speed Internet connection. Because this book assumes that have you added a WiFi *router* to your network to take advantage of your broadband Internet connection, we can allow the WiFi router to dole out TCP/IP settings to the various computers on your WiFi network.

For the WiFi router to automatically configure the TCP/IP settings for a computer (including the *IP address*), the local area connection on the computer must be configured as a Dynamic Host Configuration Protocol (DHCP) client. This means that the computer requests an IP address and other TCP/IP configuration information when it boots up. The WiFi router responds with the needed information.

▶ **KEY TERMS**

Dynamic Host Configuration Protocol (DHCP)—A protocol used by DHCP servers and clients to negotiate the dynamic assignment of IP addresses over a network. The DHCP server (such as a WiFi router) provides the DHCP client with the IP address.

DHCP client—A computer that has been configured for the TCP/IP protocol so that the IP address (and subnet mask) is automatically assigned to the computer by a device such as your WiFi router that can act as a DHCP server.

You configure a computer as a DHCP client in the **Internet Protocol (TCP/IP) Properties** dialog box, which you can access from the **Wireless Network Connection Properties** box. By default, Windows XP computers are already configured as DHCP clients. However, it doesn't hurt for you to walk through the steps of how you would configure TCP/IP properties for a WiFi adapter.

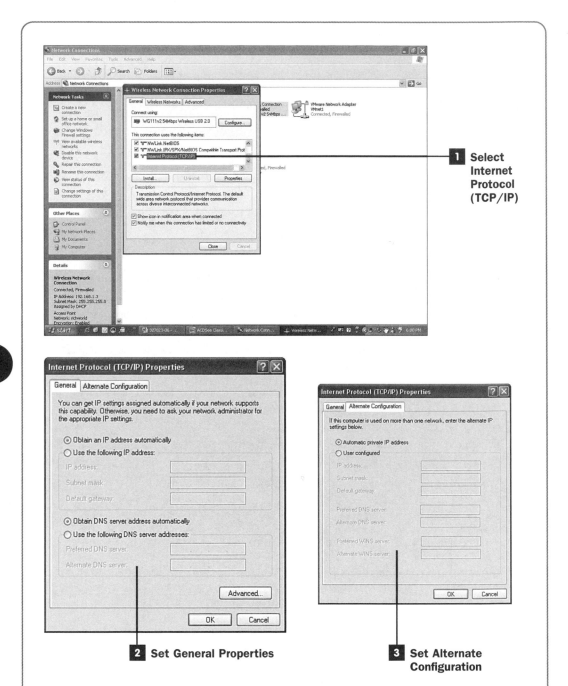

1 Select
Internet
Protocol
(TCP/IP)

42

2 Set General Properties

3 Set Alternate
Configuration

42 Configure TCP/IP Settings

1 Select Internet Protocol (TCP/IP)

In the **Wireless Network Connection Properties** dialog box for your WiFi adapter, scroll down through the list of *clients*, *services*, and *protocols* and select **Internet Protocol (TCP/IP)**. Then click the **Properties** button. The **Internet Protocol (TCP/IP) Properties** dialog box opens.

2 Set General Properties

To configure the adapter as a DHCP client, select the **Obtain an IP address automatically** option, located on the **General** tab of the **Internet Protocol (TCP/IP) Properties** dialog box . Also select the **Obtain DNS server address automatically** option. Then click the **Alternate Configuration** tab.

▶ **NOTE**

DNS stands for Domain Name Service. It is the service that translates IP addresses to "friendly" domain names—where *friendly* means "names we can easily work with." For example, when you want to go to a website such as **www.samspublishing.com**, you don't type the IP address (such as **130.5.62.1**) in your web browser window; you type the friendly name **www.samspublishing.com**. DNS servers on the Web translate the friendly name to the actual IP address, and that is why you are actually able to navigate to the correct website. Because your WiFi router communicates with the broadband device from your Internet service provider, your WiFi router knows the IP addresses of the Internet service provider's DNS servers. So you should select the **Obtain DNS server address automatically** option when you configure TCP/IP for your adapter. The DNS server IP addresses are then provided to your computers when the WiFi router leases IP address to each of the computers.

42

3 Set Alternate Configuration

The **Alternate Configuration** tab is optional, but it can be useful if you also use the computer in **Ad Hoc** *mode* (computer-to-computer mode), which requires a fixed IP address and *subnet mask*. Select the **User Configured** option and then type an IP address and subnet mask in the appropriate boxes. You can use any of the private IP address ranges for these IP address (see **37** **About Configuring PCs for Networking**). You do not have to enter the default *gateway*, DNS servers, or WINS servers. Only the IP addresses are needed for Ad-Hoc mode (since the Ad-Hoc connection only exists between the computers that are configured for Ad-Hoc mode) .

When you have finished setting the TCP/IP properties for your adapter, close the **Internet Protocol (TCP/IP) Properties** dialog box by clicking **OK**. You return to the **Wireless Network Connection Properties** dialog box.

43   Check WiFi Adapter Status

✔ **BEFORE YOU BEGIN**

40 Open Connection Properties and Enable Clients, Protocols, and Services
41 Add a Network Client or Service
42 Configure TCP/IP Settings

Now that you have configured your computer for network access and *TCP/IP* settings, you might want to check the status of your WiFi *network adapter* in the **Wireless Network Connection Status** dialog box. Not only does this dialog box allow you to check the connection duration and signal strength, it also allows you to view the *IP address* that has was assigned to the adapter by your WiFi *router*.

Being able to view the status allows you to tell whether the adapter is working correctly. Although the duration of the connection isn't all that important a setting (unless you are experiencing signal dropouts and are losing the connection), knowing whether the WiFi router has assigned an IP address to the adapter *is* important. And being able to quickly view the signal strength of the connection lets you determine how well the PC can receive the radio signals from the WiFi router.

43

▶ **TIP**

Alternatively, you can right-click the WiFi connection icon in the Notification area at the right end of the Task bar and select **Status** from the context menu to view the status of your WiFi adapter. If you are using a configuration utility that came with your WiFi adapter, choosing the **Status** option might open that utility, which can also be used to view the status and IP settings of your WiFi adapter.

1 **Open Wireless Network Connection Status Dialog Box**

In the **Network Connections** window (opened from the **Control Panel**), double-click the icon for your WiFi network connection. The **Wireless Network Connection Status** dialog box opens.

2 **View Status**

The **General** tab of the dialog box provides the current status of the WiFi adapter's connection as well as the duration of the connection and the current signal strength for the connection. The duration of the connection can be used to determine whether there has been a recent problem with the actual connection; the signal strength allows you to gauge how well the computer's WiFi adapter is connecting to the WiFi router's access point.

Click the **Support** tab to open the second page of the dialog box.

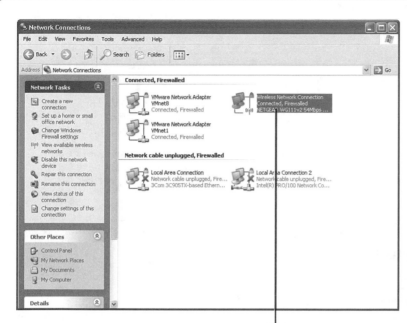

1 Open Wireless Network Connection
Status Dialog Box

2 View Status

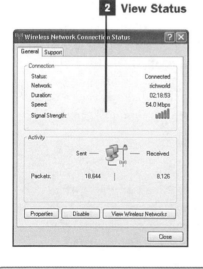

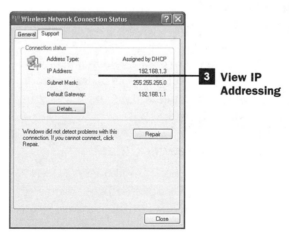

3 View IP
Addressing

3 View IP Addressing

The **Support** tab of the **Wireless Network Connection Status** dialog box shows the IP address and subnet mask assigned to the adapter by the WiFi router. It also shows the IP address of the default *gateway*, also known as your WiFi router (it is the gateway between your private WiFi network and the public network, the Internet). Click **Close** to close the dialog box.

▶ KEY TERMS

Gateway—A device that serves as an intermediary between two different types of networks. In our case, we are looking at the device—our WiFi router—that connects our private workgroup network with the public Internet. The WiFi router is the gateway.

---

44 | **Verify Workgroup Membership and Access Network Neighborhood**

✔ **BEFORE YOU BEGIN**

38 Run the Network Setup Wizard

43

After you have configured your WiFi-enabled computers (or hard-wired network computers) to be members of the *workgroup*, you can browse for these computers on the network. Locating these computers allows you to access any shared resources they might have, such as files and printers. If you can't actually view the computers in the workgroup, you have some sort of connectivity issue with either the computer you are working on or with the other workgroup computers. Viewing the workgroup computers in the **Workgroup** window allows you to make sure that all the configurations you have created in the preceding tasks in this chapter actually work.

1 Open My Network Places

Click the **Start** button and then select **My Network Places** on the **Start** menu. The **My Network Places** window opens. This window shows you any network locations to which you have created a connection. For more information on adding Network Places to your computer, see **53 Add a Network Place**.

2 Open Workgroup Window

In the **Network Tasks** list on the left side of the window, click **View workgroup computers**. The workgroup window opens.

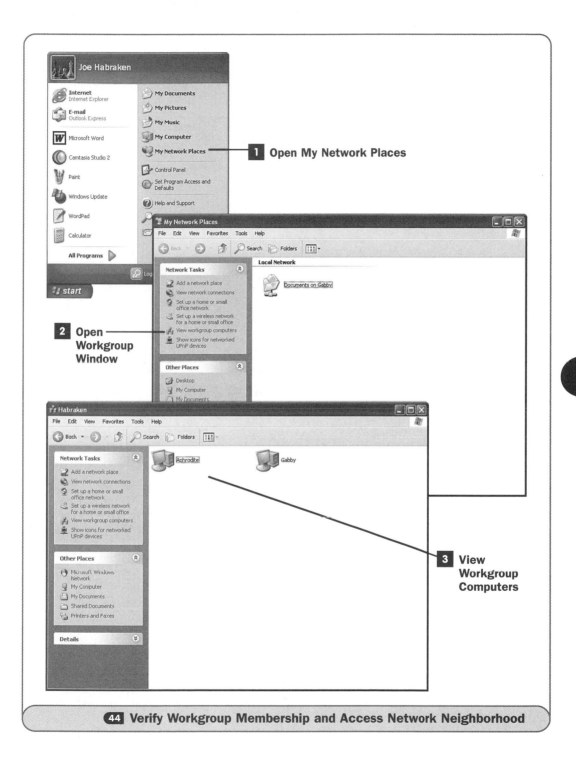

1 Open My Network Places

2 Open Workgroup Window

3 View Workgroup Computers

44

3 View Workgroup Computers

All the computers in the workgroup appear in the workgroup window. You can access any of the resources shared on these computers by double-clicking a specific computer icon. For more about sharing and accessing workgroup resources, see **45 About Sharing Network Resources**.

44

PART III

Using the Home Network

IN THIS PART

7

Sharing Network Resources

IN THIS CHAPTER:

After you have your WiFi *router* set up and the WiFi-enabled and "wired" computers on your network configured for workgroup networking, you are ready to share network resources such as folders and printers. After a resource is shared, it can be accessed by other computers in the *workgroup*. In this chapter, we take a look at how you share a particular resource such as a printer in a workgroup and we take a look at how users in the workgroup can access available resources.

---

45 About Sharing Network Resources

✔ BEFORE YOU BEGIN

- **3** Browse and Search for Files and Folders
- **4** About My Network Places
- **37** About Configuring PCs for Networking
- **44** Verify Workgroup Membership and Access Network Neighborhood

---

45

The term *network resources* is a broad term for items you can share on a network. In a Windows workgroup, you can share drives, folders (and the files in the folders), and printers. Because we are going to operate in a workgroup that doesn't have a centralized server, the types of items we can share are limited. Although we can share access to a folder that holds a software installation program and install the software by accessing the shared folder, workgroup computing does not provide for the sharing of applications. So, you can't run software that is installed on one computer over the network on another computer—even if you have shared the folder that contains the executable file for that program. It is also a violation of the software agreement to run most applications concurrently on two computers—unless you own more than one license for the software.

A shared drive or folder is referred to as a *share*. The actual access to the share is controlled by the user who actually shares the drive or folder on his or her computer.

▶ KEY TERM

Share—A drive or folder that is shared on the network.

▶ NOTE

Computers running Windows XP can share items such as printers and folders when they have been configured for workgroup networking. This requires that the **Client for Microsoft Networks** be installed and enabled on the computer and that the **File and Printer Sharing for Microsoft Networks** also be installed and enabled. You can configure these items in the **Wireless Network Connection Properties** dialog box. See **41** **Add a Network Client or Service** for more information.

In terms of network security, Windows XP Home Edition (which is what I assume you are using) is rather lax. A share is either shared or it is not shared. Once a share has been made available to the workgroup, it can be seen by *all* the members of that workgroup. The only real security is related to whether users who access the share can actually make changes to the files in the share; the decision of whether network users can modify shared files is up to the individual who creates the share in the first place.

So, workgroup networking is decentralized, meaning that each user on a computer in the workgroup can share (or not share) resources as they see fit. Decentralized peer-to-peer networking such as Microsoft workgroup networking can certainly be convenient in terms of sharing resources between workgroup computer users; however, it does not provide the secure environment supplied by a centralized network that requires users to access resources on a centralized and secure network server.

This means that securing the workgroup is more about protecting the rather unsecured network from outside intrusion. This in turn means that you must protect the WiFi network by using the security features provided by your WiFi *router* (you are securing the network medium—the WiFi radio waves—rather than the software mechanism that the Windows operating system uses to share resources). For more information about securing the network infrastructure, see **72** **About Basic Network Security**.

45

Actually sharing folders and printers in the Windows environment is extremely straightforward. Each item, such as a printer or folder, has a **Properties** dialog box (we will look at how you access these dialog boxes in **46** **Share a Printer** and **47** **Share a Folder**). These **Properties** dialog boxes each provide a **Sharing** tab, which contains the settings for sharing that particular resource.

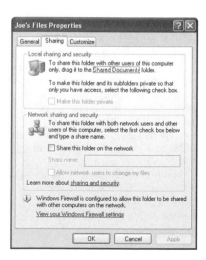

*The **Sharing** tab for a folder is used to configure a folder as a shared resource in the workgroup.*

► **NOTE**

When multiple people use the same computer, each user has a user profile, which controls access to folders created for that user on that computer. To share a folder with a person with whom you share a computer (I'm not talking about sharing a folder with other workgroup computers), you simply drag the folder from the **My Computer** window (click the **Start** button and then choose **My Computer** to open the window) to the **Shared Documents** folder that also appears in the **My Computer** window. Any user on the shared computer can then access the files in the folder that you have shared by dragging it to the **Shared Documents** folder. This type of sharing (between different users on the same computer) can take place even when a computer has not been configured for networking. So, don't confuse sharing folders locally on a computer with sharing folders on a workgroup network. For more about creating multiple user accounts on the same computer, see **⑪ Create a User Account**.

---

46 Share a Printer

✔ **BEFORE YOU BEGIN**

㊺ About Sharing Network Resources

45

A computer user who has a printer connected to her computer can share the computer with other users in the workgroup. Sharing a printer allows users on multiple computers in the network to print to a single printer. A *directly connected* printer is a printer connected to the computer by either a USB connection or a parallel connection (typically LPT1, which is the default parallel printer port). Because USB has become the most common way to connect peripherals such as printers to computers, you are probably using a USB printer (most printers no longer provide a parallel port for connecting to the computer).

► **NOTE**

As already mentioned, nearly all new printers connect to a computer by means of a USB port only. If you have an older printer, it may be connected to your computer by a parallel cable (which connects to the computer's parallel port). Many new computers come equipped with a greater number of USB ports than older computers and might not even have a parallel printer port. USB is faster in terms of connection speed, anyhow. Several manufacturers of printers such as Hewlett Packard (HP) have recently released WiFi printers. A user can connect to the printer directly through a WiFi connection. These printers are expensive, however ($300 plus), and are really designed for a user on the go who needs to print from a WiFi-enabled laptop computer to a printer without worrying about cables. In terms of connecting printers directly to a WiFi network (rather than to one of the computers on the network), WiFi adapter manufacturers, such as Netgear, also make WiFi print servers. These print servers actually look like a WiFi router or access point and provide multiple USB ports for connecting printers. The WiFi print server then connects to the WiFi network and allows any computer on the network to connect to a provided printer and print.

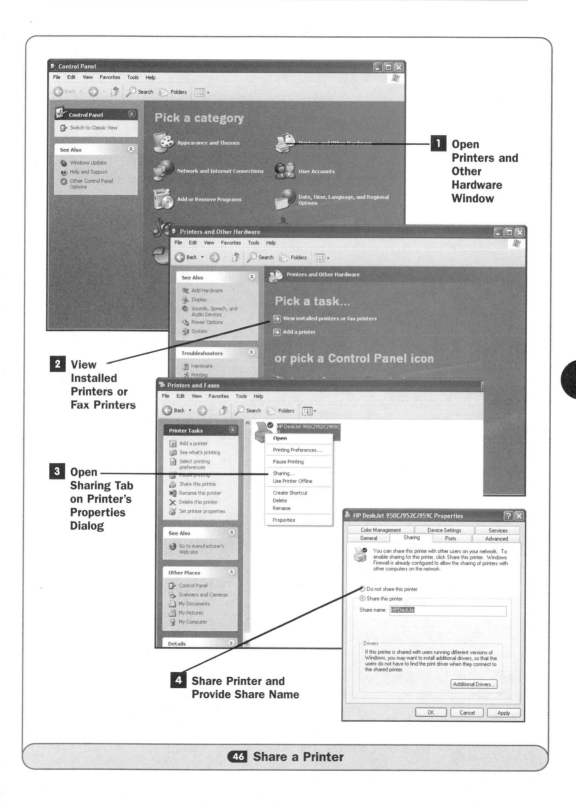

1 Open Printers and Other Hardware Window

2 View Installed Printers or Fax Printers

3 Open Sharing Tab on Printer's Properties Dialog

4 Share Printer and Provide Share Name

45

No matter how the printer is connected to the computer (USB or parallel), it is referred to as a *local printer*. The computer user shares her local printer with the other users in the workgroup, who actually refer to the printer as a *remote printer*.

▶ KEY TERMS

Local printer—A printer connected directly to the computer.

Remote printer—A printer connected to a computer in the workgroup other than the one currently being used. Users in the workgroup other than the owner of the computer to which the printer is physically connected can print to the remote printer.

The local printer is shared by the person who uses the computer to which the printer is physically connected. Other users in the workgroup can then connect to the remote printer (which is shared) over the network and print to that printer. Let's take a look at how to share the printer; refer to **51 Connect to a Shared Printer** to learn how a user connects to a remote, shared printer.

1 Open Printers and Other Hardware Window

We need to drill down through the **Control Panel** windows so that we can open the **Properties** dialog box for the printer you want to share. Open the **Control Panel** by clicking **Start** and then choosing **Control Panel**, and then click the **Printers and Other Hardware** link. The **Printers and Other Hardware** window opens.

2 View Installed Printers or Fax Printers

Click the **View Installed printers or fax printers** link in the Printers and Other Hardware window. The **Printers and Faxes** window opens.

3 Open Sharing Tab on Printer's Properties Dialog

Right-click the icon for the local printer you want to share (the icon label doesn't say the printer is local, but if you connected to a remote printer, it will typically name the computer that is sharing the printer). Select **Sharing** from the context menu that appears. The **Properties** dialog box for the selected printer opens with the **Sharing** tab selected.

▶ TIP

If the **Share this Printer** option is unavailable on the **Sharing** tab of the printer's **Properties** dialog box, and you see text that says **printer sharing must be turned on**, you must install and activate the **File and Printer Sharing for Microsoft Networks** service. The easiest way to make sure that this service is available is to run the **Network Setup Wizard** as described in **38 Run the Network Setup Wizard**.

4 Share Printer and Provide Share Name

On the **Sharing** tab of the printer's **Properties** dialog box, click the **Share this printer** option button. A share name, which is an abbreviated version of the printer's actual name (such as **Deskjet 950C**), is automatically placed in the **Share name** text box. You can retain the automatic name or you can type your own share name. The point of the share name is so that users on the network can tell which printer they are connecting to when they attach to the printer remotely. So make the share name as descriptive as possible. The share name should be no more than 31 characters (a Microsoft suggested maximum length). Although spaces are allowed in the name, I suggest that you do not use spaces, particularly if a computer in the workgroup is running an operating system earlier than Windows XP (such as Windows Me or Windows 98). These operating systems do not allow share names (such as names for shared printers) with spaces or with more than 12 characters.

After you have typed the share name for the printer, click **OK**. You return to the **Printers and Faxes** window. The printer's icon now includes a cupped hand, showing that the printer is shared on the network (the workgroup).

▶ **TIP**

We have assumed in this book that your computer and the other computers in the workgroup are running Windows XP Home Edition. However, as mentioned in step 4 of this task, earlier versions of Windows can co-exist with Windows XP in aworkgroup, but you must make allowances for these earlier versions of Windows, particularly in terms of the naming conventions you use for shares. Also, the printer-sharing feature of Windows XP is set up so that when you connect to a shared printer in a workgroup from another computer running Windows XP, the appropriate printer driver is downloaded to your computer so that you can print to the remote printer. If you have any Windows 98 or Windows Me computers in the workgroup, you must set up the printer sharing so that these computers download the correct print driver software for the operating system. On the **Sharing** tab of the shared printer's **Properties** dialog box, click the **Additional Drivers** button. In the **Additional Drivers** window that opens, use the check boxes to select the versions of the additional drivers you need (such as for Windows 95 or Windows 98). When you click **OK**, you are asked to place the Windows XP CD-ROM in your CD drive; it contains drivers for earlier versions of the Windows operating system.

47

47 Share a Folder

✔ **BEFORE YOU BEGIN**

45 About Sharing Network Resources

You can share a folder or a drive with other users on the network. Sharing a container such as a folder or a drive allows users in the workgroup to access any of the files on that drive or in that folder. It generally is not a good idea to share an entire drive because we typically have content on a drive to which we want exclusive access. It makes more sense to either place specific files in your **Shared Documents** folder (which is shared automatically on the network) or to share individual folders. Limiting the shared files and folders in this way provides you more control over the files that are actually accessible by workgroup users.

In terms of security for the file and folders you choose to share, Windows XP Home Edition allows you to designate that the access to files on a drive or in a shared folder be *read only*. Assigning read-only access to your shared files and folders means that a user on the network can access, open, and read these files but they cannot make changes to the files and save the changes directly to the source drive or folder (the drive or folder you have shared). They can, however, *copy* the file to their own computer and then edit or change the file as they see fit, including renaming the file.

▶ **KEY TERM**

Read-only access—A file or folder that can be accessed, opened, and read but that cannot be changed and saved directly to the source drive or folder. Such files and folders can, however, be *copied* and then edited or changed.

47

Sharing folder and file resources in a workgroup requires that all users on the network "play nice." Because no single administrator controls access to network resources, everyone has to behave in a manner that makes the sharing of drives, folders, and files a plus for all network users rather than a nightmare of accidentally deleted files, missing shares, and other resource problems.

In terms of removable media and "portable" USB drives, you can share CD/DVD drives and removable USB drives. However, if a user removes a USB drive from the computer, it is no longer available over the network. In terms of sharing CD/DVD drives, you can access the folders (and the contained files) for any CD or DVD that is placed in the shared drive. I actually use this technique when I need to install software (for which I have multiple licenses) to more than one computer. The installation CD can go in the shared CD drive and then I can access the installation program from any computer in the workgroup. Be advised, however, that installing software is slower over the network than actually installing the software directly on the computer using its own CD/DVD drive.

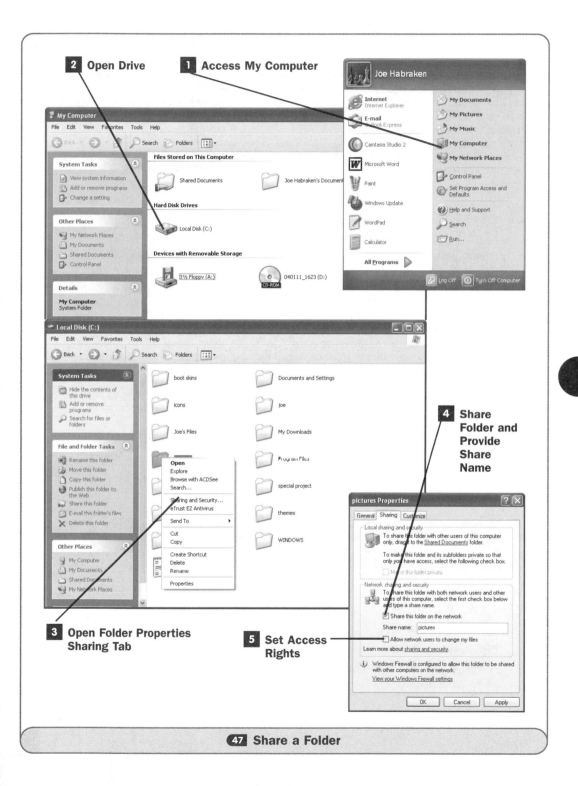

2 Open Drive   **1** Access My Computer

4 Share Folder and Provide Share Name

3 Open Folder Properties Sharing Tab

5 Set Access Rights

47

47 Share a Folder

▶ **TIP**

Although you can share folders that contain the executable files for an application, you can't run the application over the network. Applications are designed to be installed and then run from the same computer, so even though you can access the executable file for an application in a shared folder, your computer isn't configured to really run the application (and so the application won't run). Because the user license for most applications denies concurrent use of an application, you shouldn't try to get away with running more than one instance of a single user software package anyway. There are "network" versions of software applications, but these are designed to run on a network that provides specific servers that share the applications with the end-user computers on the network.

1 Access My Computer

Click the **Start** button and then select **My Computer** from the **Start** menu (you can also double-click the **My Computer** icon on your desktop if it is present). **Windows Explorer** opens, showing all your computer's drives.

▶ **TIP**

If you don't have the **My Computer** icon on your Windows XP desktop, click the **Start** button and then right-click the **My Computer** icon in the **Start** menu. Select **Show on Desktop** from the context menu that appears. The icon now appears on the desktop and can be used to access **Windows Explorer**.

47

2 Open Drive

To share a folder, you need to access the folder. Double-click the icon for a drive in **Windows Explorer**, such as your **Local Disk (C:)** drive. A list of all the folders contained in that drive appears in a new window.

▶ **TIP**

Rather than sharing an existing folder, consider creating a new folder and then sharing it. After accessing a drive on your computer using Windows Explorer, choose **File, New, Folder**. A new folder appears for the drive in the **Windows Explorer** window. Type a name for the folder. You can then share the folder as discussed in this task.

3 Open Folder Properties Sharing Tab

To share a folder in the selected drive, you must open the folder's **Properties** dialog box and then access the **Sharing** tab: Right-click the folder you want to share and select **Sharing and Security** from the context menu. The folder's **Properties** dialog box opens with the **Sharing** tab selected.

▶ **NOTE**

You can also right-click a drive icon such as the **Local Drive (C:)** icon and share the drive using the same steps as sharing a folder. However, sharing an entire drive opens up all your files to the network. Sharing a drive in this way means that all your documents and other items can be viewed by others on the network. You can make the drive read-only to negate the accidental deletion of your files, but you are still making all your personal information an open book to anyone with network access.

4 **Share Folder and Provide Share Name**

On the **Sharing** tab, click the **Share this folder on the network** check box. A default share name appears in the **Share name** text box (the default name is based on the folder name). If you want to change the share name, select the default text and type a new name. If all the computers in the workgroup are running Windows XP, you can use 31 characters (including spaces) for the share name. If your workgroup computers are running a mixture of operating systems (such as Windows XP and Windows 98), use a maximum of 12 characters for the share name and don't use spaces.

5 **Set Access Rights**

If you want to allow network users to change (meaning edit, delete, and so on) the files in the shared folder, click the **Allow network users to change my files** check box. If you want the files in the shared folder (as well as the folder itself) to have read-only access, leave the **Allow network users to change my files** check box deselected.

When you are ready to complete the folder-sharing process, click **OK**. The **Properties** dialog box closes and you return to the **Windows Explorer** window. The folder is now marked with a sharing icon (a hand holding the folder). The folder and its contents can now be accessed by other users in the workgroup. See **48** **About Accessing Network Resources** for information about accessing shared files and folders on the network.

48

48 **About Accessing Network Resources**

✔ **BEFORE YOU BEGIN**

3 Browse and Search for Files and Folders
4 About My Network Places
44 View Workgroup Membership and Access Network Neighborhood
45 About Sharing Network Resources

After network resources such as printers and folders have been shared, you and other workgroup members can access these resources. Access any available workgroup resources by opening **My Network Places**. The **My Network Places** window shows the *shares* (folders) that are currently available to the workgroup. It also identifies the host of each share by computer name. Workgroup members can access printers shared by a particular workgroup computer by opening the **My Network Places** window and selecting the **View workgroup computers** link. From this window, you can view all the resources shared by a particular computer, including printers.

If you don't see a particular share you were hoping to access, this might mean that the computer that hosts the share is currently turned off and is not available. In some cases, the host computer may be on but the share isn't showing in the **My Network Places** windows because the host computer's presence on the network hasn't reached your computer yet. Computers "advertise" their presence on the network and also advertise the shares they offer. If a computer has just been turned on, it might not appear in your **My Network Places** window because the "advertisement" hasn't reached your computer yet. In cases where you don't see a resource that you know is there, you can do a quick search for the computer using the Windows **Search** feature (available in the **Start** menu). If you still can't locate and access the other computer's shares, you might have a connectivity problem. For information on dealing with network connectivity problems, see **91** **About Network Connection Problems**.

In terms of working with printer shares, the point of accessing the remote, shared printer is to print. So you connect to the printer once (and only once), which makes the printer available to you (and your computer) as if the printer were directly connected to your computer. The printer is actually added to the Printer list on your computer. After the *remote printer* is "installed" on your computer (that is, when you have connected to it through the workgroup as explained in **51** **Connect to a Shared Printer**), the printer appears in the **Printer and Faxes** window (accessed from the **Control Panel**) as any directly connected *local printer* would. After you establish the initial connection (through **My Network Places**), the printer is available to you from that time forward or until you delete the printer from your printer settings. The only downside of printing to a remote printer is that the computer sharing the printer must be on and the printer must be on for you to print over the network.

Shared folders, as already mentioned, can be accessed from the **My Network Places** window. You can expedite the access of shared folders by *mapping* a shared folder as a network drive (as discussed in **50** **Map a Network Drive**). You can also create a network place for remotely shared folders as discussed in **53** **Add a Network Place**.

48

49 | Access Shared Folders and Open Shared Files

✔ **BEFORE YOU BEGIN**

4 About My Network Places
44 Verify Workgroup Membership and Access Network Neighborhood
48 About Accessing Network Resources

Shared folders can be quickly accessed from the **My Network Places** window. The **My Network Places** icon is available on the **Start** menu; click it to open the **My Network Places** window (which is similar to the **My Computer** window; both are actually opened using the **Windows Explorer** application, which is used to browse the contents of your computer or network). If you want to place the **My Network Places** icon on your Windows XP desktop, right-click the **My Network Places** icon on the **Start** menu and select **Show on Desktop** from the context menu that appears.

After you open a shared folder, you have access to all the files contained in that folder. You can edit, delete, and move files in a folder only if the user sharing the folder allowed workgroup users to change the files in the *share* by selecting the **Allow network users to change my files** check box on the **Sharing** tab of the folder's **Properties** dialog box. Be advised that if the files have been shared so that you can't change the files; the only way you can edit a *read-only* shared file is to copy the file to your computer, where you can then treat the file as you would any other file on your computer.

▶ **NOTE**

Although you can access files in a shared folder, you can't change any of the share settings related to the shared folder. For example, if the user who shared the folder didn't select the **Allow network users to change my files** check box when the share was created, there is no way you can change this share attribute. Only the user on the computer who created the share can change the share attributes. This also means that the user who created the share is the only one who can "turn off" the sharing on a particular shared folder. Because the sharing of folders in a workgroup is decentralized (meaning that each computer—and that computer's users—controls the resources it shares), and because workgroups do not have servers or network administrators, there is no way to override the sharing preferences sent on each individual computer or host in the workgroup.

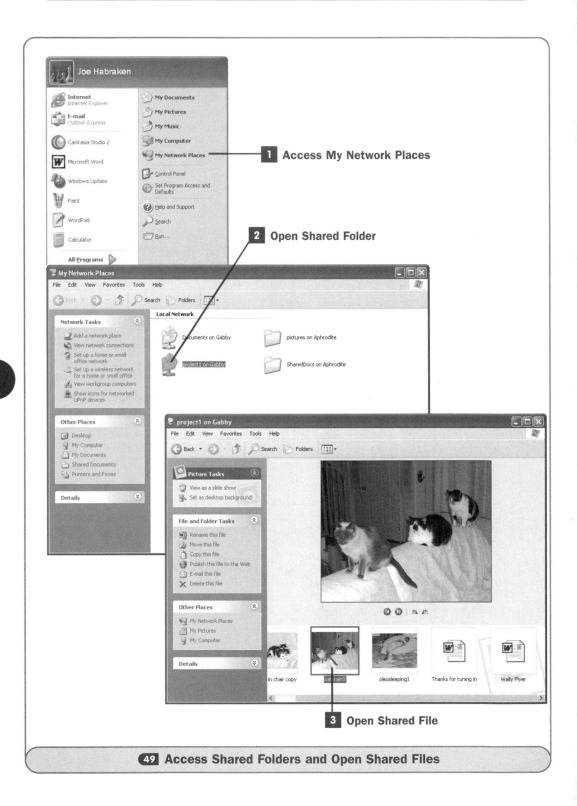

1 **Access My Network Places**

2 **Open Shared Folder**

3 **Open Shared File**

49 Access Shared Folders and Open Shared Files

1 Access My Network Places

Click the **Start** button and then select **My Network Places**. This opens the **My Network Places** window. Shares available on workgroup computers will appear in the window. You can tell which are icons for remote shares (shares not on the computer) by the fact that they have a small network "T" (an upside-down *T*, denoting a network resource) at the bottom of the icon. Shares you have shared on the computer appear as regular folders in the **My Network Places** window.

2 Open Shared Folder

To open a particular *share* (folder), double-click the icon for that folder in the **My Network Places** window. The shared folder opens, and the contents of the folder are displayed.

3 Open Shared File

Double-click any file shown in the shared folder to open that file. The file opens in the application that is configured on your computer for that file type. For example, a Word document opens in Microsoft Word; a picture opens in your default picture-editing software (which can be an application such as Microsoft Paint). If the creator of the share did not allow changes to be made to the shared files (that is, if the file has read-only access), you cannot make changes to the file unless you first save it under a new name on your computer.

▶ **NOTE**

You cannot run executable files over the network. You cannot run programs installed on another computer (other than installation programs that install the software on your computer) from shared folders.

50

50 **Map a Network Drive**

✔ BEFORE YOU BEGIN

44 Verify Workgroup Membership and Access Network Neighborhood
48 About Accessing Network Resources

Although accessing **My Network Places** and connecting to a shared folder or file is pretty easy, you can make the access to a particular share in the workgroup (say a shared folder) even easier by mapping a shared folder as a network drive. This *mapped drive* then appears as a drive in your **My Computer** window, meaning that it is listed in the same **Windows Explorer** window that shows your local drives (such as your hard drive and CD drives). After a shared folder is mapped as a network drive, you can double-click it in the **My Computer** window to access the files located in the share.

▶ KEY TERM

Mapped Drive   A shared folder or drive that is given a drive letter on your computer. Mapping a remote shared folder to a drive letter makes the shared folder accessible from **My Computer**.

1 Open My Network Places

The **My Network Places** window provides quick access to the **View workgroup computers** link, which allows you to view all the currently available computers in the workgroup. Accessing a particular computer allows you to view all the shared resources provided by that computer. The **My Network Places** window also provides quick access to your **My Computer** window, your **Shared Documents** folder, and other locations on your computer by way of the links on the left side of the window. To open **My Network Places**, click the **Start** button and then click **My Network Places**.

2 Open Workgroup Computers

In the **My Network Places** window, click the **View workgroup computers** link in the pane on the left side of the window. It may take a moment for all the workgroup computers to appear in the workgroup window on the right.

3 View Shares on Workgroup Computer

To view the *shares* provided by a workgroup computer shown in the workgroup window, double-click the icon for that computer. It may take a moment for all the shares for that computer to open in a new window.

4 Open Map Network Drive Dialog Box

After you have located the shared folder for which you want to create a network drive, right-click the shared folder and select **Map Network Drive** from the context menu. The **Map Network Drive** dialog box opens.

50

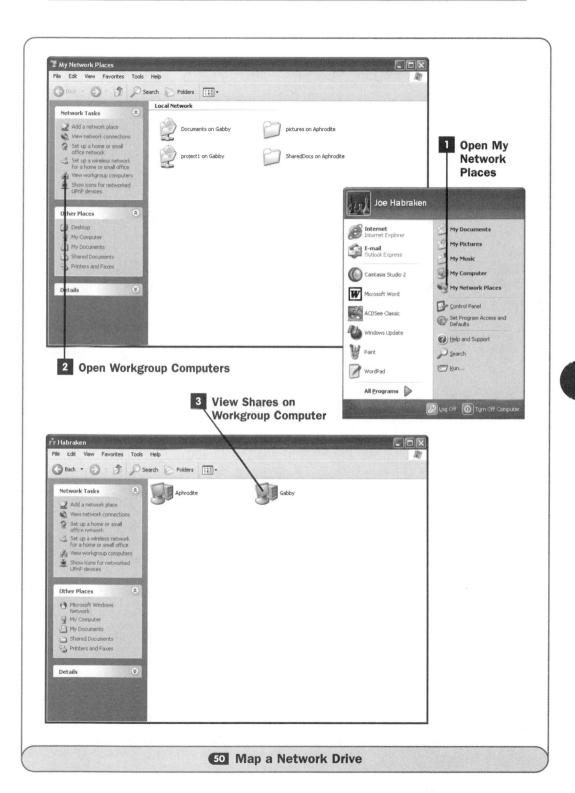

1 Open My Network Places

2 Open Workgroup Computers

3 View Shares on Workgroup Computer

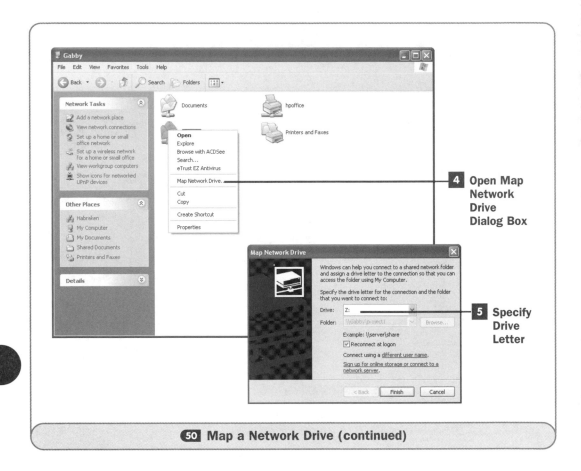

50 Map a Network Drive (continued)

5 Specify Drive Letter

A default drive letter is supplied for the new network drive that will be created for the shared folder. You can go with the default drive letter or select
another available drive letter from the **Drive** drop-down list. After selecting
the drive letter, click **Finish**. The new network drive opens, showing the contents of the shared folder. You can now access the network drive from the
drive list found in the **My Computer** window (open **My Computer** by clicking the **Start** button and then clicking **My Computer**). Or if you wish, you
can drag the mapped drive icon from the **My Computer** window onto the
Windows desktop to make a desktop shortcut to that remote resource.

▶ NOTE

The letters of the alphabet (A to Z) are used as drive letter designations (meaning you
can have a maximum of 26 drives). Certain drive letters are reserved for your local
drives. For example, A is reserved for your floppy drive, C for your hard drive, and typically D for your CD/DVD drive. If you have additional hard drives or CD/DVD drives (such

as a DVD burner), the next available drive letter is assigned to that drive (such as E). When creating a network drive (by mapping a share to a network drive), you can use any of the drive letters that have not already been assigned to local drives or network drives that you have previously mapped. Because you might want to attach removable drives to your computer from time to time, you might want to leave several drive letters (say E to H) as reserved letters for removable USB drives or other media (even digital cameras can be read as drives on the computer). So, you can start with drive letter I as the first drive letter you use to assign to workgroup shares when you map them to a drive letter.

51 Connect to a Shared Printer

✔ BEFORE YOU BEGIN

44 Verify Workgroup Membership and Access Network Neighborhood
48 About Accessing Network Resources

You can take advantage of your WiFi *workgroup* by sharing printers on the network. Sharing a printer allows users on the network to use a single printer, negating the need to buy a printer for every computer on the network. After users on the workgroup connect to a shared printer, the printer can be configured on their computers and accessed as needed in the future from applications on the computer. Although the Windows XP Help system suggests that you install the new remote printer using the **Printer and Faxes** window (accessed from the **Control Panel**), it is easier to connect to a shared printer "visually" by opening your workgroup from the **My Network Places** window and accessing the shares for a particular computer, in this case the computer that is sharing the printer. You can then connect to the printer directly in the workgroup computer's window.

1 Open My Network Places

To open the **My Network Places** window, click the **Start** button and then click **My Network Places**.

2 Access Workgroup Computers

Click the **View workgroup computers** link on the left side of the **My Network Places** window to view all the computers in your workgroup that are currently connected the network.

3 Access Shares on Workgroup Computer

After the icons for the workgroup computers appear in the workgroup window, double-click the computer that is sharing the printer to which you want to connect. The shared resources (the folders and printers) for that computer appear in the window.

51

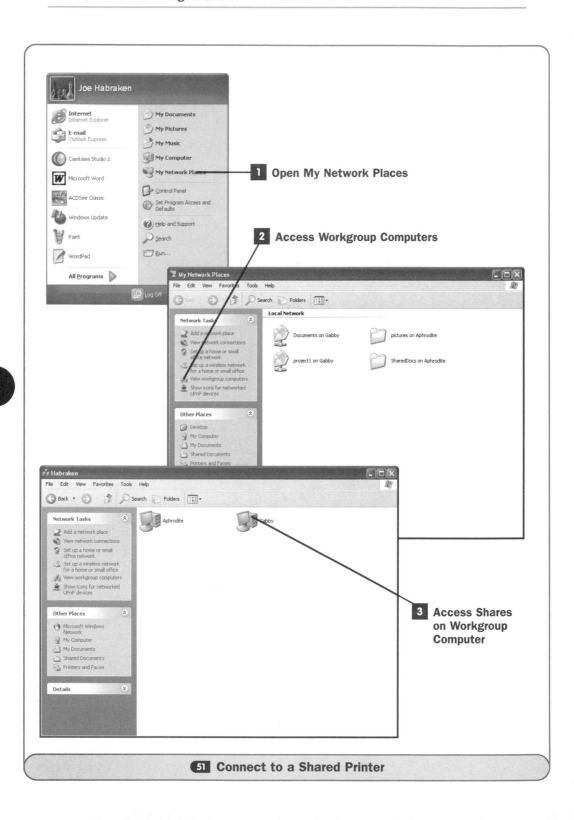

1 Open My Network Places

2 Access Workgroup Computers

3 Access Shares on Workgroup Computer

51 Connect to a Shared Printer

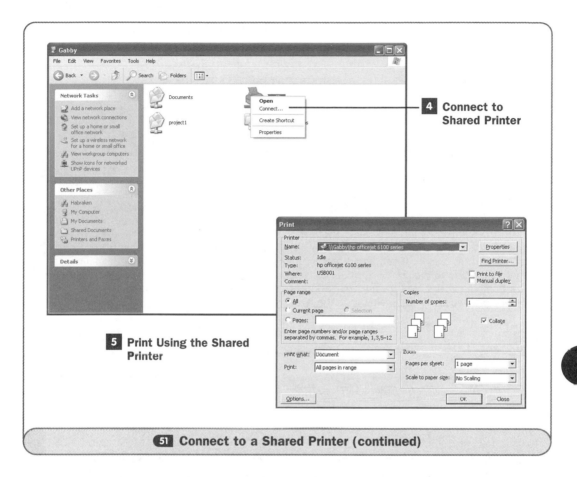

4 Connect to Shared Printer

5 Print Using the Shared Printer

51 Connect to a Shared Printer (continued)

51

4 Connect to Shared Printer

Right-click the shared printer icon and select **Connect** from the context menu. A message box appears, letting you know that a printer driver will be installed on your computer so that you can print to the shared, *remote printer*. Click the **Yes** button in the message box to install the printer driver. The driver is installed, and the printer is added to your **Printers and Faxes** configuration screen, which you can access from the **Control Panel**.

5 Print Using the Shared Printer

You can now print to the printer from any application on your computer. If this is the only printer configured for your computer, it will be designated as the default printer, and all your applications will print to the printer by default. If you have another *local printer* installed on the computer, you can print to either it or the newly connected (installed) workgroup printer. From most applications, select **File**, **Print** to open the **Print** dialog box. From the

Printer Name drop-down list box at the top of the dialog box, select the printer you want to use (whether the local printer or the remote, shared printer) and click **OK** to print. If you want, you can designate the shared printer as your default printer in the **Printers and Faxes** window.

▶ NOTE

In some cases, the printer driver will not be downloaded to your computer automatically from the computer that provides the shared printer. A message might appear, explaining that the driver could not be copied and requesting the location of the CD or other media that contains the software driver for the printer. If this happens, you will need to install the driver on your computer using the original CD or floppy disk that came with the printer. After you have installed the driver, you can print to the remote printer. To test the printer, right-click the printer's icon in the **Printers and Faxes** window (open this window from the **Control Panel**) and select **Properties** from the context menu. On the **General** tab of the **Properties** dialog box, click the **Print Test Page** button. A test page should be printed on the printer. If you do not get a printout, make sure that the printer is online and connected to the computer that is sharing the printer. If you are still having trouble printing, delete the printer from your **Printers and Faxes** window and follow the steps provided in this task to reconnect to the printer.

51

52 | **Search for Network Computers**

✔ **BEFORE YOU BEGIN**

48 About Accessing Network Resources

Because computers in a *workgroup* announce their presence (that is, they send announcement messages over the network), you might not always have an up-to-date list of workgroup computers and shared resources in the **My Network Places** window. Even if your computer has received an announcement that a workgroup member has come online, it doesn't necessarily update its list of connected computers. You can force your computer to recognize that a computer has recently come online and update its network connections list (which is the list of computers shown in the **My Network Places** window), and then you can use the Windows **Search** feature to look for the computer on the network. After the computer is located and appears in the **Search Results** window, you can double-click the computer's icon to view its shared resources such as folders and printers.

1 Open Windows Search Window

Click the **Start** button and then click the **Search** icon on the **Start** menu. The **Search Results** window opens.

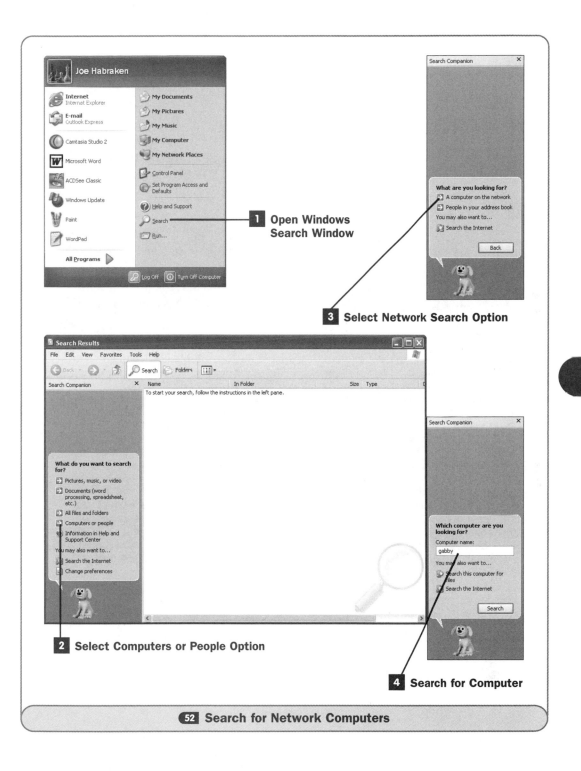

1 Open Windows
Search Window

3 Select Network Search Option

2 Select Computers or People Option

4 Search for Computer

52

2 Select Computers or People Option

To search for computers in the workgroup, select the **Computers or people** link in the **Search Companion** pane on the left side of the **Search Results** window.

3 Select Network Search Option

To search for a workgroup computer, select the **A computer on the network** link in the **Search Companion** pane of the **Search Results** window.

4 Search for Computer

Type the name of the computer you are looking for in the **Computer name** text box and click the **Search** button. The computer's name and icon will appear in the right pane of the **Search Results** window if the computer is actually on and connected to the workgroup. To access the *shares* on this computer (its shared folders and printers), double-click the computer's icon.

▶ NOTE

52

If the computer you're looking for doesn't appear in the **Search Results** list, there are a couple of things you can do. First, make sure that you typed the name of the computer correctly in the **Computer name** text box. If you remember only part of the computer's name, you can use this in the search box. If you know the first few letters of the name, type those characters. If you remember the end of the name, type an asterisk and then the remainder of the name. The asterisk acts as a wildcard for any characters that would appear before the characters provided. An asterisk can be used as a wildcard at the beginning or end of a computer name to represent any number of characters. If you need a wild card that represents a single character, use the ? (question mark). For example, if you can't remember whether the computer's name is *bill* or *bull*, use the search term **b?ll**. Also make sure that the computer is actually on and connected to the network. If you still can't see the computer, check whether the computer is actually a member of the work-group (use the **System Properties** dialog box on that computer to check its workgroup affiliation; right-click the **My Computer** icon to open the **System Properties** dialog box). If all settings seem to be correct and you still cannot see the computer on the network, take a look at Chapter 13, "Troubleshooting and Monitoring Network Connections."

53   53 Add a Network Place

✔ **BEFORE YOU BEGIN**

48 About Accessing Network Resources
50 Map a Network Drive

You can add network places to the **My Network Places** window. You might want to add icons to this window that access Internet resources such as Web folders or shares available in your workgroup.

You might wonder why you would want to create a network place in the **My Network Places** window when this is done automatically for you when you use **My Network Places** to browse the active computers in your workgroup. A network place that you create is actually a shortcut to a particular workgroup resource (such as a shared folder). After you create a new network place icon, you can drag the icon to a new location, such as your desktop. You can then quickly access the share directly from the desktop, negating the need to open the **My Network Places** window.

A network place is similar to a mapped drive in that you are creating a pointer to a specific resource at a specific place on the network. Network places you create appear in the **My Network Places** window and can be dragged onto the Windows desktop as shortcut icons. Mapped drives appear in the **My Computer** window and also can be dragged onto the desktop as shortcuts. It's up to you whether you use **Network Places** or mapped drives. However, you have only 26 (the letters of the alphabet) drive letters available. If you want to create many shortcuts to shared folders, consider using network places, which do not require a drive letter.

❶ Open the Add a Network Place Wizard

Open the **My Network Places** window by clicking **Start** and then clicking **My Network Places**. Click the **Add a network place** link in the **Network Tasks** pane on the left side of the window. The **Add a Network Place Wizard** opens; click **Next** to bypass the initial wizard screen.

52

❷ Choose Location

Click the **Choose another network location** icon in the wizard window. This option allows you to create network places for shared drives and folders in your workgroup. It also allows you to create network places for servers you can access on the Internet, such as FTP (File Transfer Protocol) sites and websites that offer file downloads. These remote shares (on the Internet) are treated the same as shares you can access from your local area network. After clicking the icon, click **Next**.

❸ Browse for Location

As already mentioned, a network place can be an Internet website or FTP site. In the case of a website, you enter the name of the website such as **HTTP://website/share**. For an FTP site, the shared name would be something like **FTP://ftpsite.com**. You can't browse for websites or FTP site shares; you must enter their exact URL. However, you *can* browse for a local workgroup *share*. Click the **Browse** button to browse for the share you want to use for the new network place. The **Browse for Folder** window opens. You will be browsing the local area network (workgroup) for the shared folder or drive you want to designate as a network place.

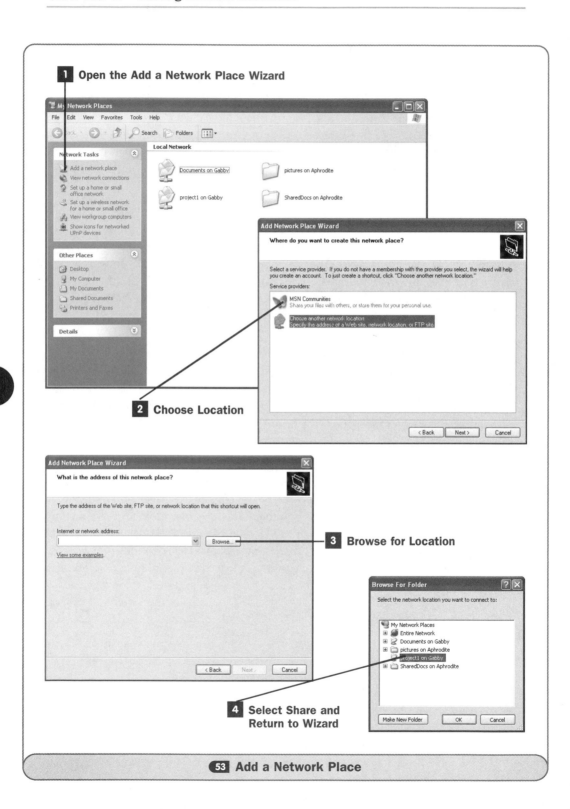

1 Open the Add a Network Place Wizard

2 Choose Location

3 Browse for Location

4 Select Share and Return to Wizard

52

53 Add a Network Place

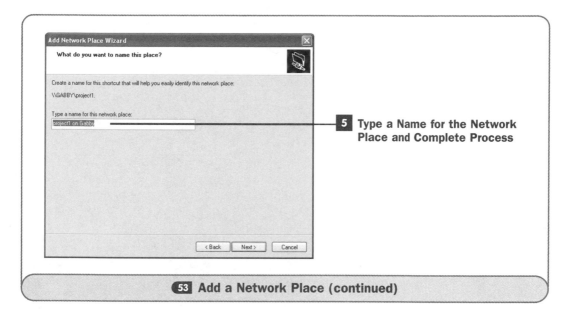

5 Type a Name for the Network Place and Complete Process

4 Select Share and Return to the Wizard

Click a workgroup share that appears in the **Browse for Folder** window to select the share you want to create the network place for. Then click **OK**. You return to the wizard, and the share name you selected appears in the **Internet or network address** text box. Click **Next** to continue.

5 Type a Name for the Network Place and Complete Process

The next wizard screen asks you to type a name for the new network place. A default name is created based on the name of the computer and the name of the share (or the name of the share in the case of a website or FTP site), but you can type a different name in the **Type a name for the network place** text box. Click **Next** to move to the final wizard screen and then click **Finish**. The new network place icon appears in the **My Network Places** window, and the associated share opens in a new window. Close the window that displays the contents of the share.

To place the new network place icon on the desktop as a shortcut to the share, drag the icon from the **My Network Places** window to your desktop. You can then close the **My Network Places** window. Now you can access the share directly from the Windows desktop by double-clicking the share's icon.

52

8

Filtering Content and Enabling Game Services

IN THIS CHAPTER:

You will find that your WiFi *router* has a number of features that allow you to control the Internet content available to users on your WiFi network. This control includes the blocking of specific Internet sites as well as access to specific Internet services such as instant messaging. Although blocking Internet access and filtering content is up to you in terms of the home network (particularly in terms of your popularity around the house), the WiFi router can also be configured so that users on the network (yes, I'm probably talking about your kids) can take advantage of online gaming without the gaming connection constituting a major security problem for the home network. In this chapter, we take a look at blocking access and services while still providing access to special services such as gaming options through *port forwarding*.

---

54 | About Content Filtering and Opening Ports

✔ BEFORE YOU BEGIN	→ SEE ALSO
21 About Configuring the Wireless Router	70 About Basic Network Security
22 Access Router Configuration	71 About Firewalls
37 About Configuring PCs for Networking	

Because the WiFi *router* sits between the home network or workgroup and the high-speed Internet connection, the router can be configured to control access to web content. This means that certain content can be blocked at the router, denying access to a particular computer in the *workgroup* or denying that access to all the computers in the workgroup. Most WiFi routers can also be configured to deny access to Internet services such as file transfer, gaming, and instant messaging.

▶ NOTE

The ability to block web content and Internet services such as email or instant messaging provides you with two ways to control the access that your users have to the different Internet communication venues (such as the Web). When you block web content, the content is blocked for all computers on your WiFi network. However, you can enter the IP address of one computer (known as the "trusted" computer) in the router's web content blocking configuration, which will allow that computer to still access the content. When you deny or block services on the network, you can specify that one or several computers are exempt from the blocking of a service or services. So, in terms of allowing exceptions, you are provided more flexibility when you block services rather than web content.

Not only can you block access to web content and Internet services, you can also design a schedule that dictates *when* the content or services are actually blocked. In a nutshell, these web-filtering and service-blocking features on the WiFi router allow you to choose what you want to block in terms of Internet content and services and when you want to block it.

▶ **NOTE**

It's important to understand the difference between the Internet and the various communication venues such as the World Wide Web and instant messaging services that operate on the Internet. The Internet is the actual infrastructure or highway that allows us to take advantage of different Internet protocols or strategies for communication on the Internet infrastructure. A service such as the Web or instant messaging is a communication strategy that runs on the Internet infrastructure. The Web is just one of the several communication strategies that can access data provided by web servers also connected to the Internet. Another example of a communication service that uses the Internet infrastructure is instant messaging, which is available from a number of different "service" providers such as Microsoft (MSN Messenger), Yahoo! (Yahoo Instant Messaging), and AOL (AIM or AOL Instant Messenger).

So, how is it that the router can actually block a user from accessing certain websites? It's because of how the Web and the Internet work. For example, the World Wide Web or "Web" is a client/server environment. Content is requested by users connected to the Internet using their web browsers (the client) and then "served up" by web servers (the server). Remember that the World Wide Web is just one service that uses the Internet infrastructure for communication.

It is the communication between the web client and the web server software that allows you to surf the Web and view the content. Because the requests from the client software (a user's web browser such as Internet Explorer) must go through the router to get to the Internet and the web servers waiting out on the Internet for content requests, the router can examine the request made by the client. If the client request asks for content that the router has been configured to block, the router does not forward the request to the Web. This means that the request for the content is blocked. Let's take a look at the specifics of how web *content* is blocked by the WiFi router, and then we can take a look at how you block Internet *services* such as gaming or instant messaging.

54

Blocking Content

When you configure the router to block web content, you are actually blocking websites based on keywords or specific website names (meaning the domain name or URL—uniform resource locator—for the site). In other words, to actually block the content from websites, you have to create a list of keywords and actual domain names.

The keyword list is used by the router as a reference; when a user on the network requests a website using a web browser, the router looks at the keyword list and compares it to the website name that is requested. If a keyword or domain name in the list matches the website name (domain name) being requested, the website is blocked.

Obviously, blocking websites by website name is fairly straightforward. For example, adding the URL **www.pornographic.com** to the keyword and site list on the router will block this specific site. Putting together a keyword list that will block sites is another matter and requires some thought.

For example, let's say you enter the word **violence** in the keyword list. Now all websites with the word *violence* in the website name will be blocked. However, this arrangement would also block a website named **www.stop-violence.org**. So, you can see that devising a keyword list that blocks the bad sites but lets the good sites in is somewhat problematic.

In terms of thinking through a keyword list for blocking certain types of websites, such as pornographic websites, your keyword list must reflect the type of language used in the website names. This means that your keyword list is going to include a lot of words that you certainly wouldn't use in public (and in most cases, even in private).

▶ **NOTE**

Whether you use your router to filter and block web content is really up to you. As the author of this book, I am certainly not advocating that you should block content; you have to decide this for yourself and the users of your network. In terms of web and Internet content, there is the issue of "free speech"; censoring content can be a slippery slope once we start down that path. Although there is a great deal of questionable and absolutely tasteless content on the World Wide Web, I believe the Internet is ultimately a good thing and probably should not be regulated by anyone, including governments. You have to decide for yourself how you are going to run your own home network, and this decision includes the concepts of filtering and blocking content (which some people would call censorship) as you see fit.

Obviously, any keyword list you devise will have to be edited over time because you don't want a keyword in the list that blocks "good" sites. Most WiFi routers provide a log feature that allows you to view the websites that have been "allowed" and "denied" by your keyword and URL list for blocking content. Viewing the log over time to see what is being blocked and what is being allowed gives you the opportunity to edit the keyword list so that the content-blocking filter does a better job at blocking only the content you don't want users on your network to view.

One more thing related to blocking content: When you block content, you are blocking the content for *all the computers* on the network. You cannot block content on a computer-by-computer basis. However, the WiFi router can be configured so that a single computer on the network can be exempt from the content blocking and filtering. This computer is referred to as the ***trusted computer*** in the block web content configuration settings for a Netgear router (your router's configuration might refer to the computer as *exempt* or use some other term). Trusted computer simply means that it can access the content that is blocked on other computers on the network by the router.

In terms of selecting the computer that will be trusted on the network, it makes sense to configure the router so that it doesn't block content for *your* computer. Typically, on a home network, you are blocking content on computers being used by your children because you want to exert parental controls over what they can see and do on the Web. This trusted or exempt computer is identified in the router's configuration settings (the block content settings) by entering the computer's IP address.

▶ KEY TERM

Trusted computer—A computer that is specified in the router's configuration settings as being exempt from the blocking of web content.

Setting up a trusted computer on the network works well if everyone using the network has their own computer. If you share a computer with someone (such as a child) who should not have access to certain websites, however, you might have to use the router's scheduling feature to block content during certain times of the day.

Blocking Services

54

Using the WiFi router to block Internet services is a little more complicated than blocking content, but only because you have to understand how different services such as email, instant messaging, and the Web actually communicate and move information on the Internet.

We have already discussed the *TCP/IP protocol* and *IP addressing* in **37** **About Configuring PCs for Networking**. The TCP/IP protocol is actually a group or "stack" of smaller protocols used to manage the different aspects of the communication between computers on a network. The IP or Internet Protocol takes care of the IP addressing scheme that we use on the network. Each computer is assigned a unique IP address, by which each computer is identified on the network when sending or receiving data.

The TCP/IP protocol stack provides two protocols that actually negotiate and manage the movement of data between computers; these protocols are the Transmission Control Protocol (TCP) and the User Datagram Protocol (UDP). Internet services or applications use either TCP or UDP or both to control the movement of data between a client such as your instant messenger or web client (your web browser) and the Internet server that supplies the type of service you are trying to take advantage of.

For example, when two computer users are "chatting" with each other using instant messaging (using a client such as AOL Instant Messenger—AIM), the data (the chat) goes from the instant messaging client to a messaging server. The data is then forwarded from the messaging server to the intended recipient (by way of their instant messaging client). The data being sent and received by the instant messaging client (using the messaging server) is actually moved on the Internet by the TCP protocol. Not only does TCP/IP supply the transport protocol, in this case TCP (some other software uses UDP instead of TCP) moves the data. To move the data, each application (such as the instant messaging software, or the Web, or your email client) negotiates the transfer of data from computer to computer using a discrete channel, which is called a *port*. For example, the port all computers use for the Web (really for the HTTP protocol that makes the Web work) is port 80. The port number used for AOL instant messaging is 5190. The port number for Real Audio (the Real player) is actually a range of ports from 6970 to 7170.

▶ NOTE

Ports used by devices to communicate on an IP network don't physically exist. They are designations in software code that direct applications to communicate on a particular port when data is being sent or received.

▶ KEY TERM

54

***Port*—A numbered communication channel or end point used by an Internet application as the avenue or doorway for negotiating data transfers between two computers.**

To review, each Internet application uses a transport protocol (TCP, UDP, or in some cases, both), and the data transfer negotiation takes place over a port. The actual list of ports available is maintained by the Internet Engineering Task Force. Port numbers can range from 0 to 65536. The ports from 1 to 1024 are reserved for certain Internet services such as the Web (HTTP) and email (POP3 and SMTP protocols) and are referred to as the *well-known ports*. Software developers creating a new program for the Internet select a port from the list (a port that is not being used by any other Internet program) so that the software can communicate on the Internet.

▶ NOTE

The Internet Engineering Task Force defined the use of port numbers for Internet data traffic. The Internet Assigned Numbers Authority (IANA), another Internet oversight agency, maintains a list of the well-known port numbers (1 to 1024) and the application/service that uses each of the well-known ports. Port numbers 1024 to 65536 are in the range of port numbers made available to software developers when they create a new Internet service or program. Many port numbers in the 1024 to 65536 range have been leased by various software developers and companies. To view a list of the well-known ports and the port numbers from 1024 to 65536 that are assigned (leased) to a particular application/service, see http://www.iana.org/assignments/port.

To block an Internet service using your WiFi router, you select a particular service such as instant messaging or the Web (HTTP) from a list of services provided in your router's configuration. The number of services listed depends on the router (and the router's manufacturer). When you select a service from the list, the transport protocol and the port for the application are configured automatically (because the router software has been programmed to know this information for the services included in the router's service list).

If you want to block a service that isn't listed in the router's service list, most WiFi routers allow you to configure a "user defined" service. To configure a service from scratch (meaning user defined), you need to know the transport protocol for the application (TCP, UDP, or both) and the port number or the range of port numbers the service uses.

You can look up the transport protocol (TCP or UDP) and the port number for many Internet services using the list provided at **http://www.iana.org/assignments/port-numbers**. You can scroll through the list or use the **Find** feature of your web browser to do a search for a particular company or application name. In cases where the IANA list does not provide you with the information you need, you might be able to get the information from the software developer's website or the website of the company that sells the product.

For example, there is a three-dimensional, collaborative software platform for the Internet (and the Web) called Muse. Muse is still being developed, so it is hard to tell what Muse will have to offer, but let's pretend that for some reason we want to block the Muse application/service for all the computers on our network using our WiFi router. To block a service, you need to know the transport protocol and the port number. If you look at the IANA list at **http://www.iana.org/assignments/port-numbers**, you will find that Muse uses both TCP and UDP protocols on port 6888. So you can configure your router to block Muse by configuring the block service feature to block service traffic using TCP and UDP on port 6888.

54

▶ NOTE

I picked Muse as an example of an application/service that was listed on the IANA list. I am not saying that Muse should be blocked. In fact, Muse looks quite interesting; read more about it at **http://www.musecorp.com/**.

As you can when blocking content, you can block services at a particular time of day using the scheduling feature provided by your WiFi router. You can block a service for all the computers on the network or you can specify the IP addresses of those computers for which you want the service blocked.

Port Used   **Protocol Used**

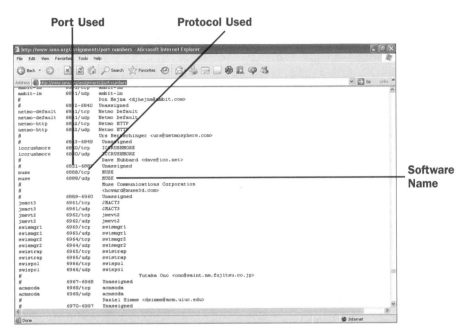

Software Name

Go to the IANA website if you need to know the transport protocol and port number used by a service you want to block using the WiFi router.

54

Gaming Issues and Workgroup Access

The WiFi router is designed to keep the internal network (your workgroup) secure from outside intrusion. We discuss the security features the router offers in **70 About Basic Network Security** and **71 About Firewalls**. But on some occasions, you want to allow users outside your private network to access services provided by your private network. For example, let's say you have web server software running on a computer and want users on the Internet to be able to view your web page. Allowing access to internal network services can also be particularly useful (and necessary) in multiplayer gaming situations where you want other gamers to be able to access your computer in a *peer-to-peer* gaming situation.

So, you want to allow outside access to your network, but you certainly don't want to open up your private internal network to outside threats. Your WiFi router can allow and control access to a resource on your network (such as a web server) using port forwarding. *Port forwarding* opens a port on the router, and the router forwards outside requests for a particular "inside" service such as a web server or file server (an FTP server) using that port. Port forwarding makes the computer on your network that is offering the service (the computer with the web server software on it) visible to computers outside the network (meaning computers on the Internet) so that those users can access your internal service and content.

▶ **KEY TERM**

Port forwarding—A method of opening ports on the WiFi router that allows outside requests for services to reach computers on the internal network supplying those services such as a web server. When you use port forwarding, your internal IP address (related to the server providing the service) can be tracked by servers on the Internet, which can be a security concern.

If you are into multiplayer gaming and want to play games such as Quake or Starcraft over your network, you must configure port triggering. *Port triggering* opens a port temporarily and also doesn't require that your internal IP address be tracked by servers on the Internet. Port triggering doesn't create a wide-open port like port forwarding does (port triggering opens and closes the port as needed) and also keeps your internal IP address private. But port triggering does allow other computers to access the service and connect to your computer, which is necessary for multiplayer gaming.

▶ **KEY TERM**

Port triggering—A way to temporarily open a port on the WiFi router when an external request for that port is received by the router. Port triggering does not leave ports open (as port forwarding does) and does not allow the IP address of the internal computer supplying the service to be known. Port triggering is used to configure computers for services such as online gaming.

55

55 **Block Access to Websites**

✔ **BEFORE YOU BEGIN**

22 Access Router Configuration
54 About Content Filtering and Opening Ports

You can block access to websites from computers in the workgroup (through the *router* to the Internet) either by web address (domain name) or using a keyword list. The number of entries you can have in your list depends on the WiFi router you have purchased. For example, the Netgear WGR614 WiFi router allows you to create a keyword/domain name list that can contain 255 entries.

If you own a Netgear WGR614 router, you could enter 255 domain names in the keyword list, which would block 255 websites. However, if you use keywords to block sites, you could conceivably build a list of keywords that could potentially block thousands of bad or inappropriate sites. If you know of particular websites you want to block, by all means enter the domain name for those sites in the list. However, the keywords you enter in the list provide the farthest-reaching possibilities for blocking the most sites.

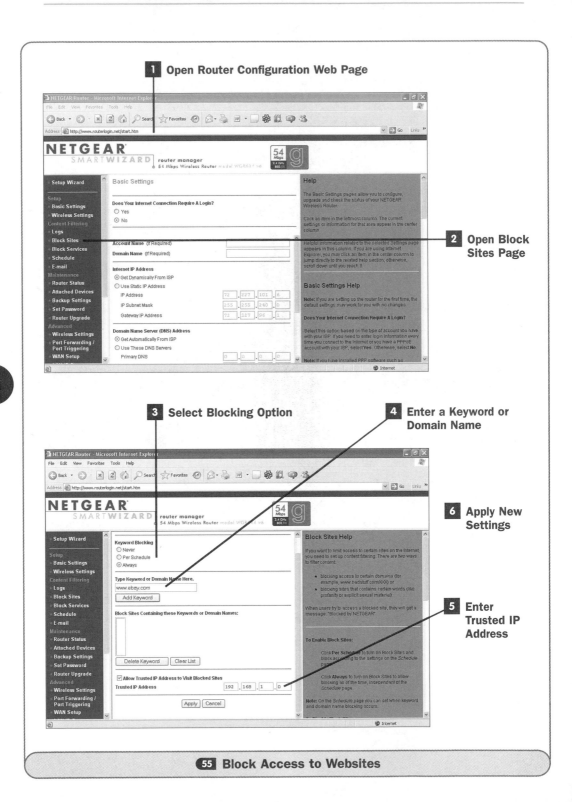

1 Open Router Configuration Web Page

2 Open Block Sites Page

55

3 Select Blocking Option

4 Enter a Keyword or Domain Name

6 Apply New Settings

5 Enter Trusted IP Address

55 Block Access to Websites

To build a keyword list for blocking access, consider the following:

- What types of websites do I want to block?

- What keywords typically appear in the domain names for these websites?

- Which websites might my keyword list block that I do not want to be blocked?

When you've started to block websites using a list of domain names or keywords, you will have to monitor your router's log to determine whether the block-access feature is actually performing as you want. For information about viewing the router's log, see **95** **View Router Log**. You might have to edit your keyword list over time to get the results you seek.

① Open Router Configuration Web Page

Open your router's configuration web page (enter the web address that was designated for your router when you installed it, and then type the administrator logon name and password for the router).

▶ **NOTE**

If you forgot the web address or the URL for your router, take a look at the documentation included with the WiFi router. This documentation also provides the logon name and default password for your router. All this information is specified by the router manufacturer and is typically the same for all the routers manufactured by a particular vendor. For example, my Netgear router uses the URL **http://www.routerlogin.net/start.htm**. The logon name is **admin** and the default password is **password**.

② Open Block Sites Page

Select the router command that opens the **Block Site** configuration page for the router. For example, on the Netgear WGR614 router configuration page, you click the **Block Sites** link on the left side of the router's main configuration page.

③ Select Blocking Option

Select an option button for blocking either **Per Schedule** or **Always** (the actual option names vary from router to router). If you select the **Per Schedule** option, you will also need to set up a filter schedule; see **57** **Set Up a Filter Schedule**.

④ Enter a Keyword or Domain Name

Type a keyword or domain name in the appropriate text box and click the **Add Keyword** button (the method of entering the keyword varies from router to router). The keyword or domain name you type is added to the list of entries your router will block.

Repeat this step to enter other keyword and domain names as needed.

▶ **TIP**

To remove a keyword or domain name from the list, select the item in the list and then click **Delete Keyword** (or a similar command on your router's configuration page). Most routers also allow you to completely clear the list and start over if necessary.

5 Enter Trusted IP Address

If you want to allow a particular computer to access blocked sites, select the **Allow Trusted IP Address to Visit Block Sites** check box. Enter the last number of the *IP address* for the computer you want to be trusted (in this example, you would change the **0** supplied to the actual ending number of the IP address) .

▶ **TIP**

55

To determine the IP address of your computer (the address assigned by the WiFi router acting as a DHCP server), you can use the **ipconfig** command, which shows you the IP address and subnet mask of your computer (and other information). On the computer you want to be trusted, click the **Start** button and then choose **Run**. In the **Run** dialog box, type **command** and press **Enter**. At the command prompt, type **ipconfig/all**. This command returns the IP address, the subnet mask, and other information about the computer, such as the IP address of your default gateway and DHCP server (which is the WiFi router). To close the command dialog box, type **exit** and press **Enter**. For more about the **ipconfig** command see **96** About Command-Line Tools and **97** Use Command-Line Tools.

6 Apply New Settings

After entering the various parameters for the blocked content feature, you must apply the settings to the router's configuration. Click the **Apply** button (or the button that applies and saves the settings for your router). The new settings will take effect immediately; access to websites from the computers on your network will be blocked according to the domain name and keyword list you created.

When a user attempts to open a website that is blocked by the router (using a web browser such as Internet Explorer), a screen opens in the web browser letting the user know that the site is blocked. For example, the Netgear router I use displays a black and red page in the Internet Explorer window that reads, **Web Site Blocked by NETGEAR Firewall**.

56 Block Access to Internet Services

✔ BEFORE YOU BEGIN	→ ALSO SEE
22 Access Router Configuration	**57** Set Up a Filter Schedule
54 About Content Filtering and Opening Ports	

Blocking services, such as FTP or instant messaging, allows you to control your network's use of particular types of applications on the Internet. For example, blocking the FTP (File Transfer Protocol) service for your network would mean that users on your network could not download files from FTP sites (which are designed as repositories for downloadable content). Blocking FTP services could block your kids from downloading illegal music files from a rogue FTP site. If you don't want instant messaging taking place on your network after 8:00 p.m., you can block the AIM service on a scheduled basis (as explained in **57** **Set Up a Filter Schedule**).

To block an Internet service from your network, you need to know whether the service transfers information using UDP or TCP (or both), and you also need to know which port the service uses to communicate. Most WiFi routers provide a default list of services you can block by simply choosing a service from the list. For example, my Netgear router provides a list that includes the following services:

- **AIM (AOL Instant Messenger)**: An extremely popular instant messaging client.

- **Age of Empires**: A popular multiplayer game from Microsoft that can be played over a network.

- **FTP (File Transfer Protocol)**: A protocol used to transfer files on the Internet.

- **HTTP (Hypertext Transfer Protocol)**: The protocol that allows your web browser to communicate with web servers and vice versa. If you block HTTP, computers on the network will not be able to browse websites. This means that you could make sure that no one surfs the Web after 9:00 p.m. if you block the HTTP service with a filter schedule.

▶ **TIP**

I think most people have embraced the popular misconception that the World Wide Web and the Internet are the same thing. Even if you block the HTTP service (which blocks web access), there are a bunch of other communication protocols that are still available for use on the Internet. Your child, for example, could still use instant messaging and email even if you block HTTP.

56

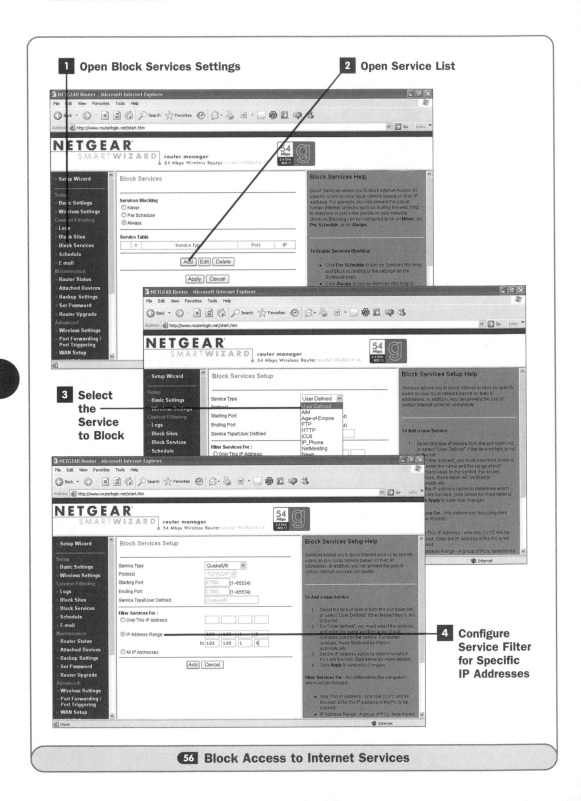

1 Open Block Services Settings

2 Open Service List

3 Select the Service to Block

4 Configure Service Filter for Specific IP Addresses

56

56 Block Access to Internet Services

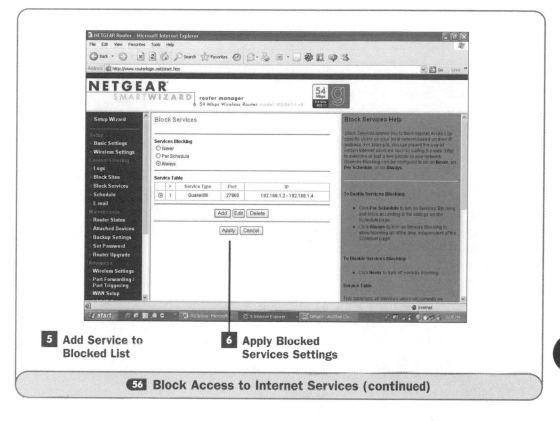

5 Add Service to
Blocked List

6 Apply Blocked
Services Settings

56

56 Block Access to Internet Services (continued)

- **Netmeeting**: A web-based communication platform from Microsoft.
  Netmeeting supports video, audio, and text communication.

- **Quake II and III**: Very popular first-person shooter games that allow multiplayer action over a network.

Selecting a service from the list provided by your router negates your having to
research the port and protocol used by that particular service. The port and protocol information are filled in for you. The list of services provided by the router
varies from router to router. Any other services you want to block (those that are
not provided on a list) must be set up manually (meaning that you must provide
the protocol—UDP or TCP or both—and the port number used by the service you
want to block) .

▶ **NOTE**

Obviously, the ability to block services is considered a parental control in terms of determining what your children can access over the Internet. I have mixed feelings about
using blocking tools to censor content and Internet access. As an alternative to blocking
content and services, consider trying to educate your children to use the Web and
Internet services such as instant messaging wisely and safely. If they understand some

of the downsides and dangers of these powerful communication tools as well as the incredible benefits and entertainment value they provide, you might make them responsible users of the Internet and therefore be able to forgo blocking content and services. The choice of whether to block content and services for your children is up to you. Remember that your kids probably spend a lot more time online than you do; even if you start blocking certain services and content, they can find ways to outsmart you by using services you haven't blocked.

1 Open Block Services Settings

Open your router's main configuration web page (type your router's URL such as **routerlogin.net** and then enter your administrative login name and password; all this information is in the documentation provided by your router and is set by the router's manufacturer). Open the router's **Block Services** feature by selecting the **Block Services** link (or similar command) on your router's command list.

2 Open Service List

Select one of the **Service Blocking** option buttons. For my Netgear router, I can choose either **Always** or **Per Schedule** (your router's configuration page will have similar options). To open the list of services offered by your router, click the **Add** button or similar command (for example, on a Linksys router, the list is a scroll list rather than a drop-down list, but you still use an **Add** button to add the service).

3 Select the Service to Block

Click the **Service type** drop-down list to display a list of all the services your router knows about. From the list, select the service to be blocked (such as AIM, FTP, or RealAudio). If you want to block a service that is not on the list, select the **User Defined** option and then enter the transport protocol (UDP or TCP) and port number for the service. You must enter both the beginning and ending port number for the service; for example, if the port number is 2600, the starting port is 2600 and the ending port is also 2600. In the **Service Type/User Defined** text box, type a name for this user-defined service (for example, if I were blocking a communication service named "glowworm," I would type **glowworm** as the service type).

▶ TIP

The IANA web site is a good place to find the port numbers for services that are not listed in the service list provided by your router. Check out **http://www.iana.org/ 198assignments/port-numbers**. This website can also provide the protocol (UDP or TCP) used by a particular service. Port information and transport protocol information for a particular service can also often be found by searching the Web. For more information on port numbers and transport protocols, see **54 About Content Filtering and Opening Ports.**

56

4 Configure Service Filter for Specific IP Addresses

After you have selected a service to block, you can enter an IP address or a range of IP addresses for computers in your network for which you want the router to block the listed service. Select one of the following option buttons:

▶ TIP

To determine the IP address of a computer (the address assigned by the WiFi router acting as a DHCP server), you can use the **ipconfig** command. On the computer for which you need this information, click the **Start** button and then choose **Run**. In the **Run** dialog box, type **command** and press **Enter**. At the command prompt, type **ipconfig/all**. This command returns the IP address, the subnet mask, and other information about the computer, such as the IP address of your default gateway and DHCP server (which is the WiFi router). To close the command dialog box, type **exit** and press **Enter**. For more about the **ipconfig** command see **96** About Command-Line Tools and **97** Use Command-Line Tools.

- **Only This IP Address:** Choose this option if you want to block the selected service for a single computer in the network. Then enter the IP address for that computer.

- **IP Address Range:** Choose this option if you want to block the selected service from a range of computers in your network (such as for all the computers used by your children). Then enter the starting and ending IP addresses of the range of computers.

▶ TIP

When you first configure your router and then bring a computer "online" on the new network, the computer you have directly connected to the router by a network cable will be the first computer to get an IP address from the router. So it will be at the beginning of the IP address range provided. Subsequent computers receive their IP addresses as you start them up and allow them to receive their IP addresses from the router. So let's say that you want to block a service for three computers that do not have IP addresses that are in sequence. Turn off the router. Use the **ipconfig/release** command to clear the IP addresses on all the computers on the network. Shut down the computers. Power up the router. Now start up the computers in the appropriate sequence so that the IP addresses that are assigned are sequential for the computers on which you want to block the service. See **96** About Command-Line Tools and **97** Use Command-Line Tools for more information about the **ipconfig** command.

- **All IP Addresses:** Choose this option if you want to block the current service for all computers on the network.

5 Add Service to Blocked List

After selecting or entering the service and selecting options related to the IP addresses for which you want to block this service, click **Add** to add the service to the blocked list.

Repeat steps 3–5 as needed to add other services to the list of blocked services.

56

6 **Apply Blocked Services Settings**

After adding the services that you want to block, click **Apply** to apply the service blocking settings to the router's configuration.

---

57 **Set Up a Filter Schedule**

✔ **BEFORE YOU BEGIN**

22 Access Router Configuration
54 About Content Filtering and Opening Ports
55 Block Access to Websites
56 Block Access to Internet Services

56

If you want to filter (that is, block) content or services for computers in your network using a schedule, you must configure the filter schedule. The filter can be configured to block services or content on certain days (or all week) and at certain times of the day.

When you use the filter schedule to block web content, the content is blocked for all computers on the network except for the *trusted computer* (the one computer on the network that is exempt from the blocking). When you use the filter schedule to block a service, the service is blocked for all the computers you specified by IP address on the router's block services configuration page. All blocked content and all services specified to be blocked are blocked by a single filter schedule. See **56** **Block Access to Internet Services** for more about the ways you specify the computers to be blocked from a particular service.

You need to configure a filter schedule only if you have selected the **Per Schedule** option for either the content or service blocking settings. You can configure only one filter schedule. So, if you designate that web content should be blocked "per schedule," and you also designate that selected services should be blocked "per schedule," both the content and the services are blocked according to the same schedule.

It actually makes sense to block content all the time (for example, you wouldn't want pornography to be available to your kids based on a schedule); to always block content, specify **Always** when you configure the router to block web content. You can then use the filter schedule more appropriately to block certain services that you don't want your kids to use late in the evening (such as instant messaging or gaming capabilities). For example, I can configure a filter schedule that will block instant messaging on Sunday through Thursday after 9:00 p.m.

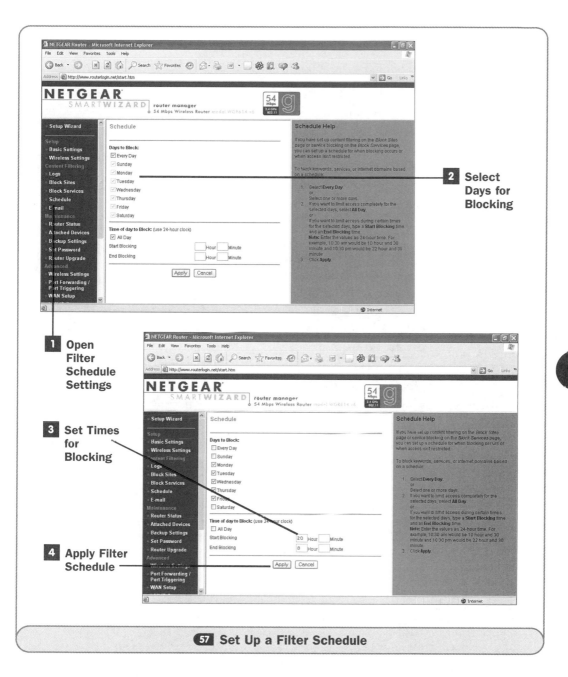

2 Select Days for Blocking

1 Open Filter Schedule Settings

3 Set Times for Blocking

4 Apply Filter Schedule

57 Set Up a Filter Schedule

The default filter schedule for most WiFi routers is **Every Day**, meaning that the content and the services you have selected to be blocked are blocked seven days a week; the default times that the content and services are blocked is **All Day**, meaning that content and services are blocked 24 hours a day.

1 Open Filter Schedule Settings

Open your router's main configuration web page (type your router's URL such as **routerlogin.net** and then enter your administrative login name and password). Open the router's **Schedule** feature by selecting the **Schedule** link (or similar command) on your router's command list. For example, on the Netgear router I use, I click **Schedule** on the command list on the left side of the Web page.

2 Select Days for Blocking

The default setting for which days the content and services will be blocked is **Every Day**. Deselect the check box for **Every Day** if you don't want to block seven days a week and instead want to block specific days, and then select the check boxes for the days on which you want to block the content or services (or both, if you have configured both).

3 Set Times for Blocking

57

If you want to specify a time range for blocking on the days you have selected, deselect the **All Day** check box and enter the **Start Blocking** and **End Blocking** times in the appropriate text boxes. Most routers use a 24-hour time setting system; the times in the morning (a.m. times) are the actual hour (8 in the morning is 8 on the 24-hour clock). Hours after noon (p.m. times) are set by adding 12 (hours) to the time, so 8 p.m. is entered as 20 (hours) on the 24-hour clock.

4 Apply Filter Schedule

After you have selected the days and set a time range, click **Apply** to add the filter schedule to the router's configuration.

▶ NOTE

Using a filter schedule allows you to block content more discretely based on a time schedule. For example, if all computers are to be turned off in the evening at 9:00 p.m., you can set a filter schedule that blocks selected content and services starting at 9 in the evening. You can then set the end blocking time for 7 or 8 in the morning. The schedule also allows you freedom in term of the days you block. You could block certain content during the school week (say, Sunday through Thursday evening) and then allow longer hours of access during the weekend. This is actually a great way to keep your kids from instant messaging while you want them to be studying.

---

58 Configure Port Forwarding and Port Triggering

✔ BEFORE YOU BEGIN

22 Access Router Configuration
54 About Content Filtering and Opening Ports

The fact that your network sits behind a *router* means that the router protects your computers from intrusion from the outside world. But there may be cases where you want to run a web server or other service from a computer on your local network and make that service available to users outside your network (meaning the Internet).

A number of popular computer games (such as Quake, Starcraft, Kali, and games from web-based game providers such as Ultima Online and MSN Gaming Zone) can be configured as multiplayer games where participants compete with each other over a network. Not only can these games be played by multiple users on your local network, but some games provide the ability to play multiplayer sessions over the Internet.

For users outside your network to access an internal web server or game that is being played on your network (they also have to have the game installed on their computer), you must supply a path for the data to move back and forth between computers running the game. Because WiFi routers are actually designed to *stop* data requests from outside the network, you must configure the WiFi router so that it allows communication between the gaming computers. This is accomplished using *port forwarding* or *port triggering*. As already discussed, port forwarding is ideal for situations where you want to run a service such as a web server on a computer in your network and make that service available to users outside of your network; port triggering is used for multiplayer gaming where at least one of the players is outside of your WiFi network.

For port forwarding and port triggering to work properly, particularly in cases where we are talking about multiplayer gaming, you must also enable the router to use *UPnP*, which stands for Universal Plug and Play. This feature helps computers on the network to discover the services that are being offered by other computers on the network and those computers outside the network.

▶ **KEY TERM**

UPnP (Universal Plug and Play—A networking architecture that aids in the communication between UPnP-compliant devices such as computers on networks and the Internet. UPnP is supported on all operating systems and by 400-plus vendors of computer hardware and peripherals who have designed their equipment to be compliant with UPnP.

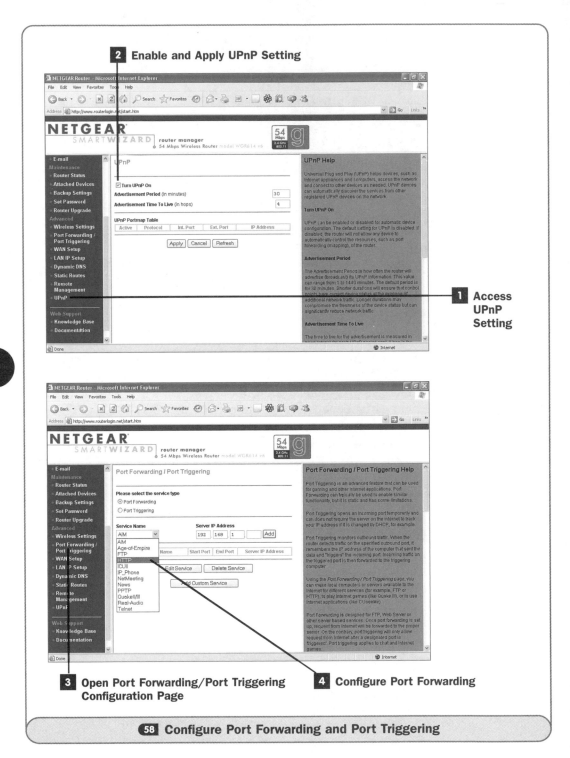

2 Enable and Apply UPnP Setting

1 Access UPnP Setting

3 Open Port Forwarding/Port Triggering Configuration Page

4 Configure Port Forwarding

58 Configure Port Forwarding and Port Triggering

5 Select Port Triggering

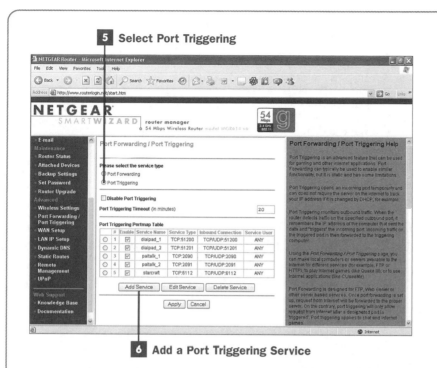

6 Add a Port Triggering Service

58

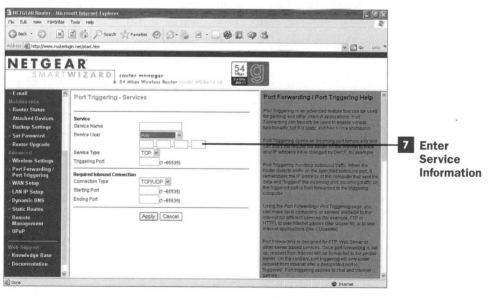

7 Enter Service Information

▶ **NOTE**

UPnP helps computers communicating over the network to determine what services are being offered by other computers on the network. Computers actually broadcast informational messages on the network, telling other computers on the network what services are being offered. Normally, a router blocks this broadcast traffic. When UPnP is enabled on your network's router, the router does not block various broadcast messages sent out by computers on your network that are offering particular services. If you use instant messaging applications on your WiFi network computers (such as AOL Instant Messenger—AIM), you will want to enable UPnP even if you are not configuring port forwarding or triggering.

1 Access UPnP Setting

Open your router's main configuration web page (type your router's URL such as **routerlogin.net** and then enter your administrative login name and password; the URL, default login name, and default password are all set by the router manufacturer, so refer to your router's documentation for this information). Open the router's **UPnP** feature by selecting the **UPnP** link (or similar command) on your router's command list. For example, on the Netgear router I use, I click **UPnP** on the command list on the left side of the web page.

2 Enable and Apply UPnP Setting

Click the **Enable UPnP** check box (or enable UPnP using the appropriate command or selection on your router's configuration page). After selecting the option for UPnP, click **Apply** (or a similar setting) to apply the setting to the router's configuration.

Some WiFi routers also provide access to additional settings related to UPnP, such as **Advertisement Period** and **Advertisement Time to Live** (*time to live* may be abbreviated to *TTL*). These settings can be left at their default settings in most cases (see the following Note). Some routers only allow you to enable UPnP and do not allow you to adjust either the period or the time to live.

The **UPnP Portmap Table** shows you the IP addresses of computers that are accessing the router and also displays the ports that have been opened by the computer or computers on the network. The Portmap Table does not provide data about your network until you have configured port forwarding or port triggering on the router (the UPnP portmap table is not available on all routers).

▶ **NOTE**

UpnP devices such as computers use *announcements* or *advertisements* to let other computers know the services they are offering, such as a gaming service. The advertisement period for UPnP messages is how often the router announces that a particular

58

service is being offered by a computer on the network. The default is every 30 minutes. The advertisement *time to live*, which is measured in *hops*, is the number of routers the advertisement can move through (it hops from router to router) before it is discarded by a router. For most small networks (nearly all in fact), the default advertisement period and the advertisement time to live settings should work just fine. If you find that some devices are having trouble connecting to a particular service, you can increase the number of hops for the time to live setting.

3 Open Port Forwarding/Port Triggering Configuration Page

Select the **Port Forwarding/Port Triggering** link or command on your router's configuration page (these commands might be on separate pages for some routers, so you might have to select **Port Forwarding**, return to the configuration command list, and then select **Port Triggering** to reach the correct pages) to open the Forwarding/Port Triggering configuration page.

4 Configure Port Forwarding

To configure port forwarding for a service offered by a computer on your network, select the service from the **Service Name** drop-down list. The services provided by the available routers vary, but they all list commonly used services such as FTP, HTTP, and popular online games such as Age of Empires (from Microsoft) and Quake (from ID Software). Then enter the last octet (the last number) of the IP address for the computer that is offering the service (remember you can use the **ipconfig** command on a computer to determine its IP address). Then click **Add** to add the service name to the service list.

If you want to add a custom service, click the **Add Custom Service** button and provide the name of the service, the starting and ending port numbers to open (for a service with only one port number, enter the same number as both the starting port and ending port), the transport protocol for the service (TCP, UDP, or both), and the IP address of the computer on your network that will be providing the service. Then click **Apply**. You will be returned to the **Port Forwarding/Port Triggering** configuration page. The services you have added appear in the service list.

You can choose other services from the service list or add custom services as needed. Remember that any time you configure a computer to offer a service and then configure the router to allow a port opening to access that service, you are creating a potential security breach on your network. Port forwarding basically provides a persistent and consistent connection to a particular port, which can be used to invade the network.

58

▶ **TIP**

You can delete or edit a service that you have added to the service list. Select the service and then click the **Delete Service** button to delete the service from the list; click the **Edit Service** button to change service parameters such as the port number and transport protocol for the service.

5 **Select Port Triggering**

To configure a service for port triggering (such as a multiplayer game running on one of your networked computers), select **Port Triggering** on the **Port Forwarding/Port Triggering** configuration page. Remember that port triggering opens a port only temporarily, while port forwarding provides a more persistent availability of an open port. Obviously, port triggering is a more secure way to allow access to a port on a computer offering a particular service.

6 **Add a Port Triggering Service**

You will find that a number of ports are already configured for triggering on the router, such as the Dialpad Internet phone service and Starcraft, a multiplayer war game. These ports are already "triggered" because they are the ports employed by the most popular gaming services used on home networks by online gaming enthusiasts. The list varies from router to router and also varies depending on when you bought your router (online games rise and fall in popularity). To add a service to the port triggering list, click the **Add Service** button.

7 **Enter Service Information**

On the **Port-Triggering Services** page (or a similar page on your router), you are required to enter information related to the service, such as the transport protocol used (TCP/UDP) and the port used by the service (typically an online game). All the information you need to configure the service for port triggering is available on the game or service manufacturer's website. For example, if I wanted to configure **Hoyle Games Online** (from Sierra) for my network, I would access the website **http://www.sierra.com/**. This site provides links and search engines that allow me to locate the information I need to configure port triggering on my router for this gaming service. Most game sites also offer forums that allow you to discuss problems and issues with other users and to get tips related to configuring router settings for a particular game. The information required to configure a new service for port triggering follows:

58

- **The Service Name**: This will be the name of the game.

- **Service User**: The default option is **Any** (meaning that anyone on the Internet can access your game on your network computer) or you can select **single address** from the **Service User** drop-down list. You then enter the IP address of the service user (the person who will be connecting to your computer) in the address boxes provided. Using the **single address** option cuts down on the possibility of unwanted users connecting to your computer, but it does require you to contact the person who will be playing the game with you so that you can exchange the IP addresses of your computers.

- **Service Type**: Select the transport protocol for the service (**TCP** or **UDP**).

- **Triggering Port**: This is the outbound port for the game. You can get the outbound port for your game from the game documentation or the game website.

▶ **NOTE**

The router listens to the outbound port for traffic from your gaming computer; when it detects data traffic, it opens up the inbound port to allow communications from the computer outside the network.

- **Connection Type**: This is transport protocol used for the inbound connection. Select **UDP**, **TCP**, or both (**UDP/TCP**). This information is available in the game's documentation or website.

- **Starting Port**: Enter the starting port for the range of port numbers that should be opened on the router for inbound traffic. This information is available in the game's documentation or on the website.

- **Ending Port**: Enter the ending port for the range of port numbers that should be opened on the router for inbound traffic. If the game uses only a single port number, enter the same number in the **Starting Port** and **Ending Port** boxes.

Click **Apply**. The new service is added to the port triggering list on the **Port Forwarding/Port Triggering** page.

You can add other services to the port triggering list as needed by repeating steps 5–7.

58

▶ **NOTE**

It is not that difficult to find the information necessary to configure port triggering for a multiplayer game. For an example, I did a search on the **activision.custhelp.com** website (the makers of Quake and Doom) to find the port numbers and transport protocol information for configuring port triggering for the Quake game. The transport protocol used is **TCP/UDP**. The port number is **28004** for both outgoing and incoming traffic. So the **Service Type** would be set to **TCP** and the **Triggering Port** would be set to **28004**. The **Connection Type** would be set to **TCP/UDP** and the **Starting Port** and **Ending Port** for the incoming port should be **28004**. Many games use the same port number for incoming and outgoing traffic. If the port numbers are different, use the incoming traffic port number for the triggering port number configuration setting.

9

Taking Advantage of Wireless HotSpots

IN THIS CHAPTER:

Having a notebook computer that is WiFi-enabled allows you to take advantage of restaurants, coffee shops, hotels, and other businesses that provide their clients with free access to the Internet through a wireless *hotspot*. In this chapter, we take a look at what WiFi hotspots are, how to find them, and how to connect to them.

59   **59 About Wireless Hotspots**

✔ BEFORE YOU BEGIN	→ SEE ALSO
32 About Configuring the Wireless Adapter	**63** About Wardriving **76** About 802.11 Security Strategies

59

Public access to the Internet through WiFi has become both a marketing tool for businesses and a major component of both urban and rural planning. Although many of us take advantage of WiFi *hotspots* in coffee shops and hotels (a hotspot being a business or other establishment that provides a "public" connection to the Internet through a WiFi access point), WiFi networks are being built for entire cities such as San Francisco and are also being implemented in the mountains of rural Appalachia by non-profit agencies.

In terms of the availability of WiFi hotspots, many businesses now provide free wireless access to the Internet. All you have to do is fire up your WiFi-enabled notebook computer within the confines of the business and connect to the WiFi access point.

▶ **KEY TERM**

Hotspot—A connection point to the Internet provided by a business or other establishment. The connection point is typically a WiFi router or access point provided by a particular business such as a coffee shop or hotel.

Some businesses provide completely "free" access to the Internet through a WiFi hotspot; others require that you subscribe to a particular provider to use the hotspot found in their establishments or pay for the service by the hour (Internet cafés usually charge for WiFi connections). For example, Starbucks requires that you subscribe to the T-Mobile Hotspot service if you want to connect to the Internet while sipping your double mocha latté (there is a subscription plan or you can pay per hour).

▶ WEB RESOURCE
http://www.starbucks.com/retail/wireless.asp
Not all Starbucks locations provide WiFi connections. For more information on Starbucks, the T-Mobile Hotspot service at Starbucks, and a locator to find Starbucks locations that provide WiFi, visit this website.

Obviously, some businesses provide WiFi access as a courtesy to their customers and use the WiFi connection as way to get you in the door so that you will buy the actual product they sell (such as a hotel room). Many business travelers expect hotels to provide WiFi hotspots with high-speed Internet connections. Hotels that provide a WiFi hotspot typically use password protection to keep folks outside the hotel from sucking up all the WiFi bandwidth that is meant for the hotel clients. Folks staying at the hotel are provided a daily user logon name and password so that they can connect to the WiFi hotspot.

Many businesses, however, don't require a logon for connection to the WiFi hotspot. You can go into the establishment, buy your lunch, and connect to the WiFi hotspot by allowing your WiFi adapter to detect the nearest (and strongest) wireless signal. As you know, WiFi *access points* (such as those built into WiFi routers) provide a range of more than a hundred feet, so you can actually park in the parking lot of a business providing a WiFi hotspot and connect without even entering the business or purchasing a thing. Again, WiFi hotspots provided by businesses are considered marketing tools, so if you feel guilty, you might want to pay back the business occasionally by buying whatever it is that they sell (a cup of coffee won't break the bank).

59

Hotspot Connection Speeds

When you use a WiFi hotspot to connect to the Internet, you might be surprised at the actual throughput that you are provided. Most 802.11g WiFi adapters provide a potential connection speed of 56Mbps; some enhanced adapters provided possible connection speeds of 108Mbps. On your home WiFi network, you might be realizing the maximum speeds if you have a router that allows a connection speed of 56Mbps or higher.

However, you will find that WiFi hotspots provide much less bandwidth because the purpose of the hotspot is to connect to the Internet and not to provide bandwidth for local area networking. For example, I can connect to a public hotspot using a WiFi adapter that provides a potential connection speed of 56Mbps, however, I might connect at only 11Mbps because the access point for the WiFi hotspot provides only 11Mbps of throughput for connecting computers.

Hotspots won't necessarily provide you with the maximum throughput that can be realized by your WiFi adapter.

Even 10 (the speed for a 802.11b connection) or 11Mbps is overkill in terms of connection speed if you think about it, because the whole point of the WiFi connection is to access the Internet. Even the fastest Internet connection rarely exceeds 700Kbps, so the 11Mbps connection is actually more than enough for me to take advantage of the full bandwidth provided by the hotspot's Internet connection.

▶ **NOTE**

The WiFi routers and access points used for public hotspots are typically more sophisticated than the WiFi equipment you buy for home networking. Higher-end WiFi routers can actually be configured so that the amount of bandwidth provided to connections is controlled by the WiFi router or access point. This would allow a hotel to provide greater bandwidth for users connecting to the Internet using the wired network in their rooms as opposed to connecting to the Internet in the lobby through a hotspot.

Hotspot Security

Because many public hotspots provide anyone with access to the Internet, the security of your data over such a connection can be an issue. If someone also connected to the hotspot is monitoring the network using eavesdropping software that collects data packets, you could be broadcasting important information into the hands of people who will use it for no good.

It is extremely satisfying to drop into a lunch spot that provides a hotspot and eat your lunch while paying your bills online over the Internet. However, your data might be going over the WiFi network unprotected. WiFi hotspots do not necessarily provide any encryption or security strategies.

So, it may be true that you get what you pay for. Hotspots that require you to pay for the service—such as the T-Mobile connections found in many Starbucks coffee shops—do take advantage of user authentication and the WPA security protocol. If you don't have to pay for access to the hotspot, assume that the connection is not secure and monitor your use of the Internet through that connection accordingly. In most cases, when you make a connection to an unsecured WiFi network, a message box opens, letting you know that the WiFi connection is not secured; connect at your own risk.

Another potential security problem when you use public hotspots is the settings on your computer related to file and print sharing. If you share files and printers on your home network, the **File and Print Sharing for Microsoft Networks** service will be enabled on your computer. So, anyone connected to the same hotspot as you can browse for connected computers and attempt to access any shared folders on those connected computers. You should disable the **File and Print Sharing for Microsoft Networks** service on your computer when you are using public hotspots to connect to the Internet. See **40 Open Connections Properties and Enable Client, Protocols, and Services** for the steps to enable/disable this service.

59

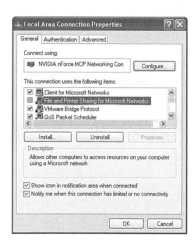

*Disable the **File and Print Sharing for Microsoft Networks** service when you are using WiFi hotspots.*

▶ **NOTE**

If you must do transactions and other important data transfers over public hotspot connections, you might want to consider buying a software product that helps secure your data. There are a number of products on the market. For example, check out **http://www.jiwire.com/spotlock.htm**. JiWire provides a WiFi security product called Spotlock, which encrypts the data going from and to your computer when you are using a public WiFi hotspot connection.

60 | **Use the Web to Locate Hotspots**

✔ **BEFORE YOU BEGIN**

59 About Wireless Hotspots

59

You can use the Web to locate WiFi *hotspots* in your area. Doing some research online before you leave home negates the necessity of driving around trying to connect to hotspots that might or might not exist. It also clues you in to the "public" hotspots that are available rather than the hotspots that are unprotected private WiFi networks. Hotspots provided by coffee houses, hotels, and other businesses are designed to handle many connections on their networks. Unprotected private WiFi networks are open to possible connection only because the network hasn't been secured by the network administrator. Public hotspots expect you to connect; unsecured private networks don't expect you to connect (and you shouldn't connect to unsecured private networks that you detect; doing so is unethical and, in some cases, might be illegal).

Because resource pages that list hotspots seem to come and go on the Web, it makes sense to do a periodic search using your favorite search engine to locate the most up-to-date lists of hotspots in your area or in an area you will be visiting or traveling through.

1 **Search for WiFi Hotspots**

Open your Web browser and navigate to your favorite search page. Enter the search term **WiFi hotspots** and run the search.

2 **Select Hotspot List Link**

A number of results will be listed when you conduct the search. Click one of the links to access that resource. For example, I might choose the search result for **http://www.wififreespot.com/**.

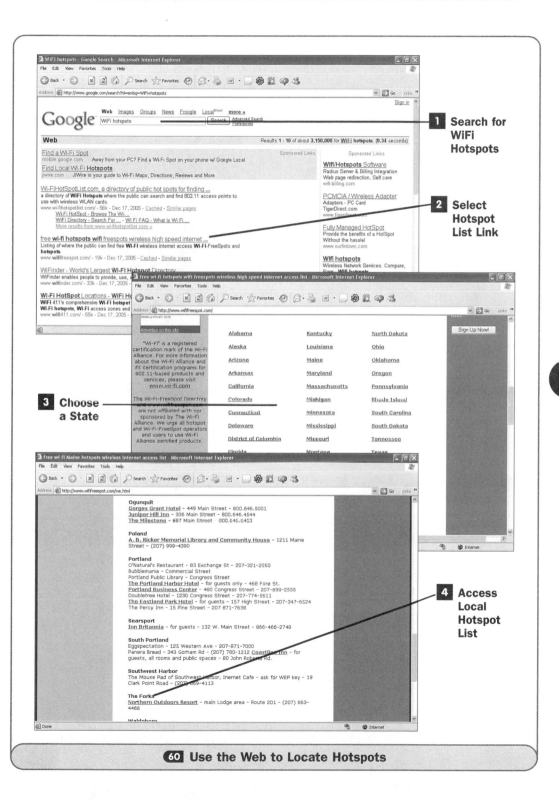

3 Choose a State

Most websites that provide a listing of WiFi hotspots will allow you to view hotspots by state or might provide a search engine that allows you to search by state and town. In the case of the **www.wififreespot.com** site, I click a particular state in the state list provided.

4 Access Local Hotspot List

The local hotspot list for the selected state is typically listed by city. For example, I can scroll down the list of hotspots in the state of Maine and view the hotspots in my town of Portland, ME. Unfortunately, most hotspot listings provide only the location of the hotspot and typically do not include information about the hotspot itself (such as whether the WiFi connection is secured and whether the connection is free or requires payment or a subscription).

If you don't feel that the website has provided a complete list or you want to look at other possibilities, use your browser's **Back** button to return to your original search list and start the process again.

60

61 Detect WiFi Hotspots and Connect

✔ **BEFORE YOU BEGIN**

59 About Wireless Hotspots
60 Use the Web to Locate Hotspots

After you have used the Web to locate WiFi *hotspots* in your area (or in a city you are planning to visit), you can actually go to a particular hotspot location and connect to the WiFi network and the Internet.

When you attempt to connect to a hotspot with your WiFi-enabled notebook computer, you might be surprised that you actually detect more WiFi networks than you expected. This is often true in large urban areas where a number of hotels or office buildings are tightly packed on a city street. If you are faced with the happy situation of detecting more than one WiFi network hotspot, you can choose the network to which you want to connect.

▶ **NOTE**

If you don't want to lug your laptop around to detect hotspots, other devices are available that can be used to detect WiFi hotspots. For example, any WiFi-enabled Palm or other personal digital assistant can be used to locate WiFi networks. If you don't want to spend the money for a WiFi-enabled handheld device, you can buy a WiFi detector that costs less than 50 dollars. For example, the Kensington WiFi Finder Plus can be used to detect WiFi connections and sells for around 30 dollars. For more about handheld computers and WiFi detectors, check out **www.handtops.com**.

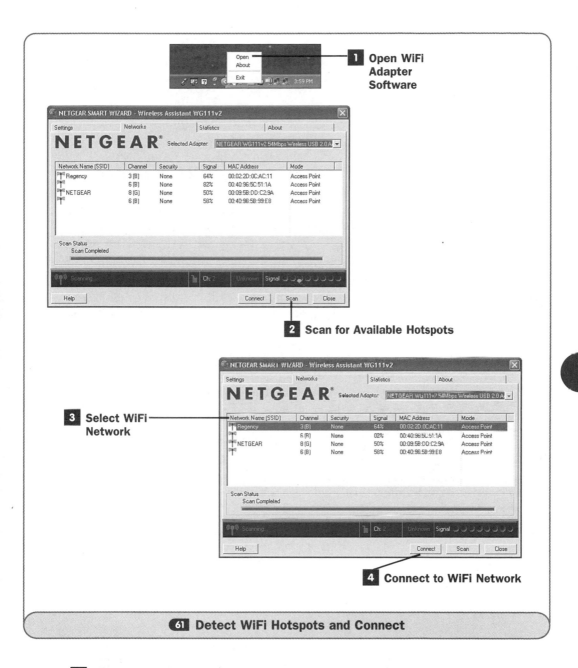

1 Open WiFi Adapter Software

2 Scan for Available Hotspots

3 Select WiFi Network

4 Connect to WiFi Network

61 Detect WiFi Hotspots and Connect

1 Open WiFi Adapter Software

Right-click the WiFi adapter icon in the System Tray and select **Open** from the context menu. Your WiFi *adapter*'s software or the **Windows Wireless Connection Monitor** opens.

2 Scan for Available Hotspots

Click the **Scan** button (or choose a similar command) to have your adapter scan for available WiFi networks. The results appear in your WiFi adapter's software window.

Hotspots that are free and readily available in terms of you connecting to them will have no security settings. So, under the **Security** column, you will see the setting **None**. If a network appears on your scan list and lists WEP or WPA as the security setting, this means that you will need the shared security *key* or the *passphrase* to connect to the network. The presence of WEP or WPA security typically means that this is a private, secure network. However, in the case of secure public hotspots such as the T-Mobile hotspots at Starbucks coffee shops, you would see that the network is secured with WPA. When you subscribe to T-Mobile, you are provided with the security information and the passphrase to configure your WiFi-enabled computer to connect to the hotspot. So, although T-Mobile provides a public hotspot available at a number of locations, it is really a private network in that you must subscribe to it to use it.

The channel you are connected on also appears in the scan window. When your WiFi adapter scans for possible connections, it cycles through all the available WiFi channels. Although it is interesting to know what channel you are currently operating on, the **channel** setting is controlled by the WiFi access point.

61

▶ TIP

When you browse the scan list provided by your WiFi adapter, it is fairly clear which of the detected networks are public hotspots and which of the networks are unsecured private networks. For example, if you are in a hotel named the Regency, the hotspot name will be **regency** or something to that effect. If you see networks listed in the scan list that are named **Linksys** or **Netgear**, you are typically looking at unsecured private networks, set up by people who have a lot to learn about securing their WiFi networks.

3 Select WiFi Network

The list of WiFi networks detected will also provide the type of security used on a particular network and the signal strength of that WiFi hotspot. Select the network to which you want to connect, in this case an unsecured public hotspot. I know that the public hotspot I want to connect to is the **regency** option because I am sitting in the lobby of the Regency Hotel. Although you might be tempted to connect to one of the other unsecured networks that provides a stronger signal, I recommend that you take the ethical high road and leave the unsecured "private" networks alone and connect to the WiFi hotspot provided by the establishment where you are sitting.

4 Connect to WiFi Network

Click the **Connect** button or select a similar command to connect to the selected WiFi network. The new settings for the connection such as the WiFi network name and the channel (and the lack of security settings) will be validated (you don't have to do anything to have these settings validated), and then the connection will become available. You can now surf the Web or use other Internet tools such as email as needed.

▶ **NOTE**

You won't necessarily know whether a WiFi hotspot works or will provide you with unsecured access until you try to connect. Some WiFi networks, such as hotel hotspots reserved for guests of the hotel, require you to enter a login name and a password when you open your web browser. You might have to get the login name and password from the hotel's front desk or the concierge.

---

62 Fine-Tune Hotspot Connection Parameters

✔ BEFORE YOU BEGIN

59 About Wireless Hotspots
61 Detect WiFi Hotspots and Connect

62

You might find that the signal strength and connection quality of a WiFi *hotspot* is less than ideal. The signal strength can actually vary during the connection depending on how many other users are connecting to the hotspot.

▶ **NOTE**

You have most likely positioned your home WiFi router and other equipment so that you get an excellent connection and signal strength when you are connected to your home WiFi network. You will find that the world of the WiFi hotspot is not as ideal as your home networking environment. WiFi hotspot signals can be weak and can even disconnect while you are online. But it does come down to the old adage that you get what you pay for—and many hotspots are absolutely free.

You can fine-tune some of your WiFi connection settings to maximize a weak or dodgy connection. Be advised, however, that changing the advanced settings for a WiFi connection can also make the connection fail. The settings you can tweak (if you are careful) are as follows:

- **Power Saving**: If you are using a laptop on battery power, you should turn on the *adapter's* **Power Saving** feature. Doing so helps conserve the adapter's power usage, and therefore preserves your laptop's batteries. On the Netgear WG111 USB adapter, the power saving options can be **Off**, **Maximum**, or

Dynamic. The **Maximum** setting is equivalent to the adapter being on all the time; the **Dynamic** setting allows the power savings to be turned on and off. I suggest that you use the **Dynamic** setting only in situations where you know that your laptop battery is low. Sometimes using the **Dynamic** setting can result in the adapter dropping the connection.

- **Preamble**: The preamble is the bit stream sent at the beginning of a connection conversation between the WiFi adapter and a WiFi access point. You can set the preamble length to **Auto**, **Long**, or **Short**. If you want to try to make a connection more reliable (connections can be dropped by your adapter, so making them more reliable helps negate the loss of the connection) or get a little more range out of your WiFi adapter, select the **Long** preamble. To fine-tune performance on a connection, select **Short** (a short preamble can provide better transfer performance, meaning the overall transfer speed can be increased for the connection). Note that changing the preamble setting can disable an existing connection.

- **Transmit Rate**: For a 54Mbps WiFi adapter, the transmit rate can be set between 1 Mbps and 54Mbps. In most cases, it makes sense to leave this setting at **Auto**. However, if there are a lot of access points in a small area, you can experience interference when you attempt to connect to a local hotspot. Lowering the transmit rate can cut down on the interference, but it also reduces the range of your WiFi adapter.

62

The other settings found in the **Advanced Settings** dialog box for your WiFi adapter should be left at their defaults. Changing these settings will not change performance or range parameters.

▶ **TIP**

The power-saving, preamble, and transfer rate settings might be labeled differently depending on the WiFi adapter you are using. The settings discussed here are those provided for the Netgear WG111 USB wireless G adapter. Make sure that you read the documentation provided with your WiFi adapter before you change any settings that are considered "advanced."

1 Open Advanced Settings

Right-click the WiFi adapter icon in the System Tray and select **Open** from the context menu to open your adapter's configuration window. Click the **Advanced Settings** button to open the **Advanced Settings** dialog box (this command varies from adapter to adapter).

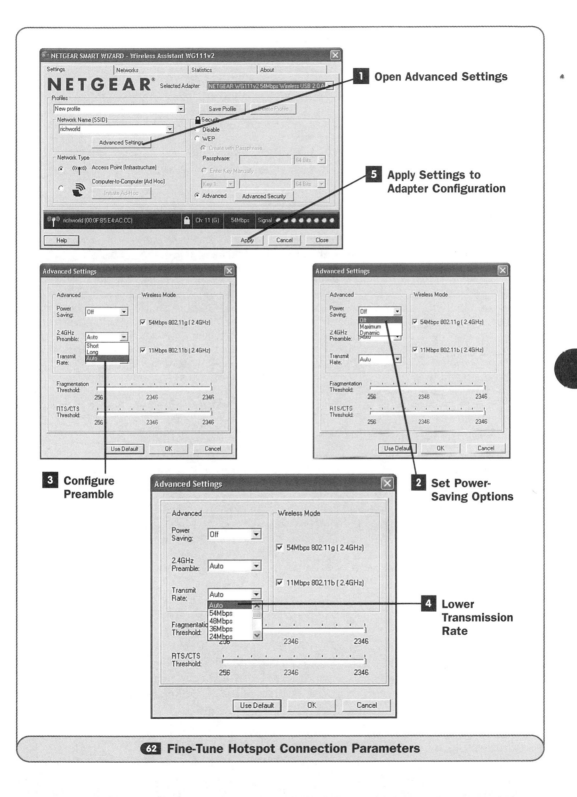

1 Open Advanced Settings

5 Apply Settings to Adapter Configuration

62

3 Configure Preamble

2 Set Power-Saving Options

4 Lower Transmission Rate

62 Fine-Tune Hotspot Connection Parameters

2 Set Power Saving Settings

From the **Power Saving** drop-down list, select **Maximum** or **Dynamic**. The default is **Off**. The **Dynamic** setting saves you the most power but can cause the adapter to disconnect when the laptop is at very low battery power.

3 Configure Preamble

Locate the **Preamble** drop-down box. The default setting is **Auto**. If you want to increase the range of the adapter, change this setting to **Long**. If you want to tweak performance, select **Short**.

▶ NOTE

When the 802.11b specifications were first designed, the WiFi preamble was transmitted at only 1 megabit per second, with the data that followed transmitted at 11 megabits per second. This preamble standard is still with us because of the backward compatibility of newer WiFi hardware (such as 802.11g hardware). A long preamble increases the stability of the connection (including the range) but will be slower than a shorter preamble. The long preamble basically negotiates a strong consistent connection between the sending and receiving devices. A shorter preamble provides faster transmission because the preamble for each data stream is shorter, and the actual movement of the data from sending to receiving device happens faster, meaning the overall connection performance is increased. However, because Ethernet connections can drop data packets during transmission, the shorter preamble might result in the connection being dropped.

62

4 Lower Transmission Rate

Locate the **Transmit Rate** drop-down list. The default setting is **Auto**. If you want to fine-tune the connection with a hotspot—for example, if you have been disconnected because of interference—you can lower the transmit rate to cut down on the local interference. Go down one menu choice at a time (say, from 54Mbps to 48Mbps) because lowering the transmission rate also lowers the range of the adapter.

After fine-tuning the advanced settings, click **OK** to return to the main configuration window.

5 Apply Settings to Adapter Configuration

Click the **Apply** button in the main adapter settings window to apply the new advanced settings to your WiFi adapter's configuration. If you find that tweaking the settings hasn't really solved any of the problems you were experiencing, return to the **Advanced Settings** dialog box and try other selections. You can also return to the default values if necessary.

▶ **TIP**

If fine-tuning any of the advanced settings for your WiFi adapter gives you connection problems, return to the **Advanced Settings** dialog box and select the **Use Default** button (or similar command) to go back to the router's default advanced settings.

63 **About Wardriving**

✔ **BEFORE YOU BEGIN**

59 About Wireless Hotspots
61 Detect WiFi Hotspots and Connect

→ **SEE ALSO**

76 About 802.11 Security Strategies

With more public and private WiFi networks coming online, computer hobbyists (okay, so I'm talking computer *geeks*) have begun to locate and then map unsecured WiFi connections. This process is termed ***wardriving***, which basically means that someone is driving around the city or town with a wireless-enabled laptop computer, trying to find and connect to unsecured wireless networks. Wardrivers often outfit their vehicles with an external wireless antennae, which makes it easier to find wireless hotspots. A handheld Global Positioning System device (GPS) is also often used to help map the actual borders of the hotspot, making future use of the hotspot for Internet access extremely easy.

▶ **NOTE**

In most cases, if an unsecured network is detected by your WiFi adapter, you will be able to connect to it. *Unsecured* means that the WiFi access point is not using **WEP** or **WPA** security. In some cases, however, *hotspots* might use secondary security that requires a logon name and password when you attempt to use the unsecured connection to browse the Web. In the case of secure hotspots or local WiFi networks found using a WiFi adapter scan, secured networks such as a T-Mobile hotspot at a Starbucks coffee shop will show that the network is secured (for example, the characters **WPA** will appear in the **Security** setting column for the detected network).

▶ **KEY TERM**

Wardriving—The process of driving around town with the purpose of identifying and mapping unsecured WiFi hotspots.

Wardriving has become such a geek fad that many people are involved in trying to locate unsecured wireless hotspots. These hobbyists are really just looking for free Internet access and will readily share information about mapped hotspots with other wardrivers over a number of sites on the Web. Some wardrivers or war walkers (meaning that you are on foot instead of driving a vehicle in order to detect hotspots) actually use a system of chalk marks on the sidewalk to mark buildings that provide unsecured and public access to the Internet through a WiFi hotspot. Look for a circle with a W inside it to locate a hotspot that has been marked by a war walker.

The problem with wardriving is that it readily identifies unsecured WiFi networks. This means that hackers are basically given a roadmap to unsecured wireless networks. If you haven't done so already, the threat that wardrivers can locate your unsecured network should make you secure your WiFi network, particularly if you live in an urban center (where wardriving is more common) with the WPA security protocol. For more about WPA, see **76 About 802.11 Security Strategies** and **78 Configure WiFi Protected Access (WPA) Security**.

Wardrivers know that the default configuration for an *access point* makes it extremely easy to promiscuously connect to a wireless network that is broadcasting its SSID and is not using either WEP or WPA to secure the network. Even if there is no SSID broadcast, wardrivers can connect to an unsecure WiFi network using the default SSID for the different popular access points available. For example, the default SSID for an access point manufactured by Linksys is **linksys**.

63

You can find websites that provide the location of WiFi hotspots—including hotspots that were not necessarily designed to be public. Other wardriving related websites provide the default SSIDs, default passwords, and other information for WiFi routers and access points; for example check out **http://www.cirt.net**. This list shows that there are 315 vendors of WiFi hardware such as access points and WiFi routers. Each vendor has its own default SSIDs and passwords.

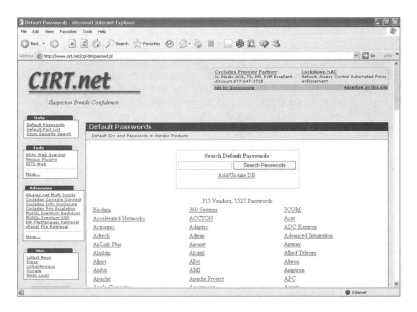

*Wardriving sites such as **www.cirt.net** provide default SSIDs and WiFi hardware default passwords.*

So, while wardrivers say that the purpose of wardriving is to catalog available WiFi hotspots, wardriving also provides information that can be used to access WiFi networks that have not been secured. A number of hacking tools are available that can be used to monitor network traffic and attempt to break the security for even secured WiFi hotspots. Definitely protect your WiFi network from unauthorized access.

63

PART IV

Protecting and Securing the Wireless Network

IN THIS PART

10

Protecting Your System and Data

IN THIS CHAPTER:

Protecting your data—meaning your documents, pictures, and other important files—is an important aspect of managing a computer whether that computer is attached to a network or not. Because sharing files on a *workgroup* network actually increases the possibility that a file will be inadvertently deleted, it makes sense to back up important data on your computer. Then if there is a problem or a loss of important data, you can restore the file or files.

And because the Windows system files as well as other files that actually make your system work correctly can become corrupt or be infected by a virus, it makes sense to take advantage of the Windows **System Restore** feature, which allows you to quickly restore your system if it begins to malfunction. In this chapter, we look at backing up and restoring data and using the **System Restore** feature.

---

64 **About Backing Up and Restoring Data**

✔ **BEFORE YOU BEGIN**

1 About the Windows XP Environment
7 Get Help in Windows
50 Map a Network Drive

64

The most efficient method of protecting important files on your computer is to regularly back up these files. A backup copy of a folder or drive is actually a single compressed file that can be restored to a computer if necessary. You can back up files to different drives such as a USB removable *flash drive* or a dedicated USB *external backup drive*. Many external backup drives now also provide for FireWire connectivity; FireWire (also referred to as IEEE 1394) is a high-speed interface available on many new computers that can transfer data as fast as 800Mbps.

► **KEY TERMS**

Flash drive—A portable flash memory drive that can be attached to a computer through a USB port. Flash drives are small and use a memory chip to hold data. They provide an excellent way to transfer limited amounts of data between computers.

External hard drive—An external storage device that can be connected to a computer using a USB or FireWire connection. USB external hard drives are actual hard drives like the one inside your computer (meaning they contain magnetic media that spins at high speeds). The hard drive has been adapted to work in an external case and to transfer data using either a USB or FireWire connection.

You can back up system setting files to a floppy disk (if you have a floppy drive on your computer). You can back up data stored on one of your local drives (such as your C: drive) and you can also back up data stored on another computer in the workgroup, such as a share that you have mapped as a drive. However, placing your backup on someone else's computer doesn't necessarily mean that your backup is safe from accidental erasure or corruption.

Having a backup copy of your computer data allows you to actually restore the data if the data is accidentally deleted (a common problem with shared folders in a workgroup) or if you have hardware problems such as a failed hard drive. For example, if your hard drive fails, you can put a new hard drive in the computer, install Windows and the other software you use, and then restore the backed-up data files to the new hard drive. All you have lost is the time it takes to put in a new hard drive and restore the files. Important data that has been backed up can also be restored to an entirely different computer, which is particularly useful if you are upgrading to a new computer.

In terms of backing up the data on your network, you have two alternatives: local backups or backups over the WiFi network. Because a workgroup network is a grouping of peer computers that share resources among the individual computers, local backups allow each computer user to select and back up the files she feels are important. Backing up locally to a backup device directly connected to a computer is a fairly fast process and does not consume network bandwidth; backing up over the network can actually slow down the network.

The other alternative is to have a device on the network dedicated to the backup process—such as a computer designated as a file server or a network backup drive that is directly connected to the WiFi network. However, if you back up to another computer on the network, you are going to tie up processing power on that computer during your backup. And because the data must travel on the network, the backup will take more time than backing up to a directly connected local device.

For example, a directly connected USB hard drive can provide a transfer rate of 480Mbs (Megabits/second), while your WiFi network can transfer data at only a maximum speed of 56Mbs (unless you are using some type of speed-boosting technology on your router and adapters, which can provide faster throughput but still not as fast as a directly connected drive). So, directly connected backup devices are always going to be faster and more reliable (because the data isn't sent over the network).

▶ **NOTE**

Large, corporate computer networks use centralized file servers as file repositories for all the users on the network. It is easy to then back up these files because the network administrator can back up the entire file server. The network administrator attaches a backup device directly to the file server to ensure a fast and glitch-free backup because the data moves directly to the backup storage device and does not have to travel over the network. In a workgroup environment, your files are actually spread across the computers in the workgroup. So, it really makes sense for each computer user to back up his own files; backing up the files locally using an external hard drive or a CD-RW drive means that you get a fairly fast backup and don't have to sit and wait while the files are sent over the network to a centralized backup device. Tying up your computer and sapping the resources on another workgroup computer on the network (not to mention sucking up network bandwidth) by doing a backup over the network probably isn't a good use of your time or network and computer resources. However, if your only way of backing up your various networked computers is using a shared drive on the network, please do so, because it is extremely important to back up files that are vital to you.

I don't want to completely jade you against network-based backup scenarios because any backup is better than no backup at all. Although backing up across the network is slower than backing up individual computers to local backup devices and media, network backup drives *are* available that connect directly to the network. Not only do they provide you with the option of backing up to a centralized network location, they provide additional storage space on the network that can be accessed by any computer in the workgroup.

For example, the SimpleTech Office Storage Server is a portable hard drive (the 160GB version costs around $250 US) that has its own Ethernet port so that it can be directly connected to the WiFi router using a network cable. The drive is then managed over the network using software that is installed on each computer in the workgroup that will need access to the drive. This type of network-attached drive provides you with centralized network storage space for files and can also be used as a network backup drive. The LaCie Ethernet Disk Mini Network Hard Drive provides both a USB connector for direct connection to a computer and an Ethernet port for direct connection to the network (using a switch or the WiFi router). The LaCie drive is actually managed using a web interface much like the interface used to manage most WiFi routers.

▶ WEB RESOURCE

www.simpletech.com
For more information about SimpleTech external drives, see the SimpleTech website.

www.lacie.com
For more about LaCie drives, see the LaCie website.

There are a number of software and hardware possibilities for backing up data on a PC in terms of backup software and the actual hardware storage device you use to hold the backup files. Let's talk about the software possibilities first.

Backup Software

Although a number of companies sell a wide variety of backup software products, I don't think that in most cases you need to buy any additional software. If you have purchased an external USB drive, most of these drives come with their own backup software. For example, the SimpleDrive External Hard Drive (a USB drive) provides backup software called StorageSync Professional. This backup software provides both file compression and encryption along with a very simple-to-use interface.

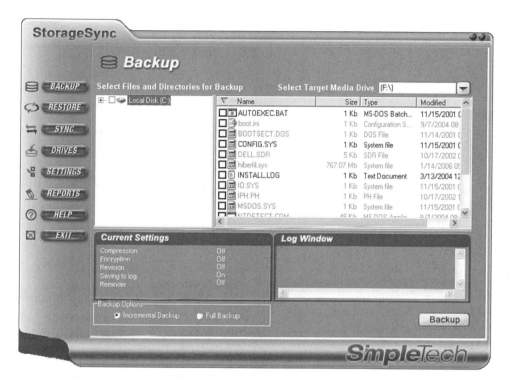

Most USB hard drives provide backup software that can be used to back up to the locally connected external drive.

The downside of the backup software that ships with USB external hard drives (such as the SimpleDrive) is that it is designed to detect USB-connected drives and then use them as the backup destination. The software generally provides no options for backing up over the network or even backing up to the local internal hard drive on the computer.

If you don't want to use the backup software that came with an external USB drive, or if you bought a drive that didn't provide backup software, you might be able to get by with the Windows Backup utility. It is an adequate backup and restore utility, and will provide you with most of the options you need to complete periodic backups of important files.

If, after reading the tasks in this chapter that provide a look at backing up and restoring data using the Windows Backup utility (which provides for a convenient example because everyone with Windows XP has access to it), you determine that you want to purchase a more "feature rich" backup software package, you will find that many are available. For example, Roxio (**www.sonic.com**) sells Backup MyPC Deluxe, which can back up and restore data, and also provides advanced features for restoring operating systems and copying CDs and DVDs. More advanced backup software such as Norton Ghost (**www.symantec.com**) can be used to create a backup "image" of your entire computer hard drive. Most external USB hard drives (large-capacity USB drives of more than 60 Gigabytes) come with a CD that contains backup and restore software you can use with the drive.

▶ **NOTE**

The Windows XP backup and restore utility can probably provide you with all the basics you need in terms of creating backups and then restoring them if disaster strikes. You can check out some of the other products available, but creating simple backups doesn't really warrant the cost of special backup and restore software. You will have to be your own judge in terms of your particular needs and the various features these backup and restore software packages offer.

As mentioned earlier, if you don't want to buy additional backup software (or don't even want to buy an external drive and are comfortable placing backups on a CD or flash drive) and don't feel you have many important files, you can probably make do with the Windows **Backup** utility that is provided free with Windows XP.

64

The **Backup** utility includes wizards that can walk you through the backup or restore procedures. The utility also lets you create automated system recovery backups, which make it easy to restore Windows system settings and other files. A wizard helps you create these system backups and then restore them if necessary. The **Backup** utility also allows you to schedule backups so that backups are made at regular intervals (once or twice a week—or more frequently if necessary).

▶ **TIP**

The biggest problem with backup and restore utilities such as the Windows **Backup** utility is that people don't use them. When their system crashes, they lament the fact that they never backed up their important files.

When most people think of backing up their system, they assume that they must leave the computer alone while the backup process is taking place. However, Windows XP's backup utility creates a volume shadow copy of your data as it creates the backup. This means that the files are backed up in the volume specified (meaning on your hard drive or some other location) as *copies* of the files' current state. So files that you have open and are working on are actually backed up or copied in the state that the backup utility finds them in during the backup. For example, if you are typing a letter in Microsoft Word and have finished two-thirds of the letter (and have the file open to work on it), when the backup takes place, two-thirds of the typed letter will be saved in the backup file. Windows XP's backup feature gives you a "real-time" backup of the files you have selected for backup whether they are currently open or not.

Backup Hardware

In terms of the hardware you will need to store your backups, what you need really depends on the number of files you want to back up. If you want to back up an entire 100GB hard drive, the contents obviously will not fit on a 512MB USB flash drive (even if the files are compressed). The backup archive files created by the Windows **Backup** utility are compressed to a certain extent to take up less space, but some file types such as sound files (such as MP3s) and digital image files really don't compress because they are saved in a format that typically uses some sort of compression anyway. To be safe (and realistic), think in terms of a 1-to-1 relationship between the size of the files to be backed up and the space needed to hold the backup file. If you are going to back up 20GB of data, for example, you should have 20GB or more of free space on the drive you will be using to store the backup.

▶ **TIP**

64

To determine the size of a particular folder (basically the size of the folder's contents), open **My Computer** by clicking the **Start** button and then choosing **My Computer**, and then double-click the drive (such as your C: drive) that contains the folder you are interested in. Right-click the folder and select **Properties** from the context menu. On the **General** tab of the folder's **Properties** dialog box, the **Size on disk** statistic provides you with the number of bytes taken up by the folder on your hard drive. Knowing the size of a folder or folders allows you to estimate the amount of space you need to back up the files in that folder or folders.

One consideration in terms of selecting a backup device (such as a USB hard drive) is that the device must be big enough (in terms of disk space available) to accommodate your backup needs. And because files can be backed up over your Windows workgroup network, consider purchasing a device that can be shared on the network and used to back up all the important files from the various computers in the workgroup. Although backing up over the network is slow and uses network bandwidth, it can be convenient because everyone on the network can use the network drive. If convenience is more important than time and network bandwidth (because a network backup is both slower and uses the network bandwidth), consider buying an external drive with an Ethernet port or use a computer with a large hard drive and a WiFi card as a file server and backup repository. Each individual on the network can back up important files to a shared backup device that is hosted by one of the computers on the network. For more about sharing drives and folders in a workgroup, see **47** **Share a Folder**.

A number of companies such as Seagate and Western Digital sell USB hard drives. These drives come in capacities as high as 400 Gigabytes and offer plenty of space for expanding the available storage space for a computer and also serve as excellent devices for backups. Because they are USB drives, they are separate from the computer; even if the computer fails, the USB drive (which has its own power source) is still functional. This means that important files that have been backed up to the USB drive could actually be restored to another computer if they are needed immediately.

64

USB hard drives, such as this Western Digital drive, are portable, large-capacity devices that are very useful for storing computer file backups.

USB hard drives (both flash drives and actual hard drives) are not the only devices available for backing up data. Some backup software (not the Windows **Backup** utility, however) allow you to back up data directly to a CD or DVD burner on your computer (the backup software backs up the data and then burns it directly to the writable CD or DVD). Tape drives (such as drives that use DAT tape) and large capacity disk drives such as Zip and Jaz drives from Iomega (**www.iomega.com**) are another option. You can remove the tape or disk backup media from the drive and store it in a safe location. Large companies typically use some sort of high-speed tape drive to store backup files because the tapes can then be taken offsite to guard against a fire or natural disaster. In terms of backing up home computer data, USB drives are probably the most economical and easy to use. You don't necessarily have to take copies of your backup files offsite (away from your home), but how you protect the personal and important data on your computer is up to you.

If your backup needs are minimal—meaning that you really back up only a few important files in your **My Documents** folder or you want to back up just your Windows system state files (the files that control your Windows configuration)—you might get by with a USB flash drive (available in a variety of sizes, typically from 256MB to 2GB or more).

▶ **NOTE**

You can forgo using an external device such as a USB hard drive or flash drive by burning your backup file to a CD or DVD. To do this, you use the Windows **Backup** utility to back up your data files to a folder on your hard drive (yes, you can back up to your own hard drive). You can then use your CD-burning software to burn the backup file to a CD. This approach allows you to have the backup file on removable media (the CD). Obviously, this method requires that you have enough free space on your hard drive to hold the backup file, and It takes an extra step to burn the file to a CD or DVD. But this method does get your backup file onto removable media so that you can restore your computer files if thc hard drive on the current computer ever explodes.

64

Types of Backups

When you back up files from your computer, you really need to back up only the files you have created (your résumé, checkbook file, Christmas card list, and so on). Backing up software files is a waste of time and storage space because software can always be reinstalled from the original software CDs.

You might think that you have to completely back up all your files each time you run the backup utility. However, you can configure the backup utility so that it backs up only those files that are new or have changed in the folders you specify. The Windows **Backup** utility allows you to customize the backup process and so that you can minimize the amount of time required to actually back up your files.

In short, the first time you back up *all* the files in the folder or folders you select; for subsequent backups, you back up only those files that have changed or are new. The various backup types supported by the Windows **Backup** utility are as follows:

- **Normal backup**: The default backup type for the Windows **Backup** utility. Use this option the first time you back up files on your computer. All the files backed up during a *normal backup* are electronically tagged (with a file switch) as having been backed up. When you edit or modify a file that has been tagged as backed up, the tag is removed (the file is no longer tagged as having been backed up). Tagging the files is important in respect to using other backup types such as daily and differential, which only back up files that have changed since the last normal backup.

▶ **KEY TERM**

Normal backup—A backup method that backs up all selected files to the backup archive file and flags the files as having been backed up.

- **Daily backup**: This type of backup copies the selected folders to the backup file. Only the files modified *on that day* are backed up. The files that are backed up are not flagged as backed up, however. This means that if you had to restore the files that had been backed up recently, you would have to restore the files from your normal backup and then restore the files from the *daily backup*. Bottom line: In most cases, I don't believe you will need to do daily backups, but please read about the other backup types listed here as well as my advice for the best-practice way to combine backups so that you can always quickly restore files if needed.

64 ▶ **KEY TERM**

Daily backup—A backup method that backs up all the files in a selected folder or folders that have changed or have been newly created on that day.

▶ **NOTE**

Files on your computer have different electronic flags associated with them. These flags or attributes can change depending on the state of the file. The **archive** attribute tells backup software whether or not a file has been backed up. When the **archive** attribute is on, a file has not been backed up. When the file has been backed up, the **archive** attribute is clear. You don't really have to worry about file attributes such as the **archive** attribute, but be advised that the backup software uses the attribute when it chooses which files to ignore and which files to copy during the backup process.

- **Differential backup**: This type of backup copies the files that have changed (meaning that the files were previously backed up) or that you have created since your last normal or incremental backup. The files are not marked as backed up. This backup type is similar to the daily backup, but it backs up *all* changed and newly created files in the selected folders.

▶ **KEY TERM**

Differential backup—A backup method that backs up all the files in a selected folder or folders that have changed or have been newly created since the last normal or incremental backup. This type of backup does not "tag" the files as having been backed up.

- **Incremental backup**: This type of backup backs up only those files that are new or that have been changed since your last normal backup. The files that are backed up during an incremental backup are marked as having been backed up, meaning that the **archive** attribute is removed from the file during the incremental backup.

▶ **KEY TERM**

Incremental backup—A backup method that backs up all the files in a selected folder or folders that have changed or have been newly created since the last normal backup. Files backed up are tagged as having been backed up.

- **Copy backup**: This type of backup copies all the files in folders that were selected for backup. The files are copied to a backup archive file whether or not the files have been backed up before.

▶ **KEY TERM**

Copy backup—A backup method that copies all the files in a selected folder or folders regardless of whether they have been backed up before.

Now you are probably wondering why there are different backup types and what you should do in terms of backing up your own data. Here is the solution I recommend: The first time you back up your data, it makes sense to do a normal backup (which is also referred to as a full backup in some backup software packages). This type of backup gets all your important files into a single backup file on a USB drive or some other media such as a tape drive. The next time you do a backup, do an incremental backup. Because an incremental backup copies only the files that are new or that have changed since the normal backup, the incremental backup goes very quickly.

Now you have to decide how often to do incremental backups—daily, every other day, or weekly. The time increment you should use depends on how often your files change. For example, you could do an incremental backup on Monday, Wednesday, and Friday of every week. And every Sunday (including the Sunday before you start the incremental backups on Monday), you can do a new normal backup.

After following the suggested backup schedule for a few months, let's say that your computer's hard drive fails one Saturday. What do you do with the backups you have made after you have a new hard drive installed on the computer? Well, first you install Windows and the other software you use from your software CDs (the discs you got when you bought the software). Then you restore the normal backup from the previous Sunday (your first normal backup), and then you restore each of the incremental backups you made on Monday, Wednesday, and Friday in sequence. This approach allows all the new and changed files from the

64

Monday, Wednesday and Friday incremental backups to be added to the hard drive with the files that were in the normal backup. The restore utility overwrites files as you restore each subsequent incremental backup until you have all your files in the same state as they were when you did the Friday incremental backup. You end up with all the files on your computer up to date as of your Friday backup; any work you did after the backup on Friday and before the drive failed on Saturday is, sadly, lost.

What I have described here in terms of a backup strategy is reasonable for a computer user who backs up a number of folders and files and uses the computer for a home business or other activity where files change frequently and new files are created often. If you use your computer for pleasure (to send emails, browse the Web, and play games), backing up files isn't as crucial. You could probably get away with doing a periodic normal backup, giving you a failsafe archive of your important files in case you need to restore them.

You really have to decide for yourself how often to back up your data and the type of backups (such as normal or incremental) to use to make the backup process efficient. Be warned that having no backup or backup strategy at all will eventually lead to the loss of files you really need.

64

A final word related to using the Windows **Backup** utility: The utility is not part of the default installation of Windows XP Home Edition. In some cases, the utility might already be installed on your computer, but that depends on how Windows XP Home Edition was installed by your computer's manufacturer (or you, if you upgraded your computer to Windows XP). To see whether the **Backup** utility is installed, click the **Start** button and choose **All Programs**, **Accessories**, **System Tools**. The **Backup** utility should appear as an icon in the **System Tools** subfolder. If you do not see the **Backup** icon, you need to install the utility.

Insert your Windows XP Home Edition CD in your CD drive. Open **My Computer** by clicking the **Start** button and then clicking **My Computer**. Right-click the CD drive icon that contains the Windows CD and select **Explore** from the context menu to open the Windows XP CD. Double-click the **VALUEADD** folder to open it. Then double-click the **MSFT** folder inside the **VALUEADD** folder. Double-click the **NTBACKUP** folder inside the **MSFT** folder. Then double-click the **NTBACKUP** installation icon. An installation wizard opens; follow the steps provided by the wizard to install the **Backup** utility. You can then remove the Windows XP CD from your CD drive. Now you can run the **Backup Wizard** as discussed in **65** **Use the Windows Backup Wizard**.

65 Use the Windows Backup Wizard

✔ **BEFORE YOU BEGIN**

64 About Backing Up and Restoring Data

The Windows **Backup** utility actually can function in two different modes: wizard mode and advanced mode. When you use the wizard mode, the utility provides the **Backup or Restore Wizard**, which walks you through the process of either backing up or restoring your files.

The advanced mode allows you to control various settings related to the backup and restore process, such as selecting the type of backup (normal, daily, or incremental) or selecting to not overwrite existing files when doing a restore. The advanced mode also provides you with the ability to schedule backup jobs so that the backups run automatically.

When you run the **Backup** utility using the **Backup or Restore Wizard**, the default type of backup that is performed is a normal backup of all the files in the selected folders. If you want to change the type of backup the next time you back up your files (such as changing from normal to incremental), you must use the advanced mode.

When you start the **Backup** utility from the **Start** menu, the software scans your system for backup drives such as USB hard drives or USB flash removable drives. Make sure that the drive you want to use as the destination for your saved archive file is attached to your computer (such as an external USB drive) before starting the **Backup** utility. If you are going to back up to a computer on the network that is sharing a drive or folder or are backing up to an external network drive, make sure that the computer or drive is available on the network (meaning the computer that shares the backup location is up and running on the network).

You can back up data from a network location to a destination drive on your computer that you specify, and you can also back up local data (data on your computer) across the network to a remote share or drive. Moving data across the network will take time, and you must decide for yourself whether backing up data over the network or from your computer to an attached drive such as a USB external drive is the better option.

The **Backup** utility is designed to prepare a Windows system (however, not Windows XP Home Edition) for automated recovery using the **Automated System Recovery (ASR) Wizard**. Because the **Backup** utility was originally designed for earlier versions of Windows, it cannot correctly restore the system recovery files to a computer running Windows XP Home Edition. So, you can basically ignore the ASR wizard and plan on using the **System Restore** feature, which is discussed in **68 Create a System Restore Point** and **69 Restore the System**.

65

▶ **TIP**

If you want the **Backup** utility to automatically start in advanced mode the next time you start it, deselect the **Always start in wizard mode** check box on the initial wizard screen.

1 Start the Backup or Restore Wizard

Click the **Start** button and select **All Programs, Accessories, System Tools**. In the **System Tools** folder, select **Backup**. The **Backup or Restore Wizard** opens. Click **Next** to bypass the wizard's initial screen.

2 Select a File Backup Option

The next wizard screen asks whether you want to back up or restore files. Click the **Back up files and settings** option button and then click **Next** to proceed to the next screen.

3 Select What to Back Up

The next screen provides options in relation to what you want to back up. Select one of the following:

- **My documents and settings**: This option backs up **My Documents** (including subfolders such as **My Pictures**) and also backs up settings related to the Windows desktop and Internet Explorer (such as cookies and your web favorites).

- **Everyone's documents and settings**: This option backs up the **My Documents** folder for *all users on the computer* as well as their system files related to the desktop, cookies, and so on.

- **All information on this computer**: This option creates a system recovery disk and backs up all the information on the computer's hard drive. The system recovery disk and the backup file created from this type of backup can be used to restore your Windows system in case of a major meltdown. This backup requires a destination drive with a lot of storage space and also takes the longest time of the backups listed here.

- **Let me choose what to back up**: This option allows you to move to an additional wizard screen where you can specify the drive and folders you want to back up. This is the best option if you are backing up only specific folders containing important files.

65

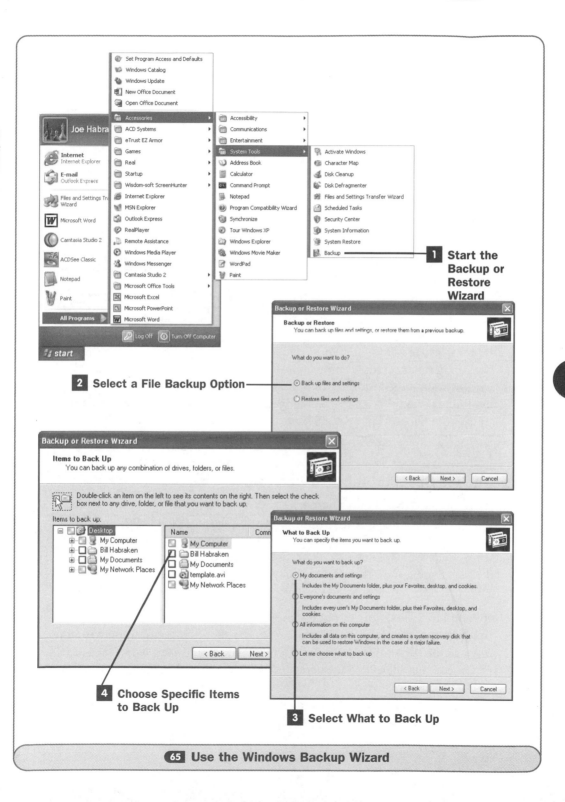

1 Start the Backup or Restore Wizard

2 Select a File Backup Option

4 Choose Specific Items to Back Up

3 Select What to Back Up

65

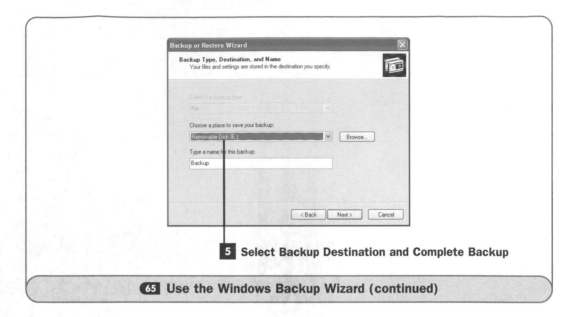

5 Select Backup Destination and Complete Backup

65 Use the Windows Backup Wizard (continued)

If you select one of the first three options, proceed to step 5 to specify the backup destination and complete the backup process. If you choose the **All information on this computer** option, you must also have a floppy disk available to complete the backup. If you select **Let me choose what to back up** as your backup option, go to step 4.

After selecting one of the **What to Back Up** options, click **Next** to continue.

4 Choose Specific Items to Back Up

If you selected the **Let me choose what to back up** option in step 3, you must select the actual locations on your computer that you want to back up. In the **Items to Back Up** screen of the wizard, select the check box for the drive, folder, or subfolder you want to back up. To expand a drive or folder to see its contents, click the plus symbol to the left of the drive or folder name. You can select multiple folders by selecting the check boxes for the folders.

If you plan to back up data from the network (meaning that you are backing up data from a remote location to the backup destination you specify in step 5), click the **My Network Places** icon to expand it and then locate the share (by name) and select it. You can actually back up any files that are contained in a remote share. Selecting a shared folder backs up the shared data over the network, so remember that backing up data across the network will take more time than a backup to a directly attached backup device.

Whether you are backing up local data or data in a share, make sure to place a check mark next to the folder, share, or filename. When you have finished making your selection, click **Next** to continue.

▶ **NOTE**

Although these steps look at selecting folders and files to be backed up using the Windows **Backup** utility, other backup software products (such as the backup software that comes with an external USB hard drive) offer similar sets of steps in terms of selecting files for backup and selecting the location for the backup. Just remember, however, that not all the backup software that comes with USB drives offers the ability to back up data over the network the way the Window s XP utility does.

5 **Select Backup Destination and Complete Backup**

The next screen provides a **Choose a place to save your backup** drop-down list box you can use to specify the destination drive (such as a USB drive) or other location for the backup. Alternatively, click the **Browse** button and browse to the location that will store your backup file.

If you want to back up your local data (drives or folders selected in step 4 that are located on your computer) to a remote network share, click the **My Network Places** icon that appears in the **Save As** dialog box (which opens when you click the **Browse** button). Locate and select the remote share in the **My Network Places** window.

You must also specify the filename for the backup. The default filename is **Backup**, but you should create a more descriptive name (for example, you can include the date, such as **backup11-20-05**). After specifying the backup filename and selecting the location for the backup, click **Next** (if you used the **Browse** option, specify a name for the backup file and then click **Save** in the **Save As** dialog box to return to the wizard); you can then click **Next** to continue).

▶ **NOTE**

Backup software such as the Windows XP **Backup** utility doesn't really see any difference between local folders (on your computer) and shared folders on the network. This means that you can back up data located remotely on the network (such as a share on another computer); you can also back up your local data to remote locations on other computers.

A final screen appears, summarizing the steps that you have completed. Click **Finish** to complete the process. The **Backup Process** dialog box opens, showing the progress of the backup. When the process is complete, you can close the **Backup Process** dialog box by clicking **Close**.

65

After you back up your data, you are safe until you have a problem; then you will have to restore your data, as explained in **67** **Restore Backed Up Data**.

▶ **TIP**

If you want to view a report related to a backup you have completed using the **Backup** utility, click the **Report** button in the **Backup Process** dialog box. The report provides the date and time for the backup (both the start time and date and the end time and date), the name of the backup file created, and the type of backup that was run (such as a normal backup). The report also includes the number of folders and files backed up. It does not provide a list of the files or folders backed up, however.

66 **Use Advanced Backup Features**

✔ **BEFORE YOU BEGIN**

64 About Backing Up and Restoring Data
65 Use the Windows Backup Wizard

65

The Windows **Backup** utility offers a lot of redudancy in terms of running backups and restores. You can use the **Backup or Restore Wizard**, which opens when you select the **Backup** utility from the **Start** menu, or you can select the settings for your backups and restores using the **Backup** utility's advanced mode.

You can access the **Backup** utility's advanced mode using the **Advanced Mode** link on the first screen of the **Backup or Restore Wizard**. Advanced mode provides access to a **Backup Wizard (Advanced)** and a **Restore Wizard (Advanced)**. These two wizards are extremely similar to the **Backup or Restore Wizard**, which was discussed in the previous task. The only benefit of using the advanced wizards is that they give you control over data verfication when the data is backed up or restored, and the advanced **Backup Wizard** provides you with the ability to select the type of backup you want to perform (normal, daily, incremental, and so on).

▶ **NOTE**

The advanced mode also provides access to the **Automated System Recovery Wizard**. However, this feature does not work correctly with Windows XP Home Edition and should not be used (back up your system info using the **System Restore** feature instead; see **68** **Create a System Restore Point**).

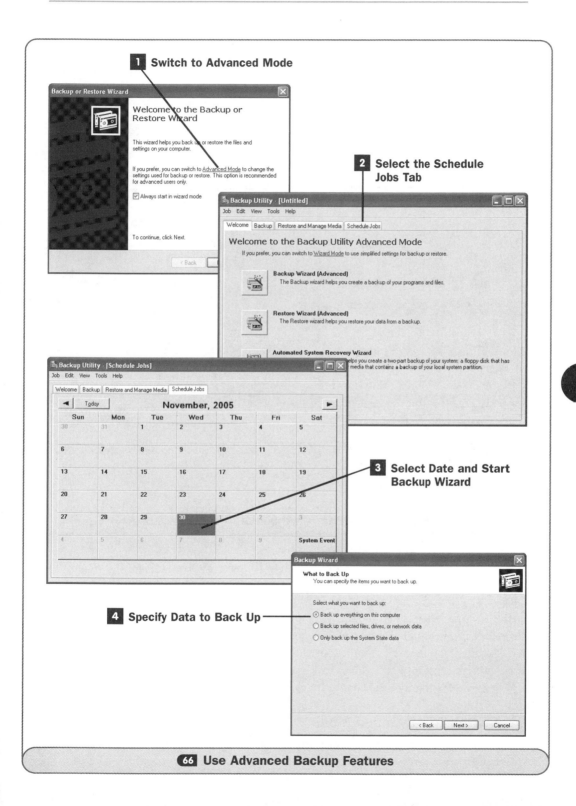

1 Switch to Advanced Mode

2 Select the Schedule Jobs Tab

3 Select Date and Start Backup Wizard

4 Specify Data to Back Up

66 Use Advanced Backup Features

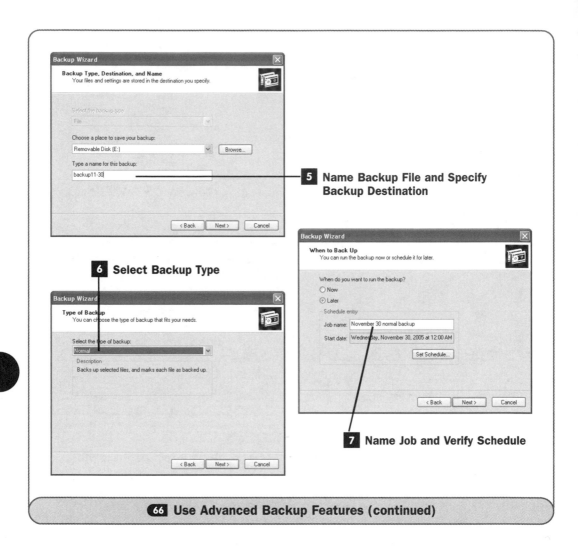

5 Name Backup File and Specify Backup Destination

6 Select Backup Type

7 Name Job and Verify Schedule

66 Use Advanced Backup Features (continued)

Because the advanced wizards provide only slightly more control over a backup or restore, and because the **Automated System Recovery Wizard** is unusable with Windows XP Home Edition, you might wonder why you would ever want to use the advanced mode. The real value of the advanced mode is that it allows you to schedule backups. You can specify all the parameters for the backup such as backup type, files to be backed up, destination for the backup, and also schedule a date and time when the backup should occur. This task explains how to schedule a backup (restore is discussed in **67** Restore Backed Up Data).

1 Switch to Advanced Mode

Start the **Backup** utility by clicking the **Start** button and selecting **All Programs, Accessories, System Tools, Backup**. On the first screen of the

Backup or Restore Wizard, click the **Advanced Mode** link. The Backup Advanced Mode window opens.

2 Select the Schedule Jobs Tab

The **Advanced Mode** window of the **Backup** utility lists the **Backup Wizard (Advanced)**, **Restore Wizard (Advanced)**, and the **Automated System Recovery Wizard**. The only difference between the advanced wizards provided on this screen and the wizard you used in **65 Use the Windows Backup Wizard** is that the advanced wizards let you select the backup type (normal, incremental, daily, and so on) and choose to have the data validated after the backup is complete. We will look at the "new steps" provided by the advanced backup wizard as we configure a scheduled backup job in this task.

Four tabs are provided on the **Advanced Mode** window of the **Backup** utility:

- **Welcome**: Lists the advanced wizards, which can be started by clicking the appropriate button.

- **Backup**: Allows you to specify the files to be backed up and the destination for the backup; also provides a **Start Backup** button to start the backup. You can set the type of backup before running the backup by selecting **Tools**, **Options**. In the **Options** dialog box, select the **Backup Type** tab and then use the drop-down list box to select the type of backup you want to perform.

- **Restore and Manage Media**: Allows you to select the media used for your backups and select the backup files to restore.

- **Schedule Jobs**: Allows you to schedule a backup by selecting a date and time and then choose the backup type, the backup filename, and the destination drive for the backup.

Click the **Schedule Jobs** tab. We can now schedule and define a backup for the computer.

3 Select Date and Start Backup Wizard

Select a date for your next backup by clicking a date on the calendar. Then click **Add Job**. The **Backup Wizard (Advanced)** starts. Click **Next** to bypass the wizard's initial screen.

4 Specify Data to Back Up

On the next wizard screen, specify the data you want to back up using the option buttons provided (**Back up everything on this computer**, **Back up selected files, drives, or network data**, or **Only back up the System State data**). If you selected the **Back up selected files, drives, or network data** option, click **Next** and specify the files using the drive and folder check boxes provided. Then click **Next** again.

5 Name Backup File and Specify Backup Destination

On the next screen, supply a name for the backup file and also specify the destination for the backup.

Use the **Drive** drop-down list to specify the drive for the backup destination (this option lists any external drives connected to your computer that were recognized when you started the **Backup** utility). If you want to specify a remote location as the backup destination (such as any shared drive, including *flash drives* and shares on other computers in the workgroup, or a specific folder on any of your local drives), click the **Browse** button. In the **Save As** dialog box that opens when you click **Browse**, click the **My Network Places** icon and then locate the remote share you want to use as the backup destination.

After you name the backup file and specify the backup destination (click **Save** to close the **Save As** dialog box, if you browsed for a location), click **Next** to continue.

66

6 Select Backup Type

On the next screen. use the **Select the type of backup** drop-down list to specify the type of backup you want to schedule; the default is **Normal**. Other options are described in the "Types of Backups" section of **64** **About Backing Up and Restoring Data**.

When you have selected the type of backup you want to perform, click **Next** to continue. The next wizard screen provides the option of verifying the data after backup, which can determine whether the backup was successful. It is up to you whether you want to verify the backup data; your decision really depends on how important the data is to you. To use it, select the **Verify data after backup** check box and click **Next** to continue.

7 Name Job and Verify Schedule

On the next wizard screen, type a job name (this required name is just a job name; it is not the backup filename). The job is scheduled to take place **Later** and the date on which the backup will be performed is listed. If you want to change the date and time, click the **Set Schedule** button to open the **Schedule** dialog box, which allows you to schedule a specific date or recurring backup day with a specific time. When you have finished setting the schedule, including the time for the backup and recurring backups, click **OK**.

You will return to the wizard. Click **Next**.

▶ **TIP**

When you set a recurring backup schedule using the **Set Schedule** dialog box, you select a particular day of the week and then a specific time on that day. Select a day of the week and a time when you know you will have the computer on but won't need to use the computer. Backing up files slows the system and makes it more difficult for you to continue working while the backup is proceeding. Again, select a day and time when the system is up and running but when you know that you are typically not using the computer.

The final wizard screen appears with a summary of the settings for the backup job. Click **Finish**. You return to the calendar on the **Schedule Jobs** tab of the **Backup** utility; the new job appears as an icon on the date you specified. When you have finished working with the advanced mode window, you can close it.

The job will run when scheduled. Make sure that the drive you use as the destination for the backup is attached to your system (such as a external *Flash drive* or USB hard drive, which is plugged into a USB drive on your computer) and is turned on before the scheduled backup runs. If you are backing up over the network to a remote share, make sure that the computer that hosts the share is on and available on the network.

▶ **TIP**

If you want to modify a backup job you have scheduled (its icon appears on the calendar on the **Schedule Jobs** tab of the **Backup** utility window), double-click the job icon on the calendar day. The **Options** dialog box for the job opens. To change the time or date for the job, click the **Properties** button on the **Scheduled data** tab of the **Options** dialog box. The **Schedule Job** dialog box opens. Use the **Schedule** tab to change the date or time and then click **OK** to return to the **Options** dialog box for the scheduled job. If you want to delete a scheduled job, click the **Delete** button on the **Scheduled data** tab of the job's **Options** dialog box. The job is deleted from the calendar.

67 Restore Backed Up Data

✔ **BEFORE YOU BEGIN**

64 About Backing Up and Restoring Data
66 Use the Windows Backup Wizard

A time may come when you need to actually use the backup files you have created using the **Backup** utility. You might have to restore data to your computer that has either been lost because of a system failure or inadvertanly deleted (which happens all too often when you share folders on a network).

The easiest way to restore data to your computer's hard drive is using the **Backup or Restore Wizard** that opens when you start the **Backup** utility. If you want, you can also use the **Restore Wizard**, which is provided by the **Backup** utility's advanced mode. Regardless of which way you go, the steps to restore the data are similar: You specify the backup file to be used during the restore process and then you specify the actual files to be restored. In cases where you have used normal backups and incremental backups, you will want to restore the data in order. This means that you restore the most recent normal backup first and then restore each of the incremental backups (in date order). Using this strategy for restoring the data ensures that you have the most up-to-date versions of your files on the computer when restores are complete.

1 Start the Backup or Restore Wizard

Click the **Start** button and select **All Programs, Accessories, System Tools, Backup**. When the initial screen of the **Backup or Restore Wizard** opens, click **Next** to continue.

2 Select Restore

On the next wizard screen, click the **Restore files and settings** option button. Then click **Next** to continue.

3 Select Backup File

On the next wizard screen, select the backup file you want to restore to the computer. You can click the file heading and expand its contents to view a list of recent backups. To view the contents of a particular backup file, expand the backup file (using the plus symbols to the left of the drives and folders). Use the check box next to an item such as a drive, folder, or file to specify the items you want to restore to the computer.

If the backup file you want to restore is not listed on the wizard screen or is on a share on another computer in the workgroup, click the **Browse** button. The **Open Backup File** dialog box opens; click **Browse** again to open the **Select File to Catalog** dialog box. Use the **My Computer** icon on the left side of the dialog box to locate backup files on your computer. To navigate to backup files held in network shares on other computers, click the **My Network Places** icon. When you have located the file you want to open; select it (whether it is on a local drive or a share on the network) and then click **Open** in the **Select File to Catalog** dialog box. Then click **OK** to close the **Open Backup File** dialog box and return to the wizard.

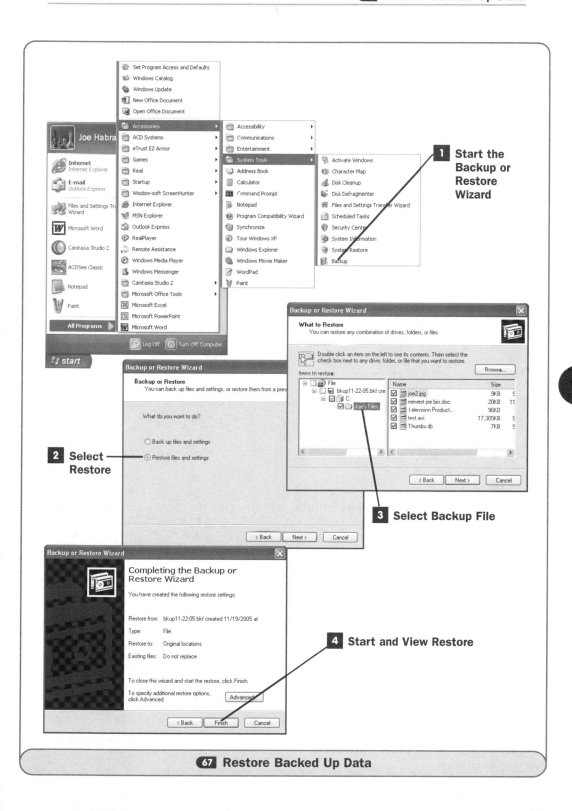

1 Start the Backup or Restore Wizard

2 Select Restore

3 Select Backup File

4 Start and View Restore

You can now select the individual items you want to restore using the appropriate check boxes (or you can select the entire backup file). When you have selected the files to be restored, click **Next** to continue.

▶ **TIP**

You can choose to restore all the files in a backup file or target the restore by selecting specific files. Expand the backup file by double-clicking it to view its contents. If you want to restore all the files in the backup file, select the check box for that backup file. If you want to restore only certain files, locate those files and select the check boxes to select the files as needed.

4 Start and View Restore

The final wizard screen provides a summary of the restore settings. Click the **Finish** button to start the restore. The **Restore Progress** dialog box opens. A progress indicator provides you with the progress of the restore. When the process is complete, you can view a report for the restore by clicking the **Report** button. The report provides the start and completion time for the restore process and also lists the number of items that were restored (it does not provide a list of the folders or files restored). To close the **Restore Progress** dialog box, click the **Close** button.

When you have restored the files to your computer, open Windows Explorer by clicking the **Start** button and then clicking **My Computer** to take a look at your hard drive and see whether the files have been restored properly. If you set up the restore correctly, the files should be found in their original folders.

▶ **TIP**

The **Backup or Restore Wizard** restores files to their original locations by default. It also replaces any files it finds at that location with the files in the backup file that have the same name. If you want to restore files to an alternative location or prevent the restore from overwriting existing files, click the **Advanced** button on the **Backup or Restore Wizard**'s final screen. This action opens a series of screens that walk you through specifying an alternative location and selecting whether files should be overwritten or not.

68 Create a System Restore Point

✔ **BEFORE YOU BEGIN**

64 About Backing Up and Restoring Data

As your computer runs over time, problems can arise with the Windows operating system. These problems can be related to files that become corrupt, the intrusion of a computer virus, or the addition of new hardware such as a printer that has a flaky software driver which makes your system go nuts. A healthy computer can become unhealthy at a moment's notice if there is a problem with the system files that keep Windows running and working properly. Although sometimes system problems are a sign of impending hardware failure (which you can't do a whole lot about other than back up your data), in many cases, you can get your system running correctly by using the Windows **System Restore** feature.

The **System Restore** feature allows you to save the system state files as system *restore points*. The system restore points are saved on your system and can then be accessed by date. When you begin to have a problem with your system, you can use **System Restore** to choose a system restore point from when you were not having any problems with the computer. Restoring to the system restore point can help you make an unhealthy system healthy again.

▶ KEY TERM

Restore point—A snapshot of your computer's settings and installed software that can be restored to your system. Restore points can be used to correct problems on your system by restoring the computer to an earlier time when it was operating properly.

System Restore automatically saves system restore points periodically. You will also find that system restore points are added when you install some software to your system. Note that **System Restore** won't help you battle viruses or spyware or other intrusive software because sometimes these attacking entities can be saved in a system restore point. You must still have a good antivirus software program on your system.

▶ NOTE

System Restore is one of those features you should know about but shouldn't obsess over. It is designed to help you get a "sick" system running again. If you don't have a problem with your system, you don't need to use **System Restore**. Although you can set system restore points occasionally if you want, remember that Windows does this for you periodically, anyway.

1 Open Control Panel Performance and Maintenance Window

Open the **Control Panel** window by clicking the **Start** button and then clicking **Control Panel**. Select the **Performance and Maintenance** icon to open the **Performance and Maintenance** window.

2 Open System Restore Window

On the left side of the **Performance and Maintenance** window, click the **System Restore** link. The **System Restore** window opens.

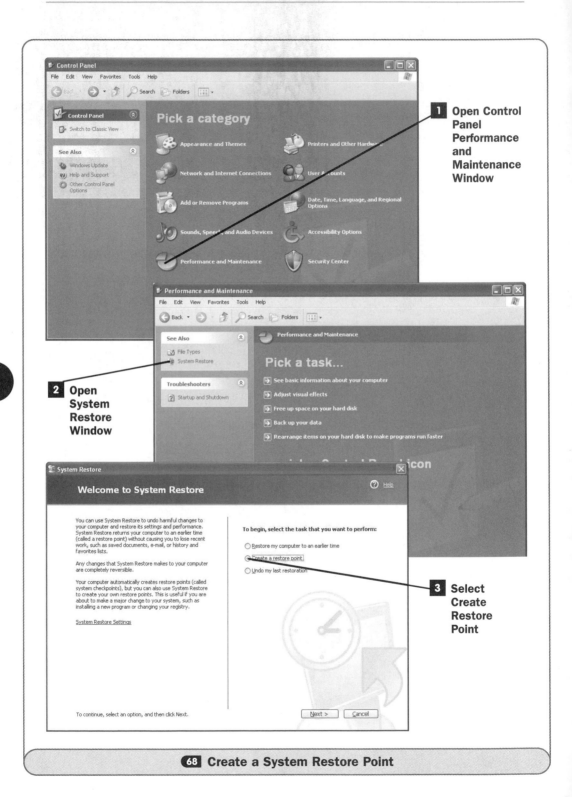

1 Open Control Panel Performance and Maintenance Window

2 Open System Restore Window

3 Select Create Restore Point

68 Create a System Restore Point

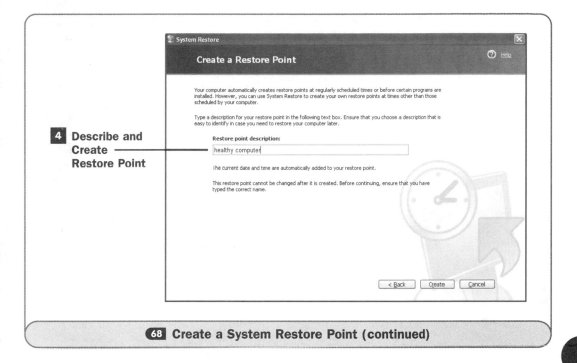

4 Describe and
Create
Restore Point

68 Create a System Restore Point (continued)

68

3 Select Create Restore Point

In the **Welcome to System Restore** window, click the **Create a restore point** option button and then click **Next**.

4 Describe and Create Restore Point

Type a description for the system restore point. You can include the date or other helpful information in the description as needed. For example, you might use the date and text such as **before scanner installation** to show that the restore point was created before you installed a scanner on your computer. After typing the description, click **Create**.

The system restore point will be created. You can close the **System Restore** window.

If you ever need to make use of the restore point you just created, turn to **69** **Restore the System** for help.

▶ **TIP**

In some situations, such as when you are attempting to remove a virus or worm that has infected your system, the instructions you receive might state that you should turn off **System Restore** in order to remove the virus or worm. To turn off **System Restore**, click the **Start** button, right-click the **My Computer** icon, and select **Properties** from the context menu. In the **System Properties** dialog box, click the **System Restore** tab and then select the **Turn off System Restore** check box. When you have removed the virus, turn **System Restore** on by repeating these steps. For more about dealing with viruses worms and other malware, see **82** About Malware.

69 Restore the System

✔ **BEFORE YOU BEGIN**

68 Create a System Restore Point

You can tell when you are having a system problem: The system slows way down, you get error messages that software windows need to close, or software fails to start. In some cases, Windows does not boot successfully and the system repeatedly restarts.

In cases where your system restarts without shutting down correctly, the system will boot and provide you with the option of booting Windows in **Safe Mode**. **Safe Mode** uses a basic Windows configuration and does not load all the drivers you have installed for your various hardware items. Safe Mode is useful because it allows Windows to at least load so that you can try to fix the problem.

After the system is up and running—whether you booted to **Safe Mode** or were able to start Windows normally—you can use **System Restore** to restore the system files to an earlier time. You should pick a *restore point* with a date *before* your system started to run poorly and you began to see that there was some sort of problem.

Be advised that **System Restore** basically "resets" the system to an earlier time. This means that drivers and other system settings are set to the earlier time. You might have to reinstall drivers for some hardware if you use **System Restore**. For example, if you added a driver and configured a WiFi USB adapter on your system and then had to restore the system to an earlier time, you will have to reinstall the driver for the adapter. Network settings that can be effected by a system restore include your default network client and TCP/IP settings. For example, if you had your system configured to use a specific IP address in the past but then changed the settings so that the IP address was received dynamically from your WiFi router, you might have to "redo" your more recent settings if you restore to an earlier time that used different settings. **System Restore** is designed to get a computer that is malfunctioning in a major way up and running again; having to reconfigure some system settings is really a small price to pay.

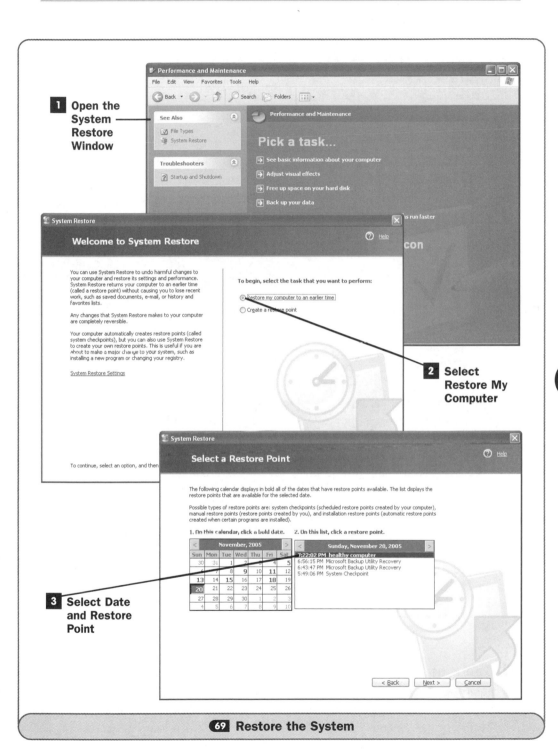

1 Open the System Restore Window

2 Select Restore My Computer

3 Select Date and Restore Point

69 Restore the System

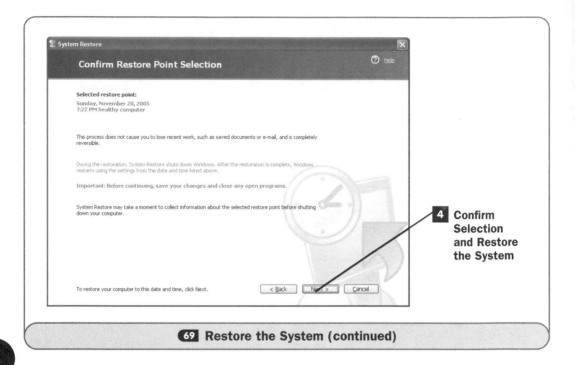

69 Restore the System (continued)

4 **Confirm Selection and Restore the System**

Any Windows updates you have added to your system after the date of the restore point are also "rolled back" by **System Restore**, so you should use **System Restore** only when you are really experiencing a problem with the Windows operating system. Files you have created and saved (such as photos you have downloaded or documents you have created and saved) *are not affected* by **System Restore**; these files will still be on your computer where you saved them after you run **System Restore**.

▶ **TIP**

Hardware driver problems and resource conflicts caused by drivers are probably the most common reason a system will begin to act up. Restoring to an earlier time removes this conflict. However, when you reinstall the offending driver, the system problem returns. Always check out the manufacturer's website for a particular device if you think the driver is causing system problems. Typically, the site provides information related to the problem because you probably aren't the only user having the problem.

1 Open the System Restore Window

Open the **Performance and Maintenance** window by clicking the **Start** button and clicking the **Control Panel** icon. Then click the **Performance and Maintenance** icon to open the **Performance and Maintenance** window. Then select the **System Restore** link on the left side of the window to open the **System Restore** window.

2 Select Restore My Computer

Click the **Restore my computer to an earlier time** option button and then click **Next**.

3 Select Date and Restore Point

Use the calendar to select a date that contains a restore point (or restore points). The dates with restore points are in bold in the calendar grid. After selecting a date on the calendar, a list of the restore points created on that date appears on the right side of the window; select one of the restore points from the list. Then click **Next** to continue.

▶ TIP

When you have a choice of multiple restore points for a date, it makes sense to select a restore point that was created *before* you began experiencing the problem. It also makes sense to select the restore point that is closest to the actual appearance of the problem (but doesn't contain the problem) because this negates the necessity of making a lot of changes in system settings and driver installations, because there probably have not been that many changes to the system since the particular restore point was created.

4 Confirm Selection and Restore the System

The next screen asks you to confirm the restore point selection. The date of the restore point and the restore point name appear at the top left of the **System Restore** window. When you are ready to begin the restore process, click **Next**.

Your computer will reboot and the system restore will take place. When Windows starts, you are notified that the system restore is complete; click **OK** to close the **System Restore** notification window. Your system will finish loading, and you can once again use your various Windows applications.

▶ TIPS

If **System Restore** does not fix the problem with your system, you have a couple of choices: You can choose a different restore point or you can use the various troubleshooters that Windows provides to help you work through software and hardware problems. Click the **Start** button and then choose **Help and Support**. From the **Pick a Task** list on the main **Help and Support** screen, select **Use tools to view your computer information and diagnose problems**. This option will walk you through different possibilities for troubleshooting the problem you are having with your system.

If you are experiencing a problem on a computer and you find that a hardware driver such as the driver for a WiFi network adapter was the culprit (and you have replaced the driver with a new driver from the manufacturer), replace that driver on any other computer on the network that might be using the same brand of adapter. Replace the driver even if the other computer doesn't seem to be having the same problem you experienced on the original computer.

69

11

Securing the Wireless Network

IN THIS CHAPTER:

WiFi networks face two potential avenues of security breaches: the WiFi medium itself (radio signals) and the persistent Internet connection that results from the home network being connected to a DSL router or broadband modem. Protecting your wireless network requires that you secure the network medium and protect the internal private network from attack by someone outside the network, meaning someone who attacks the network over the Internet.

In this chapter, we take a look at how to secure a WiFi network using wireless security strategies that use *encryption* and *security keys*. We will also look at how your WiFi *router* also provides a *firewall* that helps to secure the network from outside attack.

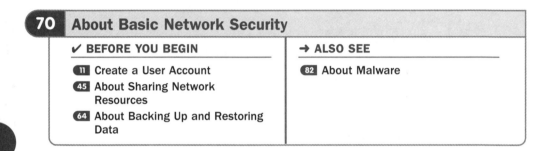

70   About Basic Network Security

✔ BEFORE YOU BEGIN	→ ALSO SEE
11 Create a User Account	**82** About Malware
45 About Sharing Network Resources	
64 About Backing Up and Restoring Data	

70

Network security—including security for a home workgroup network—revolves around protecting information, meaning network data. On a large corporate network, the data might be the social security numbers and credit card numbers for thousands of people. On your home network, the data might be your home budget file or a list of addresses for this year's Christmas cards.

Data and other network resources must be protected from internal intrusion (such as a legitimate network user who deletes important files) and external intrusion (such as a computer virus or illegal hacker on the Internet). Corporate networks spend tons of money on different security measures to protect their network data. And although network security is also important to the home network, you don't have to try to duplicate the measures taken on large networks to protect important information.

Network security, even security on a home network, is focused on network access and resource access. To protect network data, you must secure the network from unauthorized access (from the outside) and also protect data when it's accessed by an authorized user (from the inside).

In terms of locking down the network from outside intrusion, a WiFi network connected to a high-speed Internet connection device such as a DSL router or cable modem has two potential avenues for outside attacks: the WiFi infrastructure and the persistent connection to the Internet.

How does one negate (or at least greatly limit) the possibility of outside attacks on a home network? The key tool in securing the home network is the WiFi router. The router provides security options that secure both the WiFi medium or infrastructure (the radio waves used to communicate over the network) and the connection to the Internet. First let's take a look at securing the WiFi medium.

Sending data over radio signals that have not been secured is pretty much akin to leaving all the doors in your house open when you go on vacation. Your WiFi router provides you with settings and security features that can greatly enhance the overall security of the WiFi home network. Most WiFi routers offer the following settings for securing the WiFi medium:

- **Change WiFi Router Password**: Although this doesn't stop network intrusions, periodically changing your router's password does make access to the router's configuration more secure. The default passwords for router administration are typically well-known generic passwords such as **password**; the sooner you change the password that came with your router, the safer you'll be. See **73** **Change Router Password** for more information.

- **Enable/Disable SSID Broadcast**: Although disabling the broadcast of the Server Set ID (SSID) or network name by the WiFi router using a radio signal doesn't actually secure the network from outside intrusion, it does stop the WiFi router from advertising that the WiFi network exists to anyone within range who cares to listen. For more information, see **75** **Turn Off Server Set IDs (SSIDs) Broadcasts**.

- **Firewall Settings**: A firewall can protect an internal network from attacks from the outside over the persistent Internet connection. The number of firewall settings available to you depends on the router you have purchased. For more information, see **71** **About Firewalls** and **72** **Configure Router Firewall Settings**.

- **WiFi Card Access List**: The WiFi router can be configured so that only computers that have their *MAC (Media Access Control)* or hardware address for their WiFi network adapter recorded in the router's access list will be allowed to connect to the WiFi network. For more about MAC addresses and router card access lists, see **79** **About Network Interface MAC Addresses** and **80** **Create a WiFi Network MAC Access List**.

- **Key Authentication and Data Encryption**: A way to protect the WiFi network from intrusion over the network medium (the radio signals) is to require that computers attempting to connect to the network be authenticated (or approved) by the WiFi router. Data traveling on the network medium that is intercepted can also be protected if you first encrypt that data. Most WiFi routers provide two different types of WiFi security strategies: WEP and WPA.

70

For more about WEP and WPA see **76** **About 802.11 Security Strategies,** **77** **Configure Wired Equivalent Privacy (WEP) Security,** and **78** **Configure WiFi Protected Access (WPA) Security**.

When you take advantage of the different ways to protect your workgroup from outside attacks (including problems with viruses and other malware, as explained in **82** **About Malware**), you still need to protect the data from security breaches *inside* the network. This is usually a problem with the accidental deletion of important files or the fact that important data has become corrupt and unusable.

On large networks, data is protected by a network administrator who assigns each user a set of permissions related to data entry. However, because shared data is actually spread across a number of computers (shared folders reside on individual computers and are managed by the users on those computers), you really can't control users on a workgroup the way administrators of large networks can control network resources on centralized servers. So, protecting data from problems that originate on the inside of the network, such as a file being inadvertently deleted or corrupted, is really best handled by backing up the data on each individual computer (see **64** **About Backing Up and Restoring Data**).

70

Another problem with workgroup networks is that if a folder is shared in a workgroup, it is available to *everyone* in the workgroup. Therefore, it is important that the users on the network act responsibly in terms of working with shared folders and the contents of these folders. It is also important that each computer on the network have an up-to-date antivirus software product installed because it is fairly easy to spread a virus or other malware in a workgroup networking environment (see **83** **Install and Use Antivirus Software** for more about antivirus software).

The biggest security risk to networks, including small home workgroups, is intrusion by malware (such as addware and viruses) and security holes (ports) in different software applications used to connect to the Internet (such as Internet Explorer). One way to help shore up your defenses against hackers who attempt to exploit open ports on your computer is to lock these ports down and stop external access to the internal network. This is what firewalls do; they act as an intermediary between your private network and the public Internet. **72** **Configure Router Firewall Settings** looks at how firewall settings are configured on a WiFi router that supplies firewall capabilities.

▶ **NOTE**

Task **54** **About Content Filtering and Opening Ports** discussed ports, including the well-known ports for filtering Internet content and services. Ports can be exploited on your computer as a way for an outside attacker to actually take control over your computer.

71	**About Firewalls**

✔ **BEFORE YOU BEGIN**	→ **ALSO SEE**
54 About Content Filtering and Opening Ports	**96** About Command-Line Tools
70 About Basic Network Security	**97** Use Command-Line Tools

Firewalls are designed to sit between your network and the Internet and protect the internal network from outside attack. Firewalls can consist of hardware and software—such as the firewall provided by your WiFi router. Firewalls can also consist of software only—such as the Windows XP Windows Firewall.

▶ **KEY TERM**

Firewall—Software, hardware, or both software and hardware designed to prevent unauthorized access to a private network. A firewall can be used to block both incoming and outgoing data traffic.

Firewalls that are a combination of hardware and software (your WiFi router's firewall, for example) can examine data packets leaving and entering the internal network. This is why the firewall can be used to block access to web content and services, as discussed in **54** **About Content Filtering and Opening Ports**. More importantly, the firewall is designed to negate intrusions and attacks from the outside, meaning the Internet. So, how does the firewall actually determine when data packets from the outside are an attack rather than normal data traffic?

▶ **NOTE**

A large number of firewall products are on the market. Software-only firewalls—such as the Windows Firewall (a free addition to the Windows XP OS) and ZoneAlarm (for more about ZoneAlarm, a really great personal firewall, see **http://www.zonealarm.com**)— are designed as personal firewalls that protect only the computer on which they are installed. Higher-end firewalls designed to protect a small network are built in to many of the WiFi routers available from manufacturers such as Linksys and Netgear. Corporate networks employ even more sophisticated and complex firewalls that are designed to protect very large networks. These dedicated firewalls (they typically do not serve any other function, as does your multifunction WiFi router) provide more configuration options and provide a greater number of security settings compared to the simpler firewalls provided with a WiFi router designed for home and small office networking.

The firewall built in to your WiFi router inspects all the data traffic coming into and out of the local network. Each data packet is examined so that it can be matched to a specific Internet service—such as HTTP (the Web) or FTP (a file transfer). If a data packet can't be matched to an actual service connection (such as the web browsing service) that originated on the internal network, the firewall

71

will dump that packet and any other packets that can't be associated with a particular connection. So, any data traffic (the actual packets) that doesn't originate from an internal service is blocked by the firewall.

This type of packet inspection is called ***Stateful Packet Inspection (SPI)***. This is why the firewall built in to your WiFi router is referred to as an SPI firewall in the router's documentation.

▶ KEY TERM

Stateful Packet Inspection (SPI)—Data packets are inspected by the firewall and analyzed to determine their association with current network connections and service requests.

Firewalls use SPI to determine whether data packets entering the local area network from the Internet are the result of a potential attack or intrusion on the local network. One of the most common types of attacks used over the Internet is the denial-of-service attack: The attacker floods the local network (often a single computer) with so much data that the computer or network overloads and shuts down. This type of attack has been used repeatedly to take down websites on the Internet and can also be used to disrupt computers and services on a small home network. An SPI firewall can protect a network from a denial-of-service attack, so it makes sense to take advantage of the firewall provided by your WiFi router.

71

---

72 | **Configure Router Firewall Settings**

✔ **BEFORE YOU BEGIN**

22 Access Router Configuration
71 About Firewalls

The actual settings available for your WiFi router's firewall depend on the WiFi router you purchased. In most cases, the firewall settings for your home WiFi router are pretty simple; they might only allow you to turn the firewall on and off and to configure a computer to run outside the firewall in what is called the *demilitarized zone (DMZ)*. Web servers and gaming servers can be run in the DMZ so you don't have to use ***port forwarding*** or ***port triggering*** to allow users outside the network to attach to the server (not opening ports and running a single computer in the DMZ actually protects the internal network in the long run). Port triggering and port forwarding are discussed in **58** **Configure Port Forwarding and Port Triggering**.

Other settings you might have control over in terms of firewall settings relate to whether the router interface can be *pinged* from the Internet (pinging can be useful as a diagnostic tool but can open the network to potential attacks). The **ping** command is discussed in **96** **About Command-Line Tools** and **97** **Use Command-Line Tools**. Your router's firewall settings might also allow you to set the maximum packet size that can be transmitted to the network. This is called the Maximum Transmit Unit (MTU) size; it is typically configured at 1500 bytes but can be adjusted to a smaller size if required by your Internet service provider.

1 Open Router Configuration Web Page

Log on to your router as the administrator using your web browser; type the URL for your router in the browser's **Address** box and then provide the login name and password for the router when prompted for this information. You can find the URL for your router in the documentation that came with your router; routers also typically come with a quick start sheet (a one-page flyer) that provides the URL or web address for your router and the default logon name and password. If you don't have access to either of these information pages, go to the router manufacturer's website and access their support page, which should provide links to specific product pages where you can download the documentation for your WiFi router.

2 Access Firewall Settings

On the main page of the router's configuration website, select the link that takes you to the router's firewall settings. For example, on my Netgear WiFi router's configuration page, the firewall settings are on the **WAN Setup** page, so I click the **WAN Setup** link on the left side of the page. Each router's setup pages are different, so consult the router's documentation and setup manual for more information.

▶ **NOTE**

Firewall settings are typically found on a router's WAN setup configuration page because the WAN (wide area network) connection is the connection to the Internet (the Internet is a wide area network). Some routers provide you with the capability to change the connection between your network and the Internet from automatic (meaning it happens automatically through the router) to manual. A manual connection requires you to use the manual connection feature on your router to get an Internet connection up and running. The automatic connection setting is actually better because you do not have to reset the connection if it goes down or is interrupted. When the automatic setting is in force, the router automatically connects to the Internet when access is needed.

72

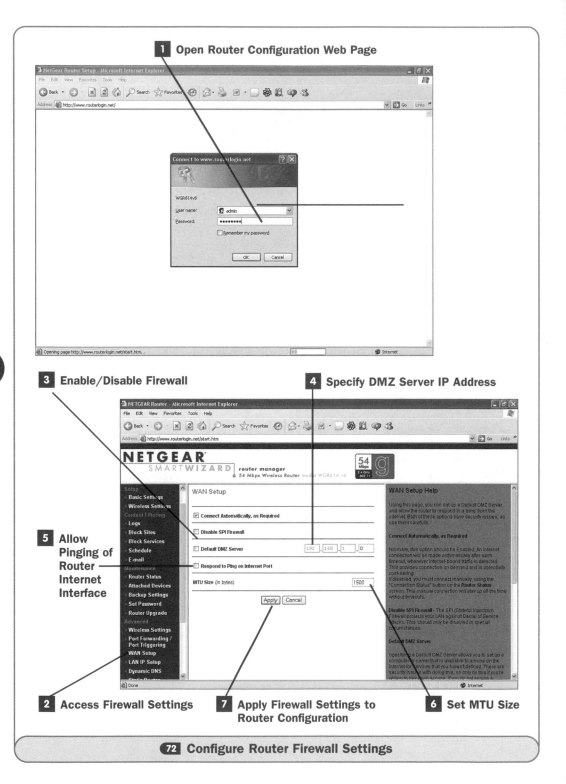

72

1 Open Router Configuration Web Page

3 Enable/Disable Firewall

4 Specify DMZ Server IP Address

5 Allow Pinging of Router Internet Interface

2 Access Firewall Settings

7 Apply Firewall Settings to Router Configuration

6 Set MTU Size

72 Configure Router Firewall Settings

🔳 Enable/Disable Firewall

Select the appropriate check box or option button to turn on your router's firewall. Some routers (such as my Netgear router) have the firewall enabled by default, and the configuration page does not provide an enable option; it only allows you to disable the firewall by selecting **Disable SPI Firewall**. Disabling the firewall opens up your network to the possibility of outside attack. There is actually no good reason to disable the firewall, even if access to gaming or other services is a problem, because all connectivity issues can be resolved with port triggering and port forwarding settings (see 🔳 **Configure Port Forwarding and Port Triggering**).

🔳 Specify DMZ Server IP Address

If you want to operate a computer or a server (such as a computer that is acting as a web server or a gaming server) outside the firewall, you can have the router place that computer in the DMZ. This means that the network is still protected from attack but that the DMZ computer could potentially be attacked. To place a computer on your network in the DMZ using a Netgear router, select the **Default DMZ Server** check box and then enter the IP address of the computer that will be placed in the DMZ. If you need to find the IP address for a computer, go to that computer and click the **Start** button and then choose **Run**. Type **command** in the **Run** box and click **OK**. In the command window that opens, type **ipconfig/all** and press **Enter**. You will be provided with the IP address and the other IP settings for the computer.

▶ **NOTE**

The DMZ isn't really a place; it is a virtual location configured by your WiFi router's firewall. The DMZ is a virtual place that resides between your protected internal network and the public Internet. Placing a computer in the DMZ allows it to communicate with the Internet without the router's firewall inspecting the data flowing to and from the computer. It is not uncommon for computers offering certain services to be placed in the DMZ. Even large corporations sometimes place communication servers in the DMZ so that they do not have to open ports on the firewall to allow access to the server.

🔳 Allow Pinging of Router Internet Interface

Ping is a command-line tool used to determine whether a connection exists between two computers or other network devices. For example, if you can't seem to connect to another computer on the network that has a shared folder, you can ping the computer using its IP address to see whether there is a connection problem. By default, most WiFi routers are configured so that the router's interface or connection to the Internet cannot be pinged. The Internet interface for you router is actually assigned its IP address by your Internet service provider. So the Internet interface on the router is really its public interface. Allowing the public interface to be pinged can open the router up to attack since it can be "pinged to death." A malicious individual on the Internet could send a barrage of ping packets or oversized ping packets that would actually bring down the router's public interface. This kind of attack is called the "Ping of Death."

Enable the router's Internet interface for pinging only if your Internet service provider (or you) needs to ping that interface to determine whether there is a connectivity problem. For my Netgear router, I select the **Respond to Ping on Internet Port** option to turn on this feature. When you have determined that the interface can be reached by a ping (from you or the ISP technician), I suggest that you disable the feature.

6 Set MTU Size

The Maximum Transmit Unit (MTU) value for Ethernet networks such as your WiFi network is 1500 bytes. Leave the MTU setting at the default unless your Internet service provider requires that a different setting be used. If you're unsure about the MTU value, contact your ISP. To change the MTU on my Netgear router, I click in the **MTU** text box and type a different value. Each router provides a slightly different configuration screen for setting the MTU.

Your Internet service provider determines the optimal MTU for the network it services by trial and error. The only way you might perceive that you don't have the correct MTU setting for your ISP connection would be a slight slowing of the connection to the Internet—and this would only be in situations where your MTU is set higher than the ISP's and your data packets have to be broken into smaller chunks for transmission. So, bottom line, call your ISP and see whether it uses a special MTU setting.

7 Apply Firewall Settings to Router Configuration

When you have set the firewall configuration for your router, you must apply or save the new settings (whether you apply or save the settings depends on your WiFi router). For example, for my Netgear WGR 614 router, I click the **Apply** button to apply and save the firewall settings.

---

73 Change Router Password

✔ BEFORE YOU BEGIN	→ SEE ALSO
22 Access Router Configuration	**74** Back Up Router Configuration

You might wonder how changing the router password can secure the network. First of all, most routers use a default password that anyone can guess. For example, Netgear uses **password** as the administrator's default password. So, the router's settings related to the firewall and other features such as content and service blocking are only as secure as the router's configuration is. If anyone in your family can hop onto the computer that is directly connected to the router (or if you have enabled remote management for the router, as explained in **81 Configure Remote Management**) and access the router's configuration, you have real potential for a major security breach—particularly if family members turn off the firewall because the online game they are trying to play isn't functioning correctly.

Before you change your router's password, you might want to back up your router's configuration. Most WiFi routers have the capability to save and back up the configuration file for the router in case there is a problem such as a forgotten administrative password (for more about backing up the configuration, see **74 Back Up Router Configuration**).

1 Access Change Password Settings

Log on to your router as the administrator using your web browser; type the URL for your router in the browser's **Address** box and then provide the login name and password for the router when prompted for this information. You can find the URL and default logon name and password for your router in the documentation that came with your router. If you have lost all the documentation for your router, go to the manufacturer's website and download a copy of the documentation.

From the router's main configuration page, access the change password setting for your router. For example, the Netgear WGR14 provides the command link **Set Password**.

2 Change Password

Enter the current password for the router. (Netgear uses the default password of **password**; Linksys uses **admin**. The default password is listed in the documentation for your router.) Then enter the new password you want to use. You must verify the new password by entering it a second time. Because a web interface is used to manage the configuration of most WiFi routers designed for home networks, rules governing the password length and the characters that can be used are pretty much non-existent. For example, on a Netgear or Linksys router, you can have a password of a single character.

73

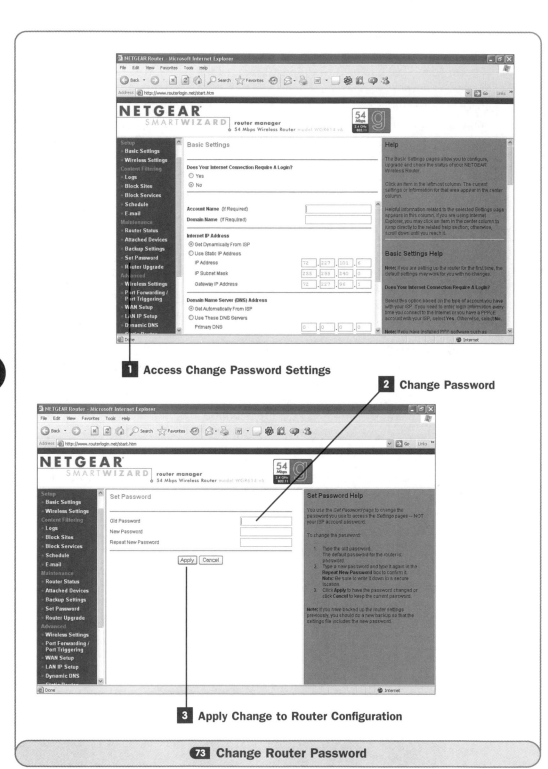

73

1 Access Change Password Settings

2 Change Password

3 Apply Change to Router Configuration

73 Change Router Password

▶ **TIP**

The whole point of having a password is to help secure the WiFi router, so I suggest that you use at least six characters (you can use any characters on the keyboard), and that you use a combination of alpha and numeric characters. Don't use the names of your spouse, dog, children, or anything else that can be guessed easily. Don't forget that you are trying to secure the router from outside intrusion (your password should have some complexity to it) and to also secure the router from folks in your house (such as kids) who might want to reconfigure the router so that it no longer blocks certain websites.

3 **Apply Change to Router Configuration**

After you have entered the old password and the new password, click the **Apply** button or a similar command to save the password change to the router's configuration.

---

74 **Back Up Router Configuration**

✔ **BEFORE YOU BEGIN**

22 Access Router Configuration

You can back up your router's configuration file. This is useful in cases where you want to try some new settings but then want to roll back the router's configuration to your tried-and-true settings. Having a backup of the router configuration file also provides you with the capability to get the router back into your preferred configuration if someone in your household has tampered with the router's settings.

The **Backup Settings** page for your router will allow you to back up the router's configuration and also restore the configuration if necessary (using the **Restore** command). You only need to back up the router when you change the router's configuration (such as after setting up the initial configuration). Do subsequent backups only after you change the router's configuration. I suggest that you back up changes that you make to the router's configuration only after you have determined that the new settings work. If new settings don't work, you can roll back the settings by restoring an earlier version of the router's configuration. You can save as many different backup files as you wish, which allows you to keep different versions of the router's configuration available. Most routers also provide a command that allows you to erase the router's configuration and roll back the configuration to the factory settings.

1 Access Backup Settings

Log on to your router as the administrator using your web browser; type the URL for your router in the browser's **Address** box and then provide the login name and password for the router when prompted for this information. You can find the URL for your router in the documentation that came with your router. If you have changed the password for the router, as discussed in **73** **Change Router Password**, use the new password you set.

▶ TIP

When you access the URL for your router, save the page as one of your favorites in your web browser. Then you can open the router's web page at any time by clicking the favorite link you have created. You can also enter the user name and the password in the logon text box and select the **Remember my password** check box. Windows will then remember the user name and password, making it easy for you to access the router. However, if Windows remembers the password for you, anyone who has access to your computer could potentially access the router. If you change the default password, make sure that you remember it or write it down in a safe place in case you need it.

74

From the router's main configuration page, click the **Backup Settings** link or similar command to access the page from which you can configure the backup process for your router.

2 Begin Backup Process

On the **Backup Settings** configuration page, click the **Backup** button or similar command. A **File Download** dialog box opens. It is the same type of download dialog box that would open when you attempt to download a file from any web page; for example if you were downloading a picture or sound file from a web page (remember that the router is configured using a web interface, so the router configuration pages are, in effect, web pages just like any other web page).

3 Select Save File Option

Click **Save** in the **File Download** dialog box. A **Save As** dialog box opens.

4 Select Location and Save Backup

Use the **Save As** dialog box to select a location for the saved file (you can save it in your **My Documents** folder on your computer or some other location, if you prefer). You can change the default name for the backup file (which is **netgear** for a Netgear router) to something a little more descriptive so that you can find the file if needed in the future. After specifying a location and a name for the file, click **Save**. The backup file will be saved to your computer's hard disk.

1 Access Backup Settings

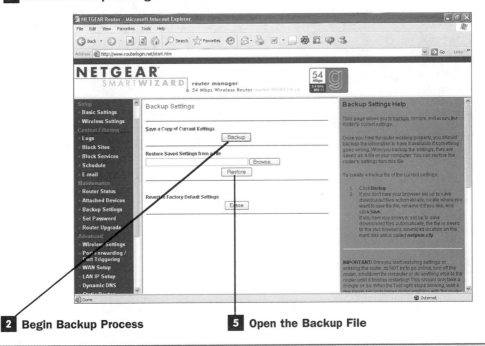

2 Begin Backup Process

5 Open the Backup File

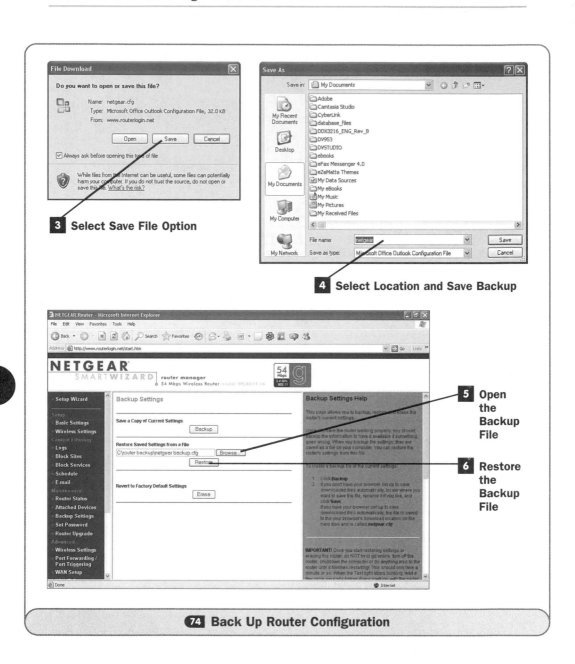

3 Select Save File Option

4 Select Location and Save Backup

5 Open the Backup File

6 Restore the Backup File

74 Back Up Router Configuration

5 Open the Backup File

You can now restore the backup file in the future (if needed) by using the **Restore** command on the **Backup Settings** configuration page.

For example, let's say that you have backed up the router and need to restore the backup configuration file. Click the **Browse** button above the **Restore** button on the **Backup Settings** page of your router's configuration. Then locate the file in the **Choose File** dialog box that opens. When you have located the proper backup file, click **Open** to return to the router configuration screen.

6 Restore the Backup File

The backup file you opened in Step 5 appears in the filename text box next to the **Browse** button. Click **Restore** to restore the configuration file to the router. A message box appears, letting you know that the current settings will be replaced by the restored settings. Click **OK** to close the confirmation box.

The router configuration will be restored (this may take a moment) and then you will be returned to the router configuration web page.

▶ TIP

If you need to reset your router and start over, your router provides an **Erase** or similar command that allows you to erase the router's configuration and then start again. For example, if all your users are having problems accessing the Web or other Internet services because you haven't configured service blocking or port triggering correctly and you can't figure out what you have done wrong, you might want to "reset" the router and start over. Having an earlier backup of the router's configuration (that actually worked correctly) negates the need for the **Erase** command because you can roll back the router to an earlier configuration; use **Erase** only as a last resort.

75

75 Turn Off Server Set IDs (SSIDs) Broadcasts

✔ **BEFORE YOU BEGIN**

21 About Configuring the Wireless Router
22 Access Router Configuration

The **SSID (service set identifier)** or network name for your WiFi network is broadcast by the router over a radio signal, making it easy for WiFi-enabled computers on your network to connect to the WiFi router and the workgroup. However, when you allow the SSID to be broadcast, anyone within range who has a WiFi-enabled computer can attempt to access the WiFi network because he can "see" that the network actually exists.

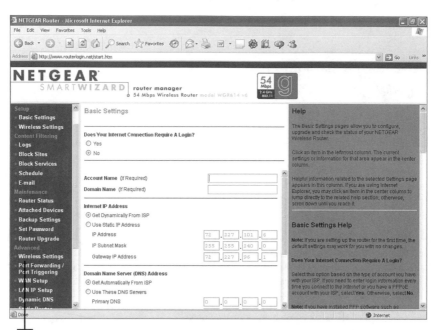

1 **Access Advanced Wireless Settings**

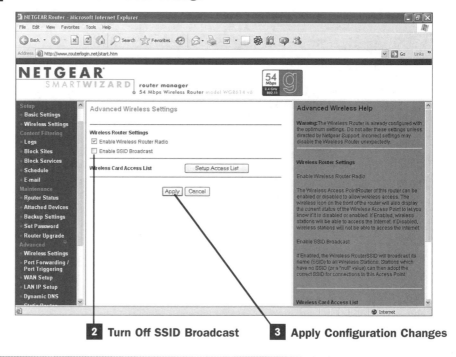

2 **Turn Off SSID Broadcast**

3 **Apply Configuration Changes**

75 **Turn Off Server Set IDs (SSIDs) Broadcasts**

Because you know the SSID for your WiFi network, you can configure the WiFi-enabled computers on your network with the SSID name. The SSID name is one of the settings required for configuring a WiFi network adapter. See **33** **Configure Adapter and Connect to the Wireless Router** for information on entering the SSID and other WiFi settings for your WiFi adapter. Because you don't require that the SSID be broadcast (you can configure your WiFi adapters with the SSID manually), turning off SSID broadcasts can at least protect your WiFi network from "amateur hackers" who might try to attach to your WiFi network when they detect the network because of the SSID broadcast.

1 Access Advanced Wireless Settings

Log on to your router as the administrator using your web browser; type the URL for your router in the browser's **Address** box and then provide the login name and password for the router when prompted for this information. You can find the URL for your router in the documentation that came with your router, or you can go to your router manufacturer's website and download the documentation for your router to learn how to access the router's configuration site.

From the main configuration page for your router, access the advanced wireless settings or whatever page contains the router's SSID broadcast settings. For example, for my Netgear router, I click the **Advanced Wireless Settings** link in the router's command list.

2 Turn Off SSID Broadcast

On the **Advanced Wireless** Settings page, deselect the check box for **Enable SSID Broadcast** (or select the setting on your router that turns off the SSID broadcasts).

3 Apply Configuration Changes

Click the **Apply** button (or a similar command) to apply the change you have made to the router's configuration.

▶ **TIP**

It is convenient to allow your router to broadcast the network SSID when you are in a situation where you have roaming users (folks with laptops) who want to scan for and then quickly attach to the network. But you aren't running a *hotspot*; you are trying to run a secure network. Because you can configure all the computers on your network with WiFi adapters manually, including the SSID name, your computers don't need to scan for the network. You don't need to broadcast the SSID—doing so is actually a security liability. So, turn it off.

76 | **About 802.11 Security Strategies**

✔ BEFORE YOU BEGIN	→ ALSO SEE
70 About Basic Network Security	**77** Configure Wired Equivalent Privacy (WEP) Security
	78 Configure WiFi Protected Access (WPA) Security

76

When the Ethernet 802.11 standards for WiFi networking were first established by the IEEE (Institute of Electrical and Electronics Engineers), it was readily apparent that security standards had to be established for wireless networking. Because the network medium is radio signals, anyone who cares to "listen" with a WiFi-enabled computer such as a laptop and some additional software for capturing data packets can eavesdrop on a WiFi network.

Obviously, you can turn off your SSID broadcast to help hide your WiFi network (see **75** **Turn Off Server Set IDs (SSIDs) Broadcasts**), but any committed hacker can still "listen" to radio network traffic on different frequencies and capture data packets. After the packets are captured, they can be deciphered; these packets contain information such as IP addresses, user names, passwords, and all sorts of stuff that the hacker can then use to gain illegal access to your WiFi network.

The first security protocol developed for WiFi networks was **WEP (Wired Equivalent Privacy)**. It was developed to secure the 802.11b WiFi standard. WEP uses two strategies for protecting the data traveling on the WiFi medium (the radio waves): shared key authentication and data encryption.

▶ KEY TERMS

WEP (Wired Equivalent Privacy)—A WiFi security protocol that encrypts data and uses shared keys for the encryption and decryption of data at the sending and receiving ends of the data transfer. WEP was originally created for use with 802.11b networks.

Authentication key—A hexadecimal character string used to validate a user or device as the intended connection point or recipient of a data stream.

Shared key authentication means that an *authentication key* is configured on the WiFi router. The authentication key is hexadecimal number that is either 64 or 128 bits long. The greater the number of bits, the more secure the key, so you will want to use a key that is 128 bits if you use WEP security.

The authentication key can be generated automatically by the router, or you can enter the number yourself (because the authentication key is in hexadecimal, if you don't know how to enter hexadecimal numbers, you might prefer to use the automatic key-generation feature). For a WiFi-enabled computer to join the network hosted by the WiFi router, that computer must be configured with the same authentication key that is configured on the router. If a WiFi-enabled computer attempts to access the WiFi network without the WiFi adapter on the computer being configured with the shared authentication key, the router denies that computer access to the network.

▶ **NOTE**

A hexadecimal number is a base-10 number. In everyday life, we use base-10 numbers—that is, we have 10 primary numbers (0–9) in our numbering system. Base-16 has 16 numbers in its numbering system—the numbers 0–9 and then the letters A–F. Because the router can generate hexadecimal keys automatically, you don't really need to know how to use the hexadecimal system. The automatically generated hexadecimal keys for WEP or WPA WiFi security are no less secure than a key you would create from scratch using the hexadecimal numbering system. When a 64-bit hexadecimal key is generated, it consists of 10 characters (but is equal to 64 bits). When a 128-bit hexadecimal key is generated, it consists of 26 characters. For example, the 10-digit key **10A8319D9D** is an example of a 64-bit hexadecimal key and the 26-digit key **10A8319D9D29DCDCC04C313AC5** is an example of a 128-bit key.

Data *encryption* is the process of coding data so that it cannot be read until it is decrypted at its final destination. So, when WEP is enabled on the network (meaning on the WiFi adapters for the individual computers and on the WiFi router), the data is encrypted by the sending computer and then decrypted by the receiving computer. WEP encrypts only the data; it does not encrypt the shared authentication keys. Unfortunately, the encryption is only in force when data is sent over the WiFi signal. The data is not encrypted if it moves from the WiFi infrastructure to a wired network. If someone is eavesdropping on your WiFi network (software is available that allows for the capture of data moving on a WiFi network), that person can take a look at the data stream and eventually determine what the authentication keys are. Once the hacker has the authentication key, he can intercept the data and decrypt it as if he were the intended recipient.

WEP also does not have the ability to generate a new authentication key after a specified amount of time. WEP also does not require user authentication when data is received and decrypted. Not authenticating the user at the other end of the data transmission opens up the data transfer to the possibility of being intercepted and decoded by someone other than the intended recipients.

▶ **KEY TERM**

Encryption—The translation of a message into a secret code. After a message is encrypted, a key or other identification method (such as a password) is needed to decipher the message.

76

Now you probably think that with data encryption and shared key authentication, there is no way a hacker can breach your network security. However, WEP uses a *static key*, meaning that the authentication key is transmitted with each data set (the key is repeated often). So, as more and more data is sent over the network, a hacker might be able to decipher parts of the key because the key doesn't change. So, the more data the hacker captures by monitoring the network (people can monitor the network even if they can't log on), the more information they can piece together over time; eventually, the hacker will have enough information to determine the key and be able to decrypt the data you assumed was secure. In fact, it is estimated that a hacker monitoring a network for less than a day can accumulate enough information about the keys to begin to decode the encrypted messages.

To shore up some of the shortcomings of WEP (which was available when 802.11b WiFi devices became available in 2000), a new WiFi security protocol was rolled out in 2002: *WPA (WiFi Protected Access)*. WPA scrambles the shared authentication keys, generates new keys at a given interval, and also has capabilities for checking whether a key has been tampered with by a computer other than the sending or receiving device. WPA also provides for the encryption of the data being transferred on the WiFi network and uses an encryption algorithm that is stronger than the WEP algorithm. WPA also requires user authentication during the process of sending *and* receiving data over the network. So, WPA addresses most of the known WEP vulnerabilities.

76

▶ KEY TERM

WPA (WiFi Protected Access)—A WiFi security protocol that encrypts data and scrambles shared keys sent over the WiFi network. WPA also requires user authentication, providing greater security than WEP, which did not require user authentication.

You can configure your WiFi router to use WEP or WPA security. Choose one or the other—you can't run both protocols simultaneously. If you choose WPA, all the WiFi devices on the WiFi network must be configured to use WPA. If you have some older devices that don't support WPA, you might have to go with WEP to accommodate those devices.

If you really want the WiFi network to be truly protected, you will want to use WPA. The configuration of WEP and WPA are similar, so in my mind you should go with WPA. Refer to **77 Configure Wired Equivalent Privacy (WEP) Security** and **78 Configure WiFi Protected Access (WPA) Security** for instructions on configuring these two security protocols on your network's router.

▶ **NOTE**

You might wonder why WiFi routers provide for WEP security, seeing as it isn't that secure. You might have some older 802.11b WiFi adapters on your network that are not compliant with the WPA standards. And because the general thought is that any security is better than no security, you should use WEP if you can't configure all your WiFi adapters and other hardware for WPA. WPA didn't actually become available on WiFi routers until 2002, so it is relatively new, and it is possible that you have some legacy WiFi hardware that isn't WPA-complaint. In fact, some new wireless gaming consoles coming out use only WEP. WPA is an option on nearly all new WiFi routers and WiFi adapters; use WPA if you can.

---

77 | **Configure Wired Equivalent Privacy (WEP) Security**

✔ **BEFORE YOU BEGIN**

22 Access Router Configuration
33 Configure Adapter and Connect to the Wireless Router

When you configure WEP on your *router*, you have the option of using a 64-bit or 128-bit *authentication key*. The more bits in a key, the more difficult the key is to decipher (say, by a hacker). The key can be generated automatically by the router (the router can actually generate multiple keys, and you can choose the one you want to use). You also can set the type of authentication to be used with WEP encryption. There are three types of authentication settings:

- **Open System Authentication**: This type of authentication (which is really no authentication at all) allows a WiFi-enabled computer to contact the WiFi router (the access point) and then connect to the WiFi network. It does not require any user authentication for the computer to connect.

- **Shared Key**: This type of authentication uses a shared key. The WiFi-enabled computer must be configured with the same shared key as the WiFi router before it can connect to the router's access point and the WiFi network. Using the shared key negates open system authentication on the network.

- **Automatic**: Some routers allow you to set authentication as "automatic." This means that a computer attempting to connect to the network can use either open system authentication or shared key authentication, depending on how the computer's WiFi *adapter* has been configured.

Depending on the WiFi router you have purchased, you might also be able to specify a *passphrase* for the WEP configuration. The passphrase can then be used to configure WiFi adapters on computers (this works best with adapters from the same manufacturer as the router). Typing the passphrase into the WiFi adapter's configuration allows the adapter to download the shared key from the router.

77

This means you don't have to manually type the shared WEP key into the adapter's configuration manually, which can be frustrating if you're using a 128-bit key, which is 26 digits long.

▶ KEY TERM

Passphrase—A text string similar to a password used to configure a WiFi device for WEP or WPA security. Because the passphrase is generated by the WiFi router, the passphrase is used in the WiFi adapters' settings to configure the device with the correct encryption key. Using the passphrase to configure the adapter negates the need to type the entire key (which isn't available for WPA) in the WiFi adapter's configuration settings.

To configure your network to use WEP security, you must first change your router's settings, and then you must configure the network adapter for each of the computers on the network.

1 Access Wireless Settings

Log on to your router as the administrator using your web browser; type the URL for your router in the browser's **Address** box and then provide the login name and password for the router when prompted for this information. You can find the URL for your router in the documentation that came with your router.

From the main configuration page for your WiFi router, click the **Wireless Settings** link or similar command to open the configuration page for the router's security settings.

2 Enable WEP

Click the **WEP (Wired Equivalency Privacy)** option button on the **Wireless Settings** page (or select the command on your router's configuration page that enables WEP security).

3 Set Authentication Type

Click the **Authentication Type** drop-down list and select **Automatic, Open System Authentication**, or **Shared Key**. The setting you select depends on the configuration requirements of the WiFi adapters used on the network.

If you select **Automatic**, the router will generate the shared key (it actually generates three keys, and you can select one of the three). You type a *passphrase* that then can be used to configure your WiFi adapters with the key (you type the passphrase in the WiFi adapter's settings, and the key is sent to the adapter by the router). You can use the **Automatic** setting if your WiFi adapter allows you to enter a passphrase in the WEP configuration settings.

77

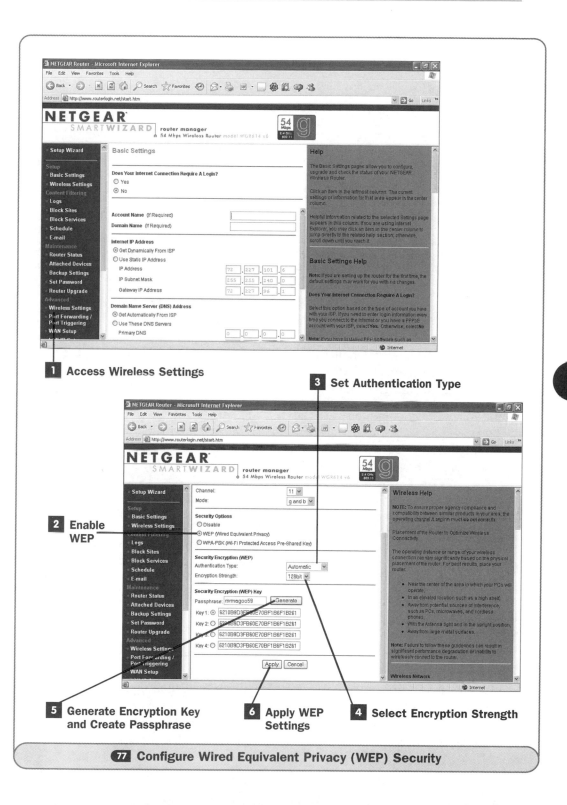

1 Access Wireless Settings

3 Set Authentication Type

2 Enable WEP

5 Generate Encryption Key and Create Passphrase

6 Apply WEP Settings

4 Select Encryption Strength

77

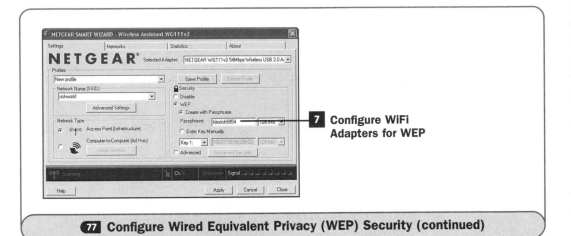

7 Configure WiFi Adapters for WEP

77 Configure Wired Equivalent Privacy (WEP) Security (continued)

77

If you select **Open System Authentication**, no key is required, so the WiFi adapters are configured for WEP but are not configured with a passphrase or a shared key. Any WiFi-enabled computer can connect to the router without authentication, but the router will encrypt the data stream sent between the devices. No shared key is required to decipher the encrypted data at the receiving end (meaning the computer).

If your WiFi adapters don't provide for using a passphrase to configure the adapter for WEP, you still have to configure the adapter with the same **Shared Key** as the WiFi router before it can connect to the router's access point and the WiFi network. Make sure that you enter the key in the adapter's configuration settings exactly as it appears in the router's configuration. No typos please!

In terms of ease of configuration and using WEP with a shared key, the best selection is **Automatic**, meaning you get to use a passphrase to configure the WiFi adapters. The second best alternative for this setting is **Shared Key** (but you have to type the shared hexadecimal key on the WiFi adapter configuration screen exactly as it appears on the router configuration screen).

4 Select Encryption Strength

You can select to use either 64-bit or 128-bit encryption. The greater the number of bits, the more difficult it is for a hacker to figure out the key. A 128-bit key is stronger than a 64-bit key. However, if you have to configure all the WiFi adapters on your network with the actual key (if they don't allow you to use a passphrase), you might want to use the shorter key as a convenience (it has fewer characters). Make your choice from the drop-down list provided.

5 Generate Encryption Key and Create Passphrase

To generate a set of encryption keys, click the **Generate** button. Four keys are generated for WEP encryption (the length of the key depends on whether you chose 64-bit or 128-bit encryption). All WiFi routers provide a similar screen for the generation of the encryption key. The multiple encryption keys are generated so that you can change the key over time to help secure the network. Because the passphrase is associated with any of the multiple keys, you can change the key at any time and not have to reconfigure your WiFi adapters (unless you have adapters that do not provide for WEP passphrase configuration). Select the radio button of the key you want to use.

To associate a passphrase with your encryption keys, type a passphrase in the **Passphrase** box. The passphrase can be from 8 to 63 characters in length. The passphrase is, in effect, a password. The greater the number of characters, the harder it is for someone to guess the passphrase. Also, passphrases that use a combination of alpha and numeric characters are more difficult to guess. The passphrase cannot contain spaces, but it can contain any characters available on the keyboard.

6 Apply WEP Settings

Click the **Apply** button to apply the WEP settings to the router's configuration.

7 Configure WiFi Adapters for WEP

After you have configured your router to use WEP security, you must configure your WiFi adapters on each of the network computers for WEP. On one of the computers in your network, open the configuration software for the WiFi adapter (right-click the WiFi adapter icon in the system tray and select **Open** from the context menu).

Select the **WEP** option button on the adapter's configuration screen. Then click the **Create with Passphrase** option button and type the same passphrase you defined in step 5 in the text box. Both Netgear and Linksys routers provide for the use of passphrases. If your router does not allow you to use a passphrase for WEP or automatically generate the WEP keys, you must manually enter the key configured on the router. If you do not have the option of setting a passphrase on your router, click the **Enter Key Manually** radio button (or similar command) and enter the encryption key configured on your router. After entering the passphrase or key, apply the new settings to the computer's WiFi adapter. This computer can now connect to the router. Repeat step 7 for each computer on the network. For more about configuring a WiFi adapter, see **33** **Configure Adapter and Connect to the Wireless Router**.

77

78   Configure WiFi Protected Access (WPA) Security

✔ BEFORE YOU BEGIN

22 Access Router Configuration
33 Configure Adapter and Connect to the Wireless Router

78

WPA (WiFi Protected Access) security provides strong encryption and authentication that can secure your WiFi network. When you configure WPA on the WiFi *router*, the only real settings you can make are selecting the option to turn on WPA and specifying a *passphrase* that is then used to configure the WiFi *adapters* on the network computers that will connect to the router. The security *authentication keys* are generated by the WiFi router at a specified interval, so you will also have to set the interval when you select WPA as your security protocol. The shorter the interval, the greater the level of security because a shorter time period is provided to a hacker who may be monitoring the network and trying to decipher the security key.

To configure your network to use WPA security, you must first change your router's settings, and then you must configure the network adapter for each of the computers on the network.

1 Access Wireless Settings

Log on to your router as the administrator using your web browser; type the URL for your router in the browser's **Address** box and then provide the login name and password for the router when prompted for this information. You can find the URL for your router in the documentation that came with your router. Alternatively, go to the router manufacturer's website, download the documentation, and consult it for the URL and the default login name and password.

From the main configuration page for your WiFi router, click the **Wireless Settings** link or similar command. This opens the configuration page for the router's security settings such as WEP and WPA.

2 Enable WPA

Click the **WPA-PSK (Wi-Fi Protected Access Pre-Shared Key)** option button in the **Security Options** portion of the **Wireless Settings** page (or similar page on your router's configuration website).

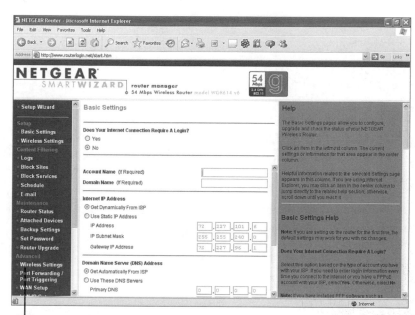

1 Access Wireless Settings

78

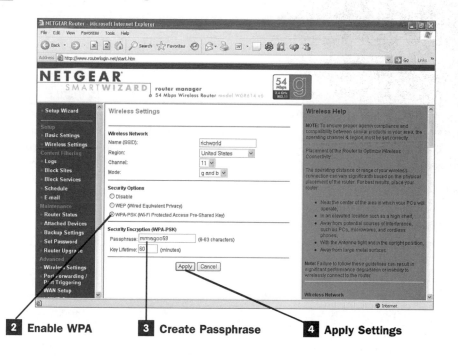

2 Enable WPA   **3** Create Passphrase   **4** Apply Settings

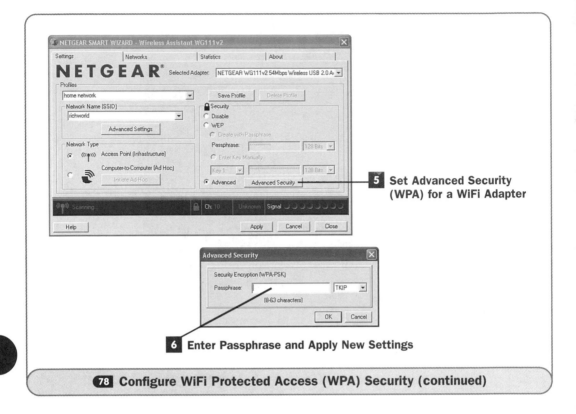

5 Set Advanced Security (WPA) for a WiFi Adapter

6 Enter Passphrase and Apply New Settings

78 Configure WiFi Protected Access (WPA) Security (continued)

78

3 Create Passphrase

WPA creates the shared keys automatically and cycles through them at a specified interval. You configure WiFi adapters and other devices on your network for WPA using the same *passphrase* you specify when you configure the WiFi router. The use of the passphrase is consistent among all WiFi routers in terms of the WPA configuration. You don't even see the keys that are generated, so you have to use a passphrase to configure your WiFi adapters.

Type a passphrase (from 8 to 63 characters). If you want to change the default interval for the key lifetime, click in the **Key Lifetime** text box and type a new value (in minutes). The shorter the key lifetime, the more secure the WiFi network. The default for most routers is a 60-minute key lifetime. Because your WiFi network probably isn't going to be the target of a host of WiFi miscreants (you are a small fish in the sea of WiFi networks), you can leave the key lifetime at its default setting. If it helps you sleep better, reduce the key lifetime to 30 minutes. A shorter lifetime will not affect data flow on the network negatively, but it will take a hacker more than an hour to decipher a shared key (and then that key will be changed, anyhow).

4 Apply Settings

After selecting the settings for WPA security, click **Apply** (or a similar command on your router) to save the new security settings as part of the router's configuration.

5 Set Advanced Security (WPA) for a WiFi Adapter

After you have configured your router to use WPA security, you must configure the WiFi adapters on each of the network computers for WPA. On one of the computers in your network, open the configuration software for the WiFi adapter (right-click the WiFi adapter's icon in the system tray and select **Open** from the context menu). To set advanced security for the WiFi adapter, select the **Advanced** option button and then click the **Advanced Security** button. The **Advanced Security** dialog box opens.

6 Enter Passphrase and Apply New Settings

Enter the passphrase you specified in step 3 for the router in the **Advanced Security** dialog box (or similar dialog box using your adapter's configuration software; for example, if you are using the **Windows Wireless Networking Properties** dialog box for your adapter, the passphrase is entered on the **Association** tab). Click **OK**. Back in the main configuration screen for the WiFi adapter, you can then apply the new settings to the adapter by clicking **Apply**.

79

---

79 | **About Network Interface MAC Addresses**

✔ **BEFORE YOU BEGIN**

22 Access Router Configuration
27 About Wireless Network Adapters

Every adapter (wired or wireless) has a unique hardware address burned onto a ROM (Read Only Memory) chip by the adapter's manufacturer. This unique address is called the *MAC (Media Access Control) hardware address*. These unique addresses are actually used by computer and networking hardware to send data between devices on a network.

▶ KEY TERM

MAC (Media Access Control) hardware address—A 48-bit hexadecimal number burned onto a ROM chip on a network adapter (for a computer on the network) or network interface card (for a router). MAC hardware addresses (also sometimes referred to as physical addresses) are used by computers and other network devices to ensure that the bit stream of data moving on the network medium is correctly identified in terms of source and destination.

You are probably thinking that IP addresses, not MAC addresses, provide the addressing system for the network. IP addresses do provide the addressing system for TCP/IP networks. However, for two devices, such as computers outfitted with network adapters, to complete a data transaction (or *data transfer*, if you prefer), the IP address is actually resolved to the MAC hardware address on the computer's network adapter. This process ensures that the data is transferred to the correct network device because the MAC address is truly unique for each device. Here's an example of a MAC hardware address: **00-50-56-C0-00-1**.

Most WiFi routers list the currently connected computers and their MAC hardware addresses on the attached devices or similarly named screen, which makes it easy to add these computers to a MAC access list. The MAC access list is typically found in the router's configuration pages by clicking the **Wireless Card Access Setup** or similar command.

If a connected computer appears on the attached devices screen, you can actually cut and paste the MAC address you want to create to the MAC access list, although you will have to move from the connected devices list to the MAC access list using the appropriate router command (typically found on the left side of the web pages used to configure and monitor the router). Oddly enough, you might find that a connected computer is not listed by the router, even though you know that the computer is connected. In this case, you need to view the MAC address on the computer and then type it into the router's MAC access list manually.

To view the MAC hardware address for a computer's network adapter, click the **Start** button and then click the **Run** command. In the **Run** dialog box, type **command** and press **Enter**. A command prompt window opens. Type the command **ipconfig/all** and press **Enter**. The IP address and subnet mask for the adapter is listed, as is the physical address (the MAC hardware address) for the adapter. When you enter the MAC hardware address in the MAC access list, you will also need the name of the computer (the host name). The host name is listed along with the IP information and the MAC address when you run the **ipconfig/all** command.

The conversion of IP addresses to MAC addresses and vice versa is something that happens completely transparently when data moves on the network. However, because MAC addresses are completely unique, you can actually use them as another way to make your WiFi network more secure. You can create a MAC access list on your WiFi router. This access list is composed of the MAC addresses from the computers you want to be able to connect to your WiFi network. Although MAC access lists are not a fool-proof system for protecting the WiFi network, they do negate the intrusion of "less-dedicated" hackers.

79

▶ **NOTE**

Securing a network (even a home WiFi network) requires you to take advantage of all the possibilities for keeping your network data private. This means that you should throw pretty much every security strategy at the network, hoping that it will be enough to keep out hackers who seem determined to break into even small networks. Using a MAC access list to "lock out" computers not included on the list is just another security strategy you might want to take advantage of. Because hackers seem to never sleep (or bathe), they can quickly find holes in almost any new strategy for securing a network.

---

80 Create a WiFi Network MAC Access List

✔ **BEFORE YOU BEGIN**

22 Access Router Configuration
79 About Network Interface MAC Addresses

Most WiFi *routers* provide you with a list of connected computers, which makes it easy to add the computers listed to the MAC access list itself. If you don't get a complete list of connected computers (this can happen sometimes for no apparent reason) or you want to add a computer to the list that is currently not listed, you must know the host names and the MAC or physical hardware addresses for the computers you want to include in the list. On each of the computers you want to include on the MAC access list, open a command prompt (click **Start**, choose **Run**, type **command**, and press **Enter**). At the command prompt, type **ipconfig/ all** and press **Enter**. This command lists the host name, IP information for the computer's network adapter, and also the MAC/physical address for the computer.

▶ **TIP**

To clear the command prompt window of the results of your most recent commands, type **clear** and press **Enter**. To close the command prompt window, type **exit** and press **Enter**.

1 Access Advanced Wireless Settings

Log on to your router as the administrator using your web browser; type the URL for your router in the browser's **Address** box and then provide the login name and password for the router when prompted for this information. You can find the URL for your router in the documentation that came with your router; alternatively, go to the router manufacturer's website and download the documentation. Each manufacturer's website provides a support page that will help you find and download the documentation for your router.

80

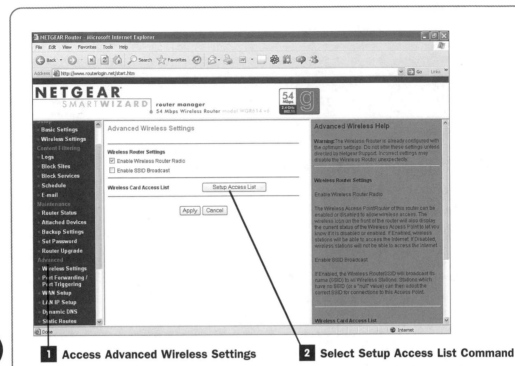

1 Access Advanced Wireless Settings   **2** Select Setup Access List Command

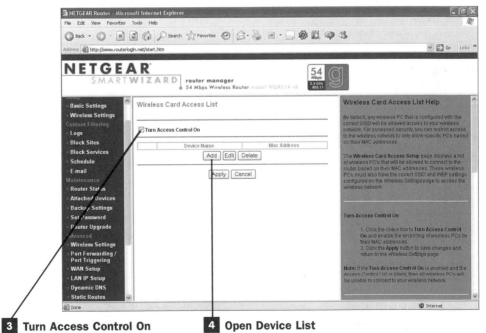

3 Turn Access Control On   **4** Open Device List

80 Create a WiFi Network MAC Access List

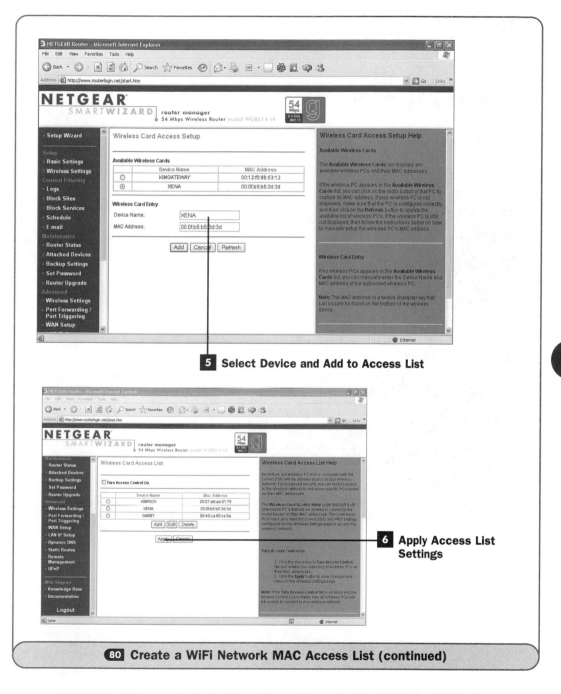

5 Select Device and Add to Access List

6 Apply Access List Settings

80 Create a WiFi Network MAC Access List (continued)

From any of your router's configuration pages, select the **Advanced Wireless Settings** command (or similar command on your router's web page). This link provides access to a command for setting up the MAC access list.

> ▶ **TIP**
> The access list setup command should be on the same configuration page as the command for enabling the router's SSID broadcasts.

2 **Select Setup Access List Command**

3 **Turn Access Control On**

For the router to actually use the access list you are going to create as a way to accept or deny access to the WiFi network, you must enable the access control feature. Select the **Turn Access Control On** check box (or similar command). Now you can build the list of computers that will be allowed to access the WiFi network through the router.

4 **Open Device List**

Click the **Add** button to open the device list. A list of currently connected computers and the MAC addresses of their network cards appears on the **Wireless Card Access Setup** page.

80

5 **Select Device and Add to Access List**

Select a device from the list by selecting the radio button for the device. If a computer (or computers) is not listed in the device list, but you know that the computer is connected to the WiFi network, type the host name and the MAC address for the computer in the appropriate text boxes. Click the **Add** button. The computer (or computers, if you selected more than one in the device list) is added to the access list.

> ▶ **TIP**
> The access list uses radio buttons for the selection of a particular device in the list. Click the radio button for a device in the list and then you can delete the device from the list using the **Delete** command; click the **Edit** command to edit the selected MAC address or device name. You can select only one device at a time.

6 **Apply Access List Settings**

The access list is updated and shown each time you add a computer to the list. You can use the **Add** button to add additional computers to the list. When you have completed entering the computers to the access list, apply the settings to the router by clicking the **Apply** button to save the access list to the router's configuration.

▶ **TIP**

To remove a computer from the access list, select the computer's option button and then click the **Delete** button. Then click the **Apply** button to apply any changes you make to the access list (such as new additions or deletions).

81　**Configure Remote Management**

✔ **BEFORE YOU BEGIN**

22 Access Router Configuration

When you first installed and configured the WiFi *router*, it was necessary to attach a computer with a "wired" network card directly to the router. The configuration of the router was then handled from the directly attached computer. Using a computer that is "wired" to the router as the configuration console for the router actually makes good sense in terms of security because only the directly attached computer can be used to access the router's configuration, even if the router administrator's password becomes known by someone other than the administrator.

However, sometimes you have to take a look at security practices and determine whether a particular practice has become an inconvenience rather than a security asset. You can configure your router for remote access, meaning that the router can be accessed by any computer or the Internet. You can choose to specify the IP address of the computer or computers that can access the router's configuration page remotely, or you can allow all computers to access the router's configuration. Of course, anyone attempting to log on to the router must provide the login name and the correct password.

The router is actually accessed remotely by the "real" IP address that the router is provided by your Internet service provider (the router gets the IP address automatically when it's connected to the DSL router or cable modem). The complete IP address and the port number extension that must be typed into a web browser for access to the router over the Internet is actually provided on the configuration page where you set up remote access. The port number **8080** must be included with the IP address to make the connection to the router. So, if the IP address of the router is **192.168.1.1**, I would type **192.168.1.1:8080** in my browser address box. I would then enter the login name and the password to access the router's configuration.

81

81

1 Access Remote Management Settings

2 Turn Remote Management On

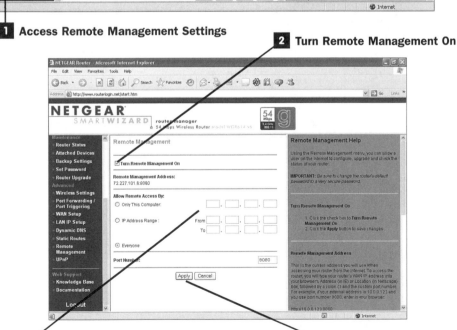

3 Specify IP Addresses for Remote Management Access

4 Apply Remote Management Settings

81 Configure Remote Management

Although remote access certainly can be useful in terms of sitting down at any computer and quickly configuring the router, it also opens up the router to another possible avenue of attack. If hackers "hijack" the router's configuration, they could change the password, allow "outlaw" computers to access your network, and turn off the WiFi radio signal feature completely, shutting down your network. So, you must decide whether remote access is a good thing or not. You certainly are not required to set up remote access if you think it will turn out to be more of a problem than a convenience.

If you decide that the conveniences of accessing your router remotely outweigh the security concerns, follow these steps to configure your router for remote management:

1 Access Remote Management Settings

Log on to your router as the administrator using your web browser; type the URL for your router in the browser's **Address** box and then provide the login name and password for the router when prompted for this information. You can find the URL for your router in the documentation that came with your router; alternatively, go to the router manufacturer's website and download the information.

From your router's main configuration page, click the **Remote Management** command (for my Netgear router, this command is on the left side of the router's configuration page; other routers will have a similar command on their configuration pages). The **Remote Management** page opens.

2 Turn Remote Management On

Click the **Turn Remote Management On** check box to enable remote management.

3 Specify IP Addresses for Remote Management Access

By default, all IP addresses on the network (everyone) can potentially access the router (meaning you can access the router over the Internet from any computer on the network). If you want to specify a single computer for remote access, click the **Only This Computer** option button and then enter the IP address of the computer. If you want to access the router remotely from several computers, click the **IP Address Range** option button and then enter the starting and ending IP addresses in the range

81

CHAPTER 11: Securing the Wireless Network

▶ TIPS

If your computers aren't in a consistent range, power off the router and use the **ipconfig/release** command to release the current IP addresses Then turn off the computer. Turn on the router, wait a moment for the router to get up and running, and then boot up each of the computers. The router should provide new IP addresses to the computers, and the IP address range should be sequential (see **97** **Use Command-Line Tools** for more about the **ipconfig** command).

You will need the "real" IP address of the router's public interface (the one connected to your broadband Internet device) to connect to the router over the Internet. If you look at the **Remote Management** configuration page for your router, you will find that the **remote management address** is listed there. You must enter this address as shown, and also include the **8080** suffix that is used to open the HTTP port on the router. Enter this information in the address box of your web browser. For example, if the public IP address was 192.5.6.7, type **http://192.5.6.7:8080** to access the router remotely.

4 Apply Remote Management Settings

After you have configured your remote management settings, you must save them to the router's configuration. Click the **Apply** button to do this.

81

12

Protecting the Wireless Network

IN THIS CHAPTER:

Taking advantage of your WiFi router's capability to secure the wireless infrastructure (using security protocols such as WPA) and protecting your network from an Internet attack using the router's firewall capabilities are only part of the battle of keeping your network and the computers on the network protected. A huge problem for nearly all computer users is the possibility of having your computer become infected with a software *virus*. Other threats include *Trojan horse* programs, *worms*, and *spyware*.

In this chapter, we take a look at the different types of infectious software that can damage your system and how you can combat them. These malicious software threats are referred to collectively as *malware*.

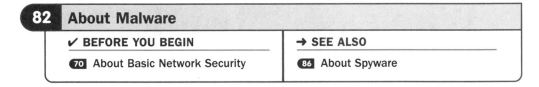

82	**About Malware**

✔ **BEFORE YOU BEGIN**	→ **SEE ALSO**
70 About Basic Network Security	**86** About Spyware

82

Keeping your network up and running after you configure your WiFi router correctly could be a fairly carefree endeavor. Now, I said "could be"; computing in general could be a much more carefree pastime if we didn't have to deal with malicious software that can disable or hijack our computers. I'm talking about *viruses*, *Trojan horses*, *worms*, and *spyware*. Malicious software such as these are often referred to collectively as *malware*. Malware would be any software designed to exploit or damage your computer. Another annoying computer incursion that we all have to deal with is spam email, and while spam doesn't really qualify as malware, it can be just as annoying.

▶ **KEY TERM**

Malware—Malicious software such as viruses, worms, and spyware.

Fortunately, the unsettling fact (actually it's *depressing* that someone with people programming knowledge would spend their time creating viruses) that there are numerous viruses, worms, and Trojan horses loose means that some excellent software tools have been developed (and continue to evolve) to protect your computer against malware. Let's take a look at the different types of malware, and then we'll walk through some tasks that explore some of the ways to protect your computer.

Viruses

A definite threat to your computer (or computers) and your network's security is the virus. A *virus* is self-replicating software code, meaning that it can make copies of itself. The fact that a virus can self-replicate means that it can spread easily from computer to computer.

▶ **KEY TERM**

Virus—Malicious, self-replicating software code that can infect computers and damage system and other files.

Viruses actually require action from you before they can infect your system. For example, if you open an infected file shared by another user or open an infected email attachment, you are going to infect your computer. The virus can then be spread from computer to computer over a network (such as your ***workgroup***) when the infected file is shared and opened. Viruses can also be spread on removable media such as floppy disks, CDs, and USB memory sticks.

Viruses come in several varieties. A number of different virus types have evolved over the years. These different types of viruses have been classified based on how they infect a computer:

- **Boot sector viruses**: Some of the first viruses were boot sector viruses, which spread through infected floppy disks or other removable storage media such as bootable CDs. When an infected disk or bootable CD is left in a computer and the computer is turned on, the computer attempts to boot to the removable media. On bootup, the boot sector virus loads in to the computer's memory. The virus can then infect the hard drive or any disks you place in the floppy drive after the computer is up and running. One of the first boot sector viruses was the BRAIN virus, which actually didn't really do any damage to the computer or files on the infected disk. However, the virus was able to spread quite quickly because floppy disks were commonly used for data storage when the BRAIN virus first appeared. Today, most computers will not boot to a CD unless you specify that the computer should do so.

▶ **NOTE**

Boot sector viruses are uncommon now. In fact, many new computers do not even come configured with floppy drives, which makes boot sector viruses a rather outdated venture for those malcontents who create viruses.

- **File viruses**: Although fairly uncommon now, file viruses actually infect an executable file such as an EXE or COM file. When the infected file is run, the file virus loads into the computer's RAM. It can then infect other executable files as they are run on the computer. A form of the file virus is the overwriting virus, which actually overwrites the executable file it infects. Examples of file viruses include the Dark Avenger virus and the KMIT virus.

- **Macro viruses:** The macro virus is a fairly recent virus type. Macro viruses are typically written in Visual Basic code and infect documents and spreadsheet data files rather than executable files. When an infected document is loaded into an application such as Microsoft Word, the virus code runs just like any other macro would in that particular application. Another scary thing about macro viruses is that they are not operating system specific. Because Microsoft Word can run on a Macintosh or a Windows-based PC, the macro virus can actually be spread between the two platforms if the infected Word document is shared. An example of a macro virus is the famous Melissa virus, a Word macro virus that automatically spread itself via email.

- **Multipartite viruses:** A multipartite virus has the characteristics of both a boot sector virus and a file virus. It can spread from the boot sector of a drive to another drive, and it can also attack executable files on the computer. Some multipartite viruses can even infect device drivers (such as the drivers for your network interface card). An example of a multipartite virus is Pastika, which is activated on only certain days of the month (typically the 21st and 22nd of the month) and can actually overwrite your hard drive.

82

The actual number of viruses in the "wild" (meaning those that are infecting computers and networks) at any one time varies, but in general, the number is increasing.

The only way you can protect your computer from virus infection is to install antivirus software on your computer and keep it up to date. Unfortunately, protection against a particular virus doesn't become part of the antivirus software capabilities until the virus "goes public." This means that there is always a lag time between the virus's appearance and the ability of the antivirus software to protect against it.

▶ **TIP**

A good place to look for information related to viruses is the SANS institute. SANS, at http://www.sans.org/, provides information on viruses and other network security issues. You can also find information on current virus and other malware threats by checking out the website of the antivirus software that you use.

Worms and Trojan Horses

Viruses aren't the only malware threats that can infect your computer. There are also worms and Trojan Horses.

A *worm* is a program that spreads itself from computer to computer on a network. It doesn't need to be activated by you as does a virus. Worms are typically specific to an operating system (such as Windows) and exploit some weakness in that operating system. Worms often exploit open ports and can actually hijack a computer and use it in denial-of-service (DOS) attacks against websites (in DOS attacks, a website is flooded by requests from the computers that have been hijacked by the worm).

► **KEY TERMS**

Worm—Self-spreading and self-activating malware software code that typically exploits a particular weakness in an operating system.

Trojan Horse—Malware that appear to be a normal program but, when executed, causes harm to your system. The fact that the malicious program is masquerading as a "normal" program is why this particular type of malware is referred to as a Trojan horse.

A *Trojan horse*, on the other hand, is a program that appears to be perfectly benign, such as a screensaver or a game. For example, the HAPPY99.EXE Trojan horse, when executed, provides a nice little fireworks display on your screen and then immediately uses mail addresses found in your computer's email client to send off copies of itself to these addresses (this is similar to how the Melissa virus is spread).

One of the earliest Trojan horses was the AIDS Information Disk Trojan, which was actually a disk sent out to medical establishments as an AIDS-awareness product. After being executed, the Trojan horse file created a hidden directory on the computer's hard drive and eventually encrypted the entire contents of the hard drive, making it unusable.

One of the biggest threats related to Trojan horses is that some can actually invade a computer and allow remote control of the infected computer by the originator of the Trojan horse (the hacker). This allows the hacker to steal personal information and also use the computer in en-masse attacks upon website servers.

83

---

83 | **Install and Use Antivirus Software**

✔ **BEFORE YOU BEGIN**

82 About Malware

Many antivirus programs are available for the Windows operating system: Norton Antivirus, Computer Associates EZ Antivirus, PC-cillin, and Kaspersky Anti-Virus, just to name a few. The antivirus software you actually use (and purchase) is really up to you. Although tests show that some antivirus programs are better at detecting and removing obscure viruses, having *any* antivirus software that is up-to-date is an important aspect of protecting your computer from *malware* invasion.

▶ **TIP**

Most broadband Internet connection providers such as Verizon, Time Warner, AOL, and others provide you with free antivirus software. Some companies even provide antimalware suites that include antivirus, antispyware, and antispam products. Check with your Internet service provider before buying antivirus software because you might be able to download it for free.

Some antivirus programs are bundled in security suites that also include antispyware, spam email filtering, and even firewall software. Examples include AVG Anti-Virus plus Firewall Edition and Norton Internet Security 2005 AntiSpyware Edition. Because Windows XP already includes a personal firewall, you don't necessarily need to purchase an antivirus suite that also provides a software firewall. However, purchasing antivirus software that includes spam filtering and antispyware capabilities does make it easy in terms of having to update only one antimalware product instead of separate products for virus detection, spyware detection, and spam filtering.

▶ **TIP**

Most antivirus software manufacturers allow you to download a trial version of the product. You can then purchase a license to continue using the product. Some antivirus programs also allow you to buy multiple licenses at a discount, which is ideal if you have several computers on the home network that need antivirus software. Remember that every computer needs its own license for the software. Don't be afraid to try different antivirus software. The products differ in terms of ease of use and effectiveness, so it is a personal choice. Check out reviews on the Web related to antivirus software and choose the best product for you and your computer.

When you run your antivirus software, you can continue to use the computer, but I think you will find that your computer will run slowly. It makes better sense to run the virus scan when you are not going to use the computer for a period of time, such as at night or during lunch.

1 Open Antivirus Software

Right-click the antivirus program icon in the Windows System Tray and select the command that opens your antivirus software; for example, the **EZ Antivirus** command opens my EZ Antivirus software window.

2 Start Virus Check

Start the virus check by clicking **Scan My Computer** or a similar command in the antivirus software window. The antivirus software will check the boot sectors of your computer's hard drive for viruses and then check all your computer's files.

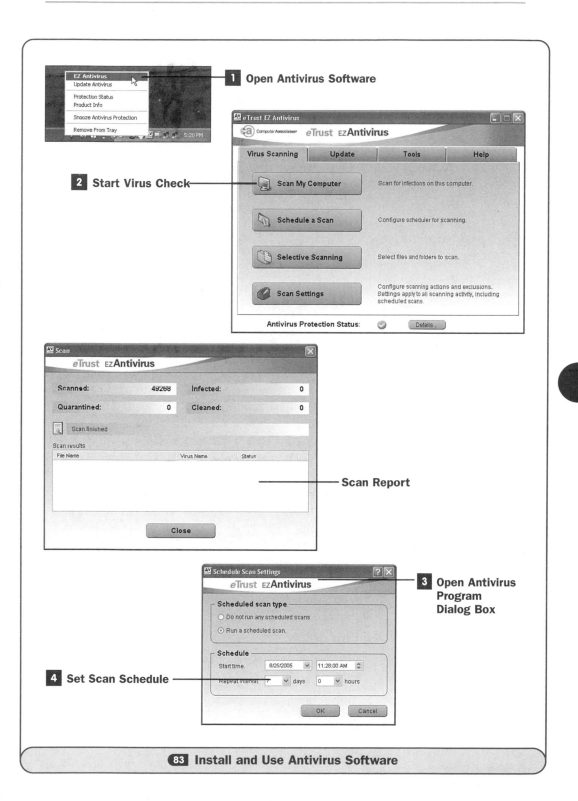

1 Open Antivirus Software

2 Start Virus Check

Scan Report

3 Open Antivirus Program Dialog Box

4 Set Scan Schedule

83

When the virus scan is complete, the software provides you with statistics related to the scan, such as the number of files that were scanned and whether or not any viruses were found and cleaned (or whether files were deleted to remove the virus). To close the message box related to the scan completion, click **OK**.

▶ **TIP**

You can specify that the virus scanner look at only selected folders or drives on your computer. Click the **Selective Scanning** button or a similar command in your virus scanner's main window and then select the drives and folders you want the program to scan.

3 Open Schedule Scan Settings

It makes sense to configure your antivirus software so that it runs periodically. You can set up your virus scan to run at a time when you are not using the computer. How you configure your antivirus software to run automatically according to a schedule varies from software to software. In the case of EZ Antivirus, I click the **Schedule a Scan** button on the program's main screen.

83

4 Set Scan Schedule

To set the scan scheduling, click the **Run a scheduled scan** option button or a similar option. Then set the start date, start time, and the repeat interval. If you want the computer to be scanned once a week, for example, set the repeat interval to 7. It is up to you to set the interval for running your virus scan. Most antivirus software provides real-time antivirus protection and alerts you if a virus or other malware attempts to invade your system. Antivirus software doesn't necessarily catch all malware on the fly, however, so I suggest that you run your antivirus software at least once a week. Run it more often if you download a lot of files from the Internet or open email attachments sent to you by people you are not familiar with.

When you have completed setting your scan scheduling parameters, click **OK** to close the dialog box.

▶ **TIP**

If a virus cannot be removed, the report provided by your antivirus software will detail this information and provide the name of the infected file or files. In some cases, you might have to update your antivirus software to clean the virus from your system. In other cases, you might have to follow special instructions provided on your antivirus company's website or download a "cleaning" program that removes the virus, *worm,* or *Trojan horse* that cannot be removed by the antivirus software.

84 Update Antivirus Software

✔ **BEFORE YOU BEGIN**

82 About Malware
83 Install and Use Antivirus Software

It is extremely important that you keep your antivirus software up to date. New *viruses* and other *malware* are cropping up all the time, and manufacturers of antivirus software are working constantly to identify and eradicate the new malware threats. Software vendors frequently release updates to your antivirus software. Keep in mind that out-of-date antivirus software is almost as bad as having no antivirus software at all.

Many antivirus software packages automatically connect to an update site to check for new information every time you turn on your computer and Windows is up and running. However, this isn't always the case, so you need to make sure that the antivirus signatures (the file used to identify and clean viruses) are up to date. This means that you should know how to manually update the antivirus software. In terms of how often you check for updates, it doesn't hurt to do so every day because the download and installation process for the update is typically fairly short. New viruses and malware pop up every day, so why not make sure that your antivirus software is up to date every day?

84

1 Start Antivirus Update

You can start the update for most antivirus software from the Windows XP desktop. Locate the icon for your antivirus software in the Windows system tray and right-click the icon. Select **Update Antivirus** or a similar command to open the antivirus update window. Some antivirus software does not put an icon in the system tray, but will provide a menu choice (which you can access after you start the software) that allows you to update the software. You will typically find this command on the **Tools** menu (or a similarly named menu).

2 Download Any Updates

The antivirus update program will connect to the software vendor's website and download any available updates. When the update files are downloaded, the software automatically installs the update files.

3 Close Update Window

When the update is complete, click **OK** to close the antivirus update window.

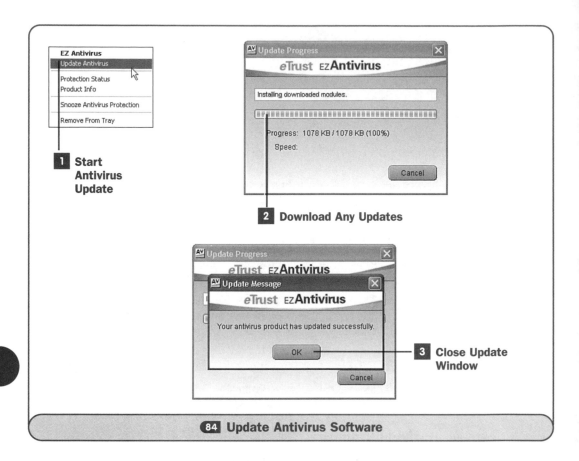

1 Start Antivirus Update

2 Download Any Updates

3 Close Update Window

84 Update Antivirus Software

▶ **NOTE**

If the antivirus software is already up to date, a message box appears letting you know that no new updates are available. In this case, you can close the update window immediately.

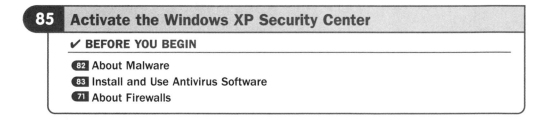

85 Activate the Windows XP Security Center

✔ BEFORE YOU BEGIN

82 About Malware
83 Install and Use Antivirus Software
71 About Firewalls

Windows XP has gone through a couple of makeovers in the form of service packs. With the Service Pack 2 (SP2) release, a new feature was added to Windows XP, named the **Windows XP Security Center**.

▶ **TIP**

If you don't have Service Pack 2 (click the **Start** button, right-click the **My Computer** option, and select **Properties** from the context menu; the **Properties** dialog box tells you the version of Windows you are running, including any service packs that have been installed), go to **www.microsoft.com** and download it. You will have to reboot your computer before the updates take effect. If you have enabled **Automatic Updates** in the **Security Center**, your system has most likely been upgraded to Service Pack 2.

Microsoft had taken some heat for the security flaws in the original Windows XP operating system. SP2 provided a new personal *firewall* for Windows as well as the **Security Center**, which monitors security settings such as whether or not your antivirus software is up to date and whether Windows automatic update is turned on. The **Security Center** can be configured to monitor security settings such as the Windows firewall or you can disable the Security Center's monitoring capabilities.

In my opinion, it makes sense to use the **Security Center** because it helps you keep your antivirus and Windows operating system up to date. The Windows firewall also provides additional protection (along with your WiFi router's firewall) for your computer.

▶ **NOTE**

85

Microsoft has been very proactive about making the Windows XP operating system more secure. Microsoft suggests that you have a personal firewall and up-to-date antivirus software, and that you make sure that the Windows XP software is up to date in terms of security updates and service packs. You can do all this from the **Security Center**. Microsoft provides you with a free firewall (so use it) and a way to keep Windows updated automatically (through the **Security Center**). You must purchase your own antivirus software. Many new computers come with a trial version (60 to 90 days) of an antivirus program. If you like this particular antivirus program (you have used it and it seems to work), purchase the software when the trial period nears completion. Do not operate your computer without antivirus software; if you do, you are just asking for trouble.

1 **Open Security Center**

From the Windows **Control Panel** (click the **Start** button and choose **Control Panel**), click the **Security Center** icon. The **Security Center** window opens.

If any of the **Security Center** components (the **Firewall, Automatic Updates,** or **Virus Protection**) are disabled, a red **Off** button appears next to that component. The **Off** button appears next to the **Virus Protection** component only if you do not have antivirus software installed on your computer or if the **Security Center** cannot identify your antivirus software as being installed.

85

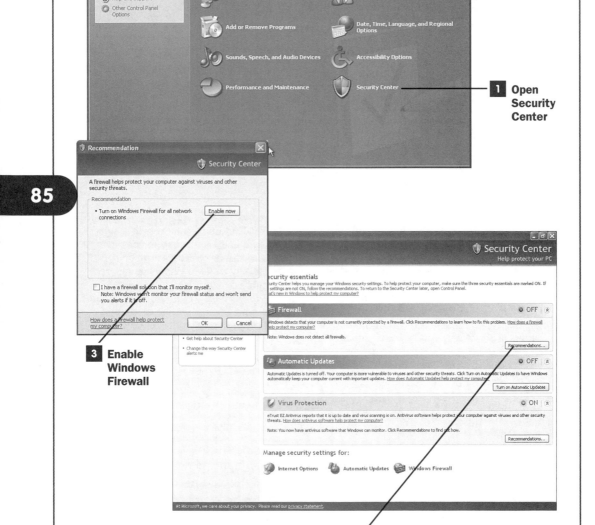

1 Open Security Center

3 Enable Windows Firewall

2 Open Firewall Recommendations

85 Activate the Windows XP Security Center

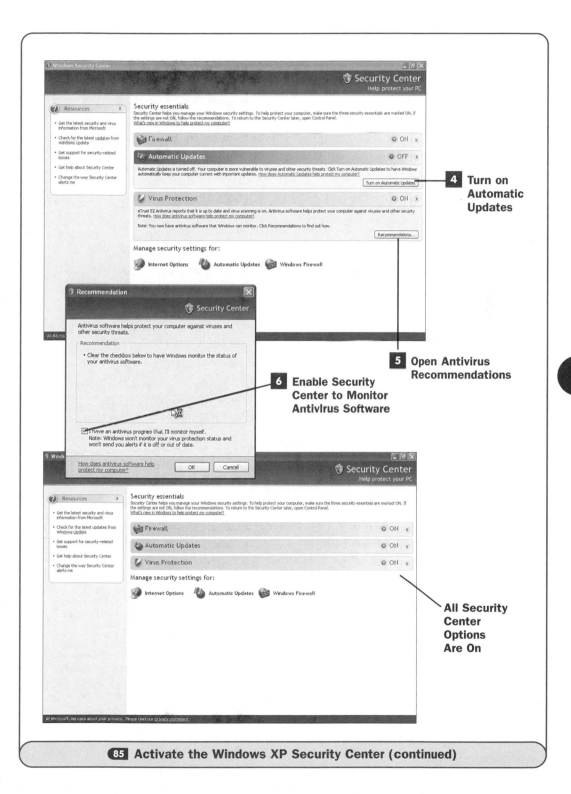

4 Turn on Automatic Updates

5 Open Antivirus Recommendations

6 Enable Security Center to Monitor Antivirus Software

All Security Center Options Are On

85

▶ **NOTE**

Some antivirus software programs aren't recognized by the **Security Center**. But that doesn't mean you need to reinstall the software or buy a different antivirus program. Just make sure that you keep your antivirus software up to date (download and install updates periodically) because the **Security Center** will not be able to alert you when your antivirus software is out of date.

▣ **Open Firewall Recommendations**

If the **Firewall** is **Off**, you should turn it on. Click the **Recommendations** button in the **Security Center**'s **Firewall** box. The **Recommendation** dialog box opens.

▶ **NOTE**

If you are using another software firewall such as a firewall that is part of your antivirus software suite, you can leave the Microsoft **Firewall** disabled. Running multiple software firewalls on the same computer can cause performance slowdowns and other problems.

▣ **Enable Windows Firewall**

To enable the firewall, click the **Enable now** button in the **Recommendation** dialog box. Click **OK** to close the message box that opens (letting you know that the firewall is now enabled) and then click **OK** again to close the **Recommendation** dialog box. The **Firewall** button is now **On** in the **Security Center** window.

▣ **Turn on Automatic Updates**

You should definitely keep your Windows software up to date because new security threats crop up often and Microsoft puts out security fixes for Windows to negate the threats. Click the **Turn on Automatic Updates** button. Windows will now provide you with an alert in the system tray whenever a new update has been downloaded and should be installed.

▶ **NOTE**

If you have configured the **Security Center** to alert you when a Windows update is available (that is, you have turned on **Automatic Updates**), Windows places an alert icon in the Windows system tray. Follow the alert's advice by clicking the alert; the update will be installed on your system automatically. Don't be afraid of the update alerts. This is not some evil genius trying to trick you into installing malware on your computer. If you really don't like automatic updates, don't enable them. It then is your responsibility to periodically go to the Windows Update website and allow the site to scan your computer and install any updates available (critical updates offered by the update website should always be installed). To go to the Windows Update website, click the **Start** button, choose **All Programs**, and then select **Windows Update**.

5 Open Antivirus Recommendations

The **Security Center** can monitor whether or not your antivirus software is up to date. If the **Security Center** finds that your software is not up to date, it will provide you with an alert in the system tray. It makes sense to allow the **Security Center** to keep track of your antivirus software and its updates.

Click the **Recommendations** button in the **Security Center's Virus Protection** box. The **Recommendation** dialog box opens.

6 Enable Security Center to Monitor Antivirus Software

Clear the **I have an antivirus program that I'll monitor myself** check box and click **OK** to close the **Recommendation** dialog box. The **Security Center** will now provide you with alerts related to the Windows Firewall, Windows updates, and the status of your antivirus software.

---

86 About Spyware

✔ **BEFORE YOU BEGIN**

82 About Malware

86

Although *viruses*, *worms*, and *Trojan horses* pose potential dangers for your home network, up-to-date antivirus software and common sense in terms of downloading and opening unknown files can go a long way toward minimizing the threat. However, a new flavor of *malware*—called *spyware*—has become the most prevalent, pervasive, and annoying threat to the personal computer.

Spyware is malware that covertly gathers information using the computer's Internet connection. Spyware is often hidden in free software and other programs that can be downloaded from the Web. Spyware can actually monitor a user's activity on the Web and gather information related to product preferences and browsing history. Some spyware can also gather information related to passwords and other transactions on the Web, including transactions where you enter a credit card number.

▶ **KEY TERM**

Spyware—Malware that infects your computer through free software and downloads from websites. Spyware gathers information related to the user, such as browsing preferences and information used in Web transactions such as passwords and credit card numbers.

A spyware infection typically has symptoms such as slower computer functionality (because the spyware uses the computer's system resources, including memory) and a seeming slowing of the Internet connection. The problem with spyware is that it actually edits the Windows registry and makes itself part of the Windows configuration, just as "normal" programs do when they are installed.

An even more insidious type of spyware, called a rootkit, actually activates during your system bootup; rootkits are difficult to detect because they are up and running before antispyware and antivirus software loads. Spyware rootkits can install all sorts of hidden files on your system and even intercept data from the network.

Spyware has really become a big problem both in terms of your computer's performance (spyware saps system resources) and the fact that personal information can be stolen—particularly if you use your computer for online purchases. Some antispyware software suggestions are provided in **87 Install AntiSpyware**

▶ TIP

Your computer can also become infected with *adware*, software that is included as part of free software or a service on a particular website. Adware can create those annoying pop-up ads. Adware can be removed from your system using some of the same tools that remove spyware from your system. However, to run some free software, such as Imesh and Morpheus (both peer-to-peer music file sharing applications that install adware on your system), you might have to put up with the adware, which is basically a "cost" of using software for which you've made no monetary payment.

86

87   Install AntiSpyware

✔ BEFORE YOU BEGIN

82 About Malware
86 About Spyware

If you surf the Web a lot (including the downloading of files), and you also use the Web for online purchases, I suggest that you install antispyware software on your computer. *Spyware,* which can be installed on your computer without your knowledge, can slow your computer's performance and, in extreme situations, lead to identity theft, particularly if information you enter for online purchases such as a credit card number is "recorded" by the spyware.

A number of antispyware products are available. Most of these products run like an antivirus program and will examine the Windows **Registry** (a database of Windows settings and installed software) for any spyware additions to your installed software. Some of these antispyware products also provide real-time protection and block the installation of spyware on your system. As with antivirus programs, you need to keep your antispyware software up to date so that it can remove (or block) the most recent forms of spyware. Some antispyware products that work well are listed here:

- **Spybot (Search and Destroy)**

  http://www.safer-networking.org

  Spybot is a free antispyware product (although you should provide a dona-tion to the authors if you use it). Spybot provides real-time antispyware capa-bilities, and the creators provide timely updates. You might think that a "free" product can't possibility get the job done, but Spybot does work quite well.

- **Ad-Aware**

  http://www.lavasoftusa.com/software/adaware

  Ad-Aware comes in different varieties, including the free Personal edition and the $26.95 Plus edition. The free version does a good job removing spyware (and adware) already on your system. You need the Plus edition, however, to get real-time protection that stops spyware from being installed on your sys-tem as you browse the Web.

- **Microsoft Windows AntiSpyware**

  http://www.microsoft.com/downloads/

  As of the writing of this book, Windows AntiSpyware is currently in Beta, meaning that a final version of the product is due sometime in the coming months. Windows AntiSpyware does a good job even in its Beta version and provides real-time protection from spyware; it also allows you to remove spyware already on your system.

In this task, we will download, install, and use the Windows AntiSpyware soft-ware because it is currently available to all Windows XP users without charge.

1 Open Microsoft AntiSpyware Download Page

Open your web browser and go to the Microsoft AntiSpyware download site at **http://www.microsoft.com/downloads/details.aspx?FamilyID= 321cd7a2-6a57-4c57-a8bd-dbf62eda9671&displaylang=en**. Because the actual download pages for Microsoft add-ons can change over time, you can also go to **http://www.microsoft.com** and search for the AntiSpyware down-load page.

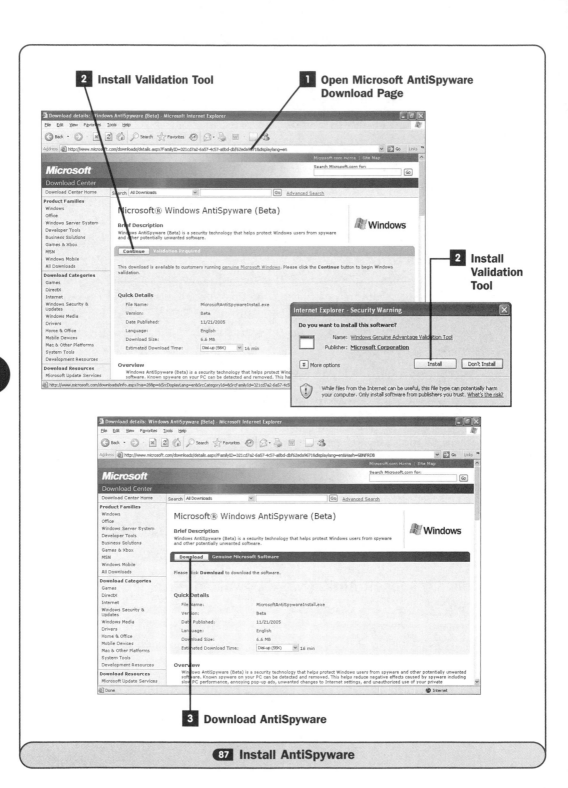

2 Install Validation Tool

1 Open Microsoft AntiSpyware
Download Page

2 Install Validation Tool

3 Download AntiSpyware

87 Install AntiSpyware

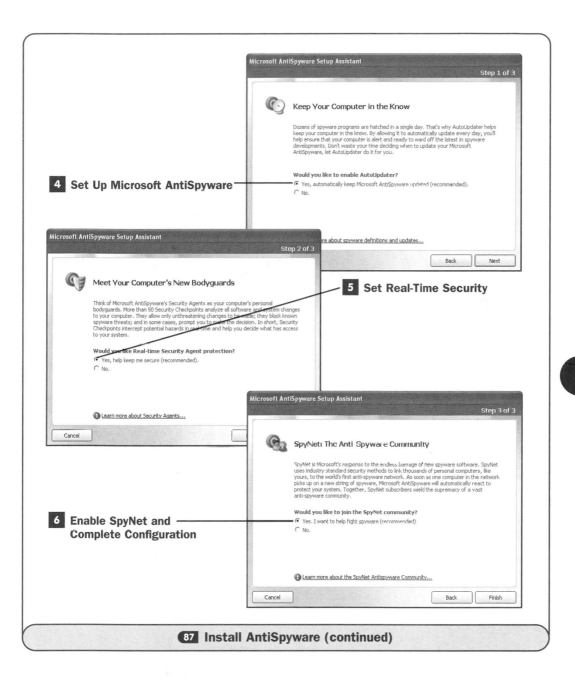

4 Set Up Microsoft AntiSpyware

5 Set Real-Time Security

**6 Enable SpyNet and
Complete Configuration**

87 Install AntiSpyware (continued)

Before you can download the AntiSpyware software, you must update your
system with a validation tool that checks whether your system is running an
"official" (meaning registered) version of Windows XP. Click the **Continue**
button. A **Security Warning** dialog box opens.

2 Install Validation Tool

In the **Security Warning** dialog box, click the **Install** button. The validation tool will be installed, and the download page for the Microsoft AntiSpyware software opens.

3 Download AntiSpyware

Click the **Download** button. A **File Download** dialog box opens. Click **Run** to install the software after it is downloaded to your system. In the second security dialog box that opens, click **Run** again. The Microsoft AntiSpyware Wizard opens. Follow the steps to complete the software's installation.

4 Set Up Microsoft AntiSpyware

After the installation, a wizard opens that helps you set up Microsoft AntiSpyware. Click the **Next** button to bypass the initial screen. On the next screen, make sure that the **Yes, automatically keep Microsoft Antispyware updated** option button is selected and then click **Next** to continue.

5 Set Real-Time Security

On the next screen, make sure that the **Yes, help keep me secure** option button is selected. This option enables the software's ability to block the installation of spyware as you surf the Web. Click **Next** to continue.

6 Enable SpyNet and Complete Configuration

The next screen provides the option of being part of Microsoft's **SpyNet**, which is a peer-to-peer network that shares information related to spyware. In theory, when one member of the SpyNet is threatened by new spyware, all member computers of the SpyNet can react to this threat by blocking it. If you want to be part of the SpyNet, make sure that the **Yes, I want to help fight spyware** option button is selected. Then click **Finish**. A screen appears that provides a link you can click to start scanning your system with the installed AntiSpyware software.

▶ **NOTE**

Whether or not Microsoft's SpyNet will prove to be a major blow to spyware is up in the air. Peer computing—where computers can share information and other things such as files—isn't new to the Internet (just think about all those file-sharing applications out there, such as the first incarnation of Napster). Whether or not SpyNet could be hijacked by hackers and used to infect computers rather than protect them is unknown at this point, so it is up to you if you want to jump onto the SpyNet bandwagon or not.

---

88 **Use AntiSpyware**

✔ **BEFORE YOU BEGIN**

82 About Malware
86 About Spyware
87 Install AntiSpyware

After you have installed the Microsoft Windows AntiSpyware software, you can use it to scan your system for existing spyware. If spyware is already on your system, AntiSpyware removes it and cleans up the Registry (spyware places entries in your Windows Registry database just as the software that you install does).

You can configure the AntiSpyware software to check for updates automatically at an interval that you set; you can also set the type of alerts you want to receive as the AntiSpyware runs in the real-time mode.

1 **Run Microsoft AntiSpyware**

Double-click the **Microsoft AntiSpyware** icon on your Windows desktop or click the **Run Quick Scan Now** link on the AntiSpyware's **Setup Assistant**. The AntiSpyware window opens, and the software begins a scan of your system.

88

2 **Close Scan Results Window**

When the scan is complete, a **Scan Results** window opens. It displays the number of spyware items detected, the number of processes and registry key scanned, and the total time it took to run the scan. Click **Close** to close the results window.

▶ **NOTE**
If spyware is detected during the scan, the AntiSpyware program removes the spyware automatically along with the Registry information that was entered by the spyware.

3 **Open AntiSpyware Options**

To set options for the AntiSpyware software, such as when the AntiSpyware is updated, choose **Options**, **Settings** from the AntiSpyware menu bar. The **Settings** window opens.

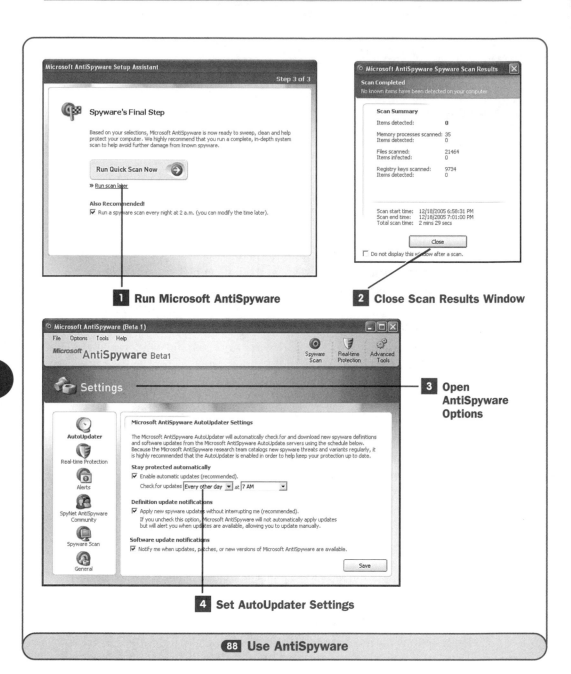

1 Run Microsoft AntiSpyware

2 Close Scan Results Window

3 Open AntiSpyware Options

4 Set AutoUpdater Settings

88 Use AntiSpyware

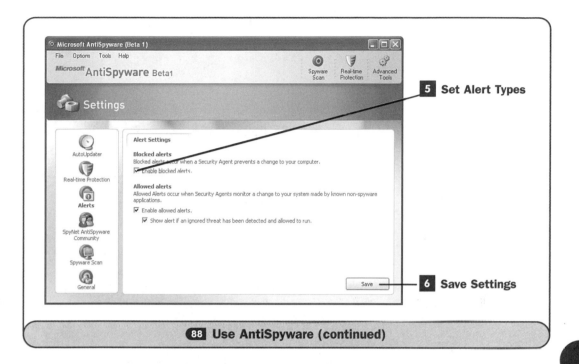

5 Set Alert Types

6 Save Settings

88 Use AntiSpyware (continued)

88

4 Set AutoUpdater Settings

To set the timing of autoupdates for your AntiSpyware installation, select the **AutoUpdater** icon on the left of the **Settings** window and then use the **Check for updates** drop-down boxes to set the interval at which you want the program to check for updates (**system startup**, **Daily**, **Every other day**, or **Every week**) and the time when you want to perform the updates.

5 Set Alert Types

Click the **Alerts** icon on the left of the **Settings** window. To receive alerts in your system tray when spyware is blocked, select the **Enable blocked alerts** check box. If you want to receive alerts when changes are made to programs and utilities that you have installed on your computer, click the **Enable allowed alerts** check box. If you check this option, you will receive an alert every time installed software on your computer is updated over the Internet. It's up to you whether you want to see all these updates, because they certainly are not revealing a problem or infection by spyware.

6 Save Settings

When you have completed making changes to the AntiSpyware settings, click the **Save** button. A message box opens, letting you know that your settings have been saved. Click **OK**. You can now close the AntiSpyware window or run a scan as needed by clicking the **SpyWare Scan** icon on the left of the application window.

▶ **NOTE**

Other settings are available in the AntiSpyware **Settings** window. However, most of these options, such as **Real-time Protection**, **SpyNet AntiSpyware Community**, and **Spyware Scan**, are informational, rather than a grouping of important settings.

---

89 **About Spam Email and Outlook Express**

✔ **BEFORE YOU BEGIN**

82 About Malware

Spam email has certainly become a plague. Everyone with an email account receives spam eventually. And if you use your email address to register for website memberships and to download software or other files, your email address may be sold to others, and so the deluge of spam email grows over time.

88

Some spam email can contain *viruses* and other *malware*. You may even get spam email that looks like it is from a legitimate website such as eBay that requests you go to a web location and update your personal information. In this example, the web site you go to isn't actually the eBay website, so when you enter your information, it is stolen. The process of sending out emails that look official and take you to websites that are not actually affiliated with the company or service mentioned in the email is known as *phishing*. Phishing actually leads to many cases of identify theft.

▶ **KEY TERM**

Phishing—The process of trying to fool people into giving up personal information, including credit card numbers, by directing them to a website using an official-looking email that purports to be from a legitimate website or web service.

Phishing isn't the only hazard related to email. Spam can also be sent that contains viruses or other malware attachments. For example, you might click a filename to open a photo or run a program, and your computer might become infected by the attached malware.

Different email clients, Outlook Express being an example, do provide some protection against spam email. This is accomplished by identifying spam email and creating rules that move suspected spam directly to the trash. Email from certain senders can also be blocked by configuring a blocked sender list.

Some email clients such as Microsoft Outlook (which is part of the Microsoft Office suite and is kind of Microsoft Outlook Express's big brother) provide a built-in spam filter that uses different rules to identify email as junk. The junk email is then placed in a **Junk** folder, where you can review the email.

Outlook Express doesn't provide a **Junk** folder by default, but you can set up rules that either move suspect email to a folder you create (a spam folder) or delete the message (or messages) automatically. For help creating rules that filter your email to minimize spam messages, see **90** **Configure Outlook Express Rules**.

90 Configure Outlook Express Rules

✔ BEFORE YOU BEGIN

82 About Malware
86 About Spyware
87 Install AntiSpyware

The Outlook Express email client provides only minimal spam protection by itself, because you have to create the rules that move the spam from your **Inbox** to a specified folder or to the trash. But the spam protection provided by Outlook Express rules is better than no protection at all, and you should be aware of how to configure email rules or block senders.

For more complete protection against spam, you might want to purchase a spam blocker program. There are a number available. Some antivirus software such as Computer Associates's EZ AntiVirus also offers spam protection such as EZ Anti-Spam, which provides spam protection for Outlook Express and Outlook. One of the best antispam products on the market is Mail Frontier Desktop, which provides antispam and antiphishing capabilities to Microsoft Outlook Express and Microsoft Outlook.

▶ NOTE

In the Windows environment, Outlook Express and Outlook are the two most commonly used email clients. So, you will find that most antispam products are designed to work with these two Microsoft email clients.

Products such as Mail Frontier Desktop also use a set of rules to identify and deal with spam, such as moving it to a special spam folder. Because spam products such as Mail Frontier Desktop are updated periodically with new rules and also have the ability to learn from your interaction with your email (you can add blocked senders and also specify mail as being spam), spam is actually dealt with more effectively the longer you use the antispam product.

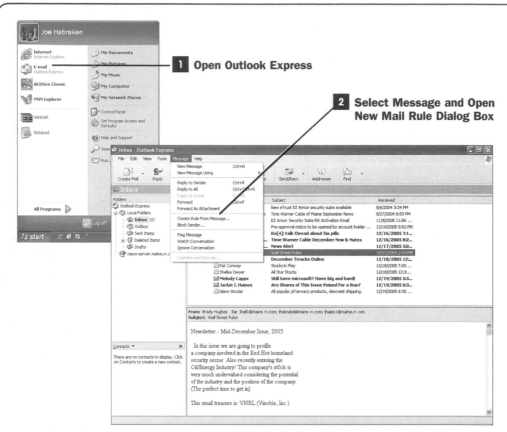

1 Open Outlook Express

2 Select Message and Open New Mail Rule Dialog Box

90

3 Specify Rule Conditions and Actions

4 Add Sender to Blocked List

90 Configure Outlook Express Rules

▶ **TIP**

Devising rules that will help cut down on spam email is an ongoing process. Take a look at the spam you receive and determine whether certain words are consistently used in this message that you do not necessarily see in regular email. You can then use these words as a way to construct a rule to negate that particular type of spam. However, spammers are pretty smart; they will misspell keywords to keep antispam rules and antispam software from flagging a message as spam. So, although you can never stop all the spam, occasionally revising your message rules can help to keep some of the annoying clutter out of your email inbox.

In terms of general rules related to spam, I suggest that you never open email attachments from senders you do not know. Also, never respond to a spam email, particularly to remove your email from their sender's list. In many cases, spam is sent as a domainwide message, and you receive it because it blankets all the email addresses in a particular domain. Answering that spam message places your email address on their list, which only leads to more spam.

1 Open Outlook Express

Click the **Start** button and then choose the **E-Mail** option to open Outlook Express.

2 Select Message and Open New Mail Rule Dialog Box

In your Outlook Express **Inbox**, select a spam message. You can create a rule that blocks future emails from the sender of the selected spam email.

Select **Message, Create Rule from Message** from the menu bar. The **New Mail Rule** dialog box opens.

3 Specify Rule Conditions and Actions

In the **New Mail Rule** dialog box, specify the condition for your rule and then specify the action that should be taken when your condition is met. For example, to act on spam email from the sender of the email you selected in step 2, click the **Where the From line contains people** check box in the **Select the Condition for your rule** list.

You must also select an action for the rule to take. You can move the mail identified by the rule to a specified folder or you can delete the message (the message is actually moved to the Outlook Express **Deleted Items** folder). Select an action such as **Delete it** from the **Select the Action for your rule** list.

A description is created for the new rule and appears in the bottom area of the **New Mail Rule** dialog box.

90

To edit the name for the new rule, click the **Name of the rule** text box and type a name. When you have completed creating the new rule, click **OK**. A message box opens, letting you know that the rule has been added. Click **OK** again.

▶ **TIP**

You can also create rules from scratch in Microsoft Outlook Express. Select **Tools, Message Rules, Mail**. You can create as many rules as you need. Rules don't have to be configured just to help deal with spam email; you can create rules that move email from certain senders to a designated folder. This would allow you to use a rule to put business or personal email directly in a particular folder.

4 **Add Sender to Blocked List**

Another way to keep spam out of your **Inbox** is to add spam senders to your blocked list. Emails from senders on the blocked list are not accepted by Outlook Express. Start by opening an email message from someone you want to block from ever sending you email again.

From the menu at the top of the message window, select **Message, Block Sender**. The sender's email address is added to the blocked sender list and no email messages from this email address will be allowed through to your **Inbox**. Click **OK** to close the message box that verifies the fact that the sender has been added to the blocked list.

90

You can repeat this step as needed to add other senders to the blocked email list.

▶ **NOTE**

The blocked sender list won't necessarily cut down on spam because spammers don't typically use the same sender address over and over again. They "spoof" any number of sending addresses so that you really don't know where the email is coming from. However, blocking senders can stop marketing or advertising email from some solicitors and companies that use a consistent email address or domain name to send out email advertisements. Having the capability of blocking certain senders is better than not having the capability at all.

13

Troubleshooting and Monitoring Network Connections

IN THIS CHAPTER:

Keeping a home WiFi network up and running requires some basic network troubleshooting skills and often just common sense. In this chapter, we take a look at how you can monitor your WiFi network and use troubleshooting techniques to diagnose and fix connectivity problems on the network.

91   About Network Connection Problems

✔ BEFORE YOU BEGIN

21 About Configuring the Wireless Router
32 About Configuring the Wireless Adapter
37 About Configuring PCs for Networking

Network connectivity problems can plague even the smallest, simplest network such as a home WiFi workgroup. To troubleshoot connectivity and resource access issues effectively, you need to work through a logical set of steps that allow you to systematically eliminate each possible cause for a connectivity problem such as the inability of a computer in the workgroup to access the Internet or print to a shared printer. Connection problems on small networks are typically caused by one of three possibilities: hardware problems, software problems (including incorrect configuration settings), and user error.

Let's assume that user error is not a problem on your network and that the users know how to log on to their computers, can locate network resources using **My Network Places**, know how to use Microsoft Internet Explorer to navigate the Web, and can use their email clients. Let's also assume that you back up important data in shared folders (see **64** **About Backing Up and Restoring Data**) and take advantage of Windows **System Restore** to protect your Windows system settings (see **68** **Create a System Restore Point**).

With user error removed from the troubleshooting equation, you are left with hardware and software problems. Hardware and software checklists for general connectivity troubleshooting follow; then we'll take a look at adapter and router fixes and some specific troubleshooting techniques related to TCP/IP networks.

▶ **TIP**

If you are experiencing interference from a digital phone system (you will also typically have problems with the phones because the WiFi network and the cordless phone system are "competing" on the same channel), change the WiFi network channel on the WiFi router and then configure the WiFi network adapters to connect to the network on the new channel.

Hardware Problems

Hardware problems typically take the form of a simple and fixable problem such as an unplugged WiFi router; other hardware problems are related to a device such as a WiFi network adapter that is malfunctioning or has failed (meaning it is dead). If you have a connectivity problem such as an inability to connect to the Internet or to a shared resource on the network such as a printer, try some of these hardware troubleshooting suggestions:

▶ **TIP**

If you think you are experiencing a hardware problem, contact the technical support team for your router, and they will walk you through a diagnosis of the problem.

- **Check the WiFi router**: The *router* is the central connecting point for the entire network. If the WiFi router is not functioning correctly, all the users on the network will have a problem. The problem with the router can be caused by either an actual hardware defect or an incorrectly configured router (see **21** About Configuring the Wireless Router).

If the router's power light is not on, check the router's power cord (and your electrical outlet). On most routers, the power light is a solid color such as green when the router is powered on (and the power supply is connected correctly). WiFi routers also have LAN port lights and typically an Internet port light. The LAN port lights show activity on the LAN ports on the router's switch. They are typically green and numbered (although they can be yellow). The Internet port shows the activity on the router's connection to your Internet connection. The Internet port light can be green or some other color and blinks as data moves from the network to the Internet (through your broadband device) and back to the network.

If these lights are not active (blinking) and you are experiencing problems with a wired LAN or the Internet connection (the connection to your broadband device), check any network cables used for these connections to make sure that they are attached correctly. You can also try a different cable if you suspect that the cable is the problem. Although this may sound idiotic, sometimes unplugging the cable from both devices (such as the router and your broadband device), reversing the cable, and then plugging it back into the devices can get the connection up and running (the problem may be due to bad connectors on the cable or a short in the cable, but hey, it works).

▶ **TIP**

If you turn on the router and all the lights stay on after power up (meaning that they are steadily on and not blinking), turn off the power and then turn on the power again. If the router lights continue to remain steadily on, you are probably looking at a defective device.

91

- **Check the broadband device**: If you are unable to connect to the Internet and the WiFi router seems to be functioning correctly, check the status lights on the broadband device (the cable modem or the DSL modem; the lights on these devices vary from device to device). There will typically be a PC Activity LED indicator that blinks, meaning that the connection between the WiFi router and the broadband modem is active. Check the power adapter (and connection) for the broadband device and the connection between the router and the broadband device. If the broadband device is malfunctioning, your WiFi router will not be assigned an external IP address for connection to the Internet. You can check the router's configuration by logging onto the router. See **23 About Internet Settings** for more information on setting up the router to connect to the broadband device.

▶ TIP

A broadband connection can also be malfunctioning because of a problem being experienced by your Internet service provider. Call the help number for your ISP; many ISPs provide a recorded message when you call the technical support number to let you know they are currently experiencing technical problems. In most cases, if you use a broadband connection from your cable television provider, the television and the Internet connection will be down at the same time.

91

- **Check the computer's WiFi adapter**: Both internal and external WiFi adapters have a "ready" light, which will be on when the card is powered on (the light can be amber or green, depending on the adapter and the connection speed; amber is often used for 10Mb connections and green is used for 100Mb connections on a switchable 10/100 LAN adapter). If you don't see the blinking light (look at the adapter), the adapter might have an intermittent problem. If the intermittent problem becomes a chronic problem, replace the adapter.

Because Windows XP is a plug-and-play operating system, a truly "dead" device will no longer be listed as an installed device in the Windows **Device Manager** (to open the **Device Manager**, click the **Start** button, right-click the **My Computer** icon, and select **Properties** from the context menu; click the **Device Manager** button on the **Hardware** tab of the **System Properties** dialog box).

If a device is malfunctioning because of a hardware driver problem, there will be a yellow warning icon or a red alert icon next to that device's name in the **Device Manager** list. You can attempt to reinstall the device driver or update the driver to take care of the problem. See **30 Install Adapter Software Utility** and **31 Check WiFi Adapter Installation** for more information on installing adapter software and drivers.

Use the **Device Manager** to view the status of a device such as a WiFi adapter and to reinstall, roll back, or update the device driver.

For internal WiFi network adapters, check to make sure that the antenna is
connected correctly and that the adapter is seated correctly on the motherboard (you have to open the computer case to check this). For a USB WiFi
adapter, check whether or not the USB device is attached securely to a USB
port on your computer. If you connect your USB WiFi adapter to your computer using a USB cable, check the cable connections and also check to see
whether a replacement cable fixes the problem.

▶ **TIP**

Sometimes hardware devices such as WiFi routers and broadband devices such as cable
modems just need to be reset. Turn the device off, wait a couple of minutes, and then
power up the device. Check the various indicator lights to see whether the restart has
helped to solve the problem. Sometimes rebooting a computer on the network will also
allow the computer to receive an IP address and connect to the network.

Software Problems

You can see from the discussion in the previous section that hardware and software problems overlap because all hardware devices depend on software to actually work. So, when you rule out actual "physical" hardware problems (meaning
defective devices or bad network cables), you are left with software issues. Software problems can be the result of incorrect configuration settings or improperly
installed software and software drivers.

▶ **TIP**

If you have configured your WiFi router for WEP or WPA, a WiFi-enabled computer won't be able to connect unless it is configured with the shared *authentication key* or the *passphrase*. So, if a user on your network can't connect a computer to the WiFi network, check the WiFi adapter's configuration. See **32** **About Configuring the Wireless Adapter** and **33** **Configure Adapter and Connect to the Wireless Router**.

It is obviously essential that the software settings on the WiFi router be correctly configured for your WiFi network to work. Another major source of connectivity problems related to software configuration problems is the TCP/IP settings on the computers that participate in the WiFi network.

If a computer is not configured to automatically receive its IP address from the WiFi router, it won't be able to participate on the IP network. In some cases, even a PC configured to receive its IP address automatically will not have an IP address from the WiFi router. For example, if the router is off and a PC boots up, Windows will assign an IP address to the computer automatically. So, once the router is powered up, the PC "thinks" it doesn't need an IP address from the WiFi router. You can reboot the computer to remedy this problem or use the **ipconfig/release** and the **ipconfig/renew** commands at the Windows command prompt (click the **Start** button, choose the **Run** icon, type **command**, and click **OK** to get to the Windows command prompt). For more about configuring a PC's TCP/IP settings, see **42** **Configure TCP/IP Settings**.

▶ **TIP**

If a PC isn't configured with the **Client for Microsoft Networks** or the **File and Printer Sharing for Microsoft Networks** service, the PC won't be able to participate on your workgroup network; see **40** **Open Connection Properties and Enable Clients, Protocols, and Services** for information on configuring a PC for workgroup networking.

Many WiFi adapters also include software utilities as well as the driver for the adapter. If you are having problems with the software, use the **Control Panel**'s **Add or Remove Programs** applet to remove the software installation. You can then reinstall the software. Also check the adapter manufacturer's website to see whether an update is available for the software or whether an update is available for the adapter's hardware driver. Both bad software and a flaky driver can cause problems with the adapter.

▶ **TIP**

Hardware devices such as WiFi adapters and WiFi routers also have built-in software (software on ROM memory chips) that allows the device to function. If you have problems with a device, upgrading the "firmware" (the built-in software) can help solve the problem. See **98** **About Upgrading Router Firmware and Adapter Drivers** for more about firmware upgrades.

Here are some final thoughts on troubleshooting: The more information you have related to computers and other devices on the network, the better your chances of diagnosing and fixing a problem. Take a look at **93** **Check Router Status**, **94** **View Attached Devices**, and **95** **View Router Log** to learn how to gain information related to the activity and connections on your WiFi network.

---

92 **Reset WiFi Adapter**

✔ BEFORE YOU BEGIN	✔ SEE ALSO
32 About Configuring the Wireless Adapter	**61** Detect WiFi Hotspots and Connect
33 Configure Adapter and Connect to the Wireless Router	

Even when you know that a computer is configured correctly (that is, its TCP/IP and WiFi settings are set appropriately) and that the WiFi network is operational (meaning that the WiFi *router* is allowing connections to the network and the Internet), you might have a computer that won't connect to the network. WiFi *adapters* can be quite finicky, and sometimes you just have to reset them to get a connection.

There isn't exactly a reset switch or reset command, but you can reset the WiFi adapter by using the **Repair** command. This command can be accessed through the context or shortcut menu that opens when you right-click the WiFi adapter icon in the Windows system tray.

A WiFi adapter that is having a problem connecting to the WiFi network might show a yellow exclamation symbol on the WiFi adapter's icon in the Windows system tray. A WiFi adapter that is not connected will show a red X on the WiFi adapter icon, meaning that no connection is present. You can attempt to make a connection with this adapter or use the **Repair** command so that Windows can check the adapter configuration and reset the various settings before attempting a connection.

92

1 Open WiFi Adapter Context Menu

Right-click the WiFi adapter icon in the Windows system tray on the right end of the Windows taskbar. The context menu opens.

2 Repair WiFi adapter

Click the **Repair** command on the context menu. Windows disables and then re-enables the WiFi adapter (status dialog boxes appear to let you know the status of the repair process).

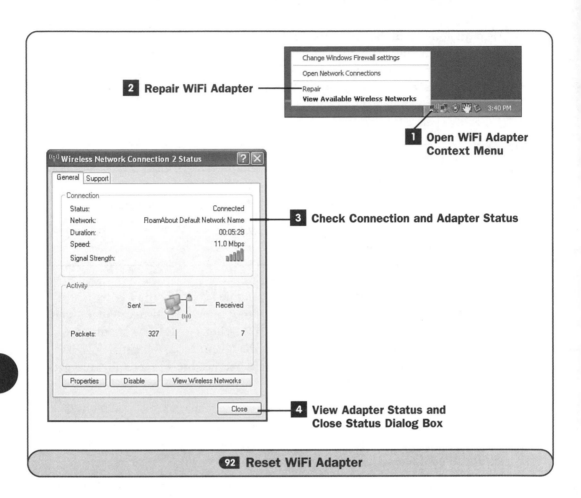

92

92 Reset WiFi Adapter

If this process repairs the adapter, the adapter will connect to the WiFi network that it is configured for (or will connect to the first available WiFi network, if you have it set up to connect to any network).

3 Check Connection and Adapter Status

After a connection has been established to the WiFi network, you can check the connection strength and the adapter's status. Double-click the adapter icon in the system tray. The **Wireless Network Connection Status** dialog box opens.

4 View Adapter Status and Close Status Dialog Box

You can check the speed of the connection and the signal strength. If the speed is lower than you normally experience connecting to the WiFi network, you might have a hardware problem with the adapter. You can view the available wireless networks and reconnect if you want to attempt to connect at a faster speed or greater bandwidth. The connection speed and signal strength can be quickly viewed by placing your mouse on the WiFi adapter icon in the Windows system tray. To view these statistics in the adapter's configuration window, double-click the icon in the system tray. To see the available networks, click the **Scan** button; all nearby networks broadcasting SSIDs (both secure and unsecured WiFi networks) will appear in the **Scan** list.

When you have finished viewing the status of the connection, click **Close** to close the **Wireless Network Connection Status** dialog box.

93 Check Router Status

✔ BEFORE YOU BEGIN

21 About Configuring the Wireless Router
22 Access Router Configuration
91 About Network Connection Problems

Checking the *router*'s status provides you with a snapshot of the router's configuration and the current status of the WAN and LAN connections to the router. This is particularly useful when you are trying to troubleshoot connection problems on the network.

The status information includes the "outside" IP address that has been provided to your WiFi router and LAN as well as wireless port information such as whether or not the WiFi router is configured as a *DHCP server* (providing IP addresses to the network clients on the WiFi network). The router status information also shows the channel that the WiFi network is communicating on and provides the LAN port address of the router, which can be used to see whether a connection exists between the computer and the router by using the **ping** command (see **96** About Command-Line Tools and **97** Use Command-Line Tools for more information on **ping** and other useful commands).

▶ NOTE

So, how does the router status information help us troubleshoot network connectivity problems? Well, here's just a sample of the information that can be gleaned from the status statistics found on the router's **Connection Status** page: If there isn't an "external" IP address showing in the status information, you don't have a connection between the router and the broadband device or there is a problem with your Internet service provider. If DHCP is disabled on the router (that is, if the setting reads **DHCP Off**), you'll see this in the router status statistics on the Status Connection page. This means that network clients are not receiving IP addressing and other TCP/IP configuration settings from the router, which would prevent these computers from communicating on the network.

1 Access Router Status Screen

Log on to your router as the administrator using your web browser; type the URL for your router in the browser's **Address** box and then provide the login name and password for the router when prompted for this information. You can find the URL for your router in the documentation that came with your router; there is typically a quick start sheet provided with your router (a one-page flyer) that provides the URL or web address for your router and the default logon name and password. If you don't have access to either of these bits of information, go to the router manufacturer's website and access the support page. This page will provide links to specific product pages where you can download the documentation for your WiFi router.

From the main router page, select the **Router Status** link (or a similar command) to open the router status page. The status page typically provides the current version of the router firmware and the status of the Internet port (sometimes called the WAN port), the LAN port, and the Wireless port.

IP addresses and MAC hardware addresses are listed for the Internet and the LAN port. The Wireless port information includes the SSID for the WiFi network, the channel being used, and the wireless mode. To troubleshoot connection issues, check to see that the Internet port has a valid IP address (an address from your Internet service provider). Also check the Wireless port area to make sure that the Wireless AP setting is **On** (otherwise there is no wireless network because the router isn't handling the radio signals).

If a setting is incorrect, change the setting so that it is correct. For example, if you have all your WiFi adapters configured to a WiFi network with an SSID of **POPEYE** and your router's SSID is **BLUTO**, reconfigure the router. If the Wireless AP setting is off, turn it on. If your router is configured for WEP security and you have configured all your WiFi adapters for WPA security, either change the router's settings or change all the adapters' settings.

▶ TIP

When you have the router and your WiFi adapters configured, and the WiFi network is running fine, document the router and adapter configuration settings. Go to any router configuration or adapter configuration screen and press the **Print Screen** key (or similar key) on your keyboard. This key takes a snapshot of your Windows desktop and the configuration page you have open. Open a word processing program such as Microsoft Word or Windows Wordpad (it's on the **Accessories** submenu on the **Start** menu) and paste the snapshot or screen capture you took with the **Print Screen** key into a new document. Print out the page. Repeat this process for the other configuration pages. You now have hard copies of the router's configuration and the configuration for your WiFi adapters. Compare these hard copies to the device configurations when you are troubleshooting WiFi network problems and suspect that there has been a negative change to a configuration.

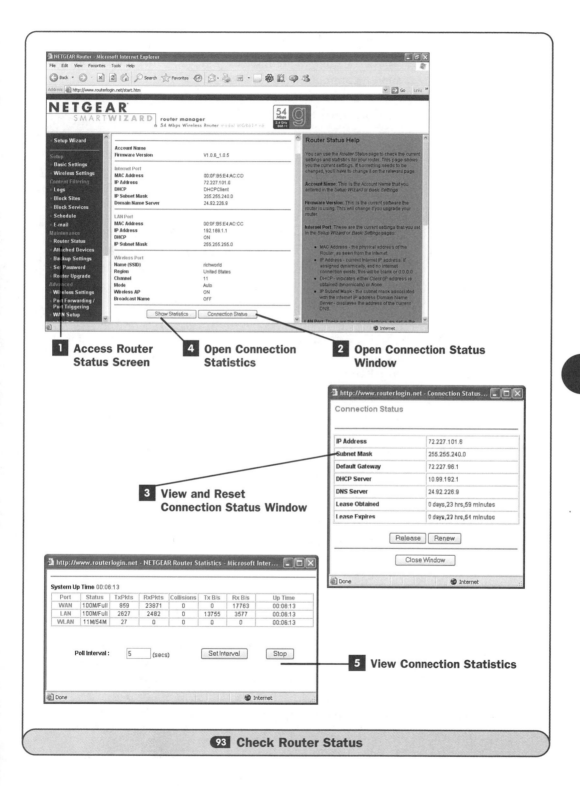

1 **Access Router Status Screen**

4 **Open Connection Statistics**

2 **Open Connection Status Window**

3 **View and Reset Connection Status Window**

5 **View Connection Statistics**

2 Open Connection Status Window

To view more information related to the Internet port, click the **Connection Status** button (or similar command on your router).

3 View and Reset Connection Status Window

Take a look at the **Connection Status** information. It includes the public IP address, the subnet mask, the default gateway, and other TCP/IP configuration information that is provided to the WiFi router by your Internet service provider.

Computers on the network cannot connect to the Internet if the router doesn't have a valid IP address (for example, if all zeros are listed); you can attempt to reset the TCP/IP settings in the **Connection Status** window by clicking the **Release** button to release the current TCP/IP settings. Then click the **Renew** button to request new TCP/IP settings, including a new IP address from the DHCP server maintained by your Internet service provider. If you get a new IP address and other TCP/IP settings, any Internet connectivity problems should be resolved for the computers on the network. If you don't get a valid IP address (meaning that you see all zeros for this setting), the DHCP server maintained by your ISP may be down or your broadband device is not providing a connection to the ISP.

To close the **Connection Status** window, click the **Close Window** button.

4 Open Connection Statistics

To view the actual data traffic to and from the router (meaning from the computers on your network), click the **Show Statistics** button in the **Router Status** window.

5 View Connection Statistics

The connection statistics show you the connection speed and status for each interface (WAN or Internet, LAN, and WLAN or WiFi). If a particular connection speed is very low or zero, there is a problem on that router interface or you have incorrectly configured the router.

TxPkts is the number of packets transmitted on the interface, and **RxPkts** is the number of packets received on the interface. If you find that packets are not being transmitted, you could have a problem with the router or the connection to the broadband device. If packets are not being received on the interface (such as the WAN port), the Internet connection might be down.

93

Most router statistics will also show the **TX B/s** values for the WAN and LAN ports, which is the outbound data traffic. The **Rx B/s** is the current bandwidth or inbound transmission on a particular interface. So, the **TxPkts** and the **Tx B/s** show outbound data, and the **RxPkts** and **Rx B/s** show inbound traffic.

Click the **Stop** button to stop the collection of data in the **Statistics** window, which provides you with a "snapshot" of the data. Clicking this button does not shut down any of the router interfaces.

▶ **NOTE**

Ethernet networks (even WiFi networks) are designed for computers and other devices to sit and listen for data traffic; when a computer or other device doesn't detect any traffic, it transmits its data. When more than one device transmits simultaneously, this can result in collisions. Collisions are actually somewhat common on Ethernet networks, so if you see some collisions listed in the statistics, don't be alarmed. If you see a huge number of collisions, you might have a network card that is malfunctioning and spraying packets out onto the network. This results in high traffic and a lot of collisions. You can fix this problem by replacing the bad network card.

When you have finished viewing the router statistics, which are updated every 5 seconds by default (you can type any interval in seconds into the **Poll Interval** text box), click the **Close** button on the **Statistics** window.

94

94 | **View Attached Devices**

✔ **BEFORE YOU BEGIN**

22 Access Router Configuration
91 About Network Connection Problems

✔ **SEE ALSO**

32 About Configuring the Wireless Adapter
42 Configure TCP/IP Settings

If a user is having a problem connecting to a network resource (such as a shared folder) or the Internet, you can begin the troubleshooting process for the connection problem by seeing whether the computer in question is connected to the WiFi router. If the computer is not connected to the router, the problem could be that the computer's WiFi adapter is having a problem, its configuration is not correct, or the WiFi router might be configured incorrectly (it could even be configured to block web access for that computer).

Most WiFi router configuration pages have a screen that provides a list of the currently connected computers. This screen is accessed through the main configuration page for your router.

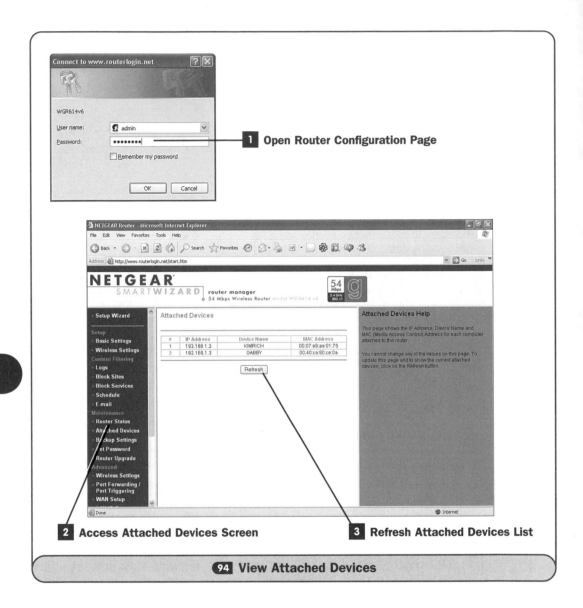

94 View Attached Devices

1 Open Router Configuration Page

Open your web browser, enter the URL for your router in the address box, and press **Enter**. Then enter the logon name and password for your router. You can find the URL for your router in the documentation that came with your router; routers typically come with a quick start sheet (a one-page flyer) that provides the URL or web address for your router and the default logon name and password. If you don't have access to either of these information sources, go to the router manufacturer's website and access the support page, which will provide links to specific product pages where you can download the documentation for your WiFi router.

2 Access Attached Devices Screen

When you are on the main configuration page for your router, click the **Attached Devices** link (or similar command). The **Attached Devices** page opens, showing the currently connected devices (the WiFi-enabled computers and printer currently connected to the router).

3 Refresh Attached Devices List

If a computer has just recently come online (meaning that has just booted up), you can refresh the **Attached Devices** list to view all currently connected devices. Click the **Refresh** button as needed.

If a computer that should be attached is not shown on the **Attached Devices** list, the computer may have a WiFi adapter problem—the adapter might not be configured to attach to the network or might not have the correct TCP/IP settings. For information about configuring a WiFi adapter, see **33 Configure Adapter and Connect to the Wireless Router.** If a computer with a "wired" connection to the router is not on the list, the LAN cable might be bad or the Ethernet adapter on the computer might be incorrectly configured or faulty. For configuring workgroup networks and TCP/IP on either a WiFi-enabled or cable connected computer, see **41 Add Network Client or Service** and **42 Configure TCP/IP Settings**

95

---

95 View Router Log

✔ BEFORE YOU BEGIN	→ SEE ALSO
22 Access Router Configuration **91** About Network Connection Problems	**54** About Content Filtering and Opening Ports **55** Block Access to Websites **56** Block Access to Internet Services

If you are using the content filtering features provided by your router (see **54 About Content Filtering and Opening Ports** and **55 Block Access to Websites** for more information), you might be inadvertently blocking access to Internet sites or services depending on how you have configured the content filtering. Content filtering is a double-edged sword, and you really have to think through how you configure content filtering if you want to provide different levels of access to the users on your network.

1 Open Router Configuration Page

95

2 Access Logs Screen   **3** Refresh Logs Screen and/or Send Log

95 View Router Log

You can see the content filtering statistics (how access to the router is being allowed or blocked) by viewing the router log. If you see that access to a particular website or service such as email is being blocked by the router and you did not intend this filtering, check the content filtering settings you have configured.

1 Open Router Configuration Page

Open your web browser, enter the URL for your router in the address box (the URL, login name, and password are available in your router's documentation), and press **Enter**. Then enter the logon name and password for your router.

2 Access Logs Screen

On the router's main configuration page, click the **Logs** link (or a similar command on your router). The **Logs** screen opens.

3 Refresh Logs Screen and/or Send Log

To view the most current data being collected in the log, click the **Refresh** button.

If you want to take a snapshot of the current log and send the data to your email account so that you can read through it more carefully (and detect any problems in terms of sites or services unintentionally blocked), click the **Send Log** button (or similar command). This action will send the log to the email address you have configured in the router's email notification settings.

The log provides you with a look at all the data traffic between your network and the Internet. If you see that a connection to a certain website was denied by the router, and you hadn't intended on blocking access to that site, check your **Block Sites** configuration to see whether a keyword you entered is blocking that site. If you see that instant messaging traffic is originating on a computer after 9:00 in the evening, and you have asked your kids not to use instant messaging after 9, you might want to consider using the service-blocking feature to block access to instant messaging and then configure a schedule for that blocked service so that instant messaging is available only until the time you set (and on the days you set). For more about configuration issues related to blocked sites and services, see **55** **Block Access to Websites, 56** **Block Access to Internet Services,** and **57** **Set Up a Filter Schedule.**

▶ TIP

To use the email log feature, the router must be configured for Email Notifications. This feature can be found on the **E-mail configuration** page of the router's configuration screen, which is opened using the **E-mail** link or a similar command. Select the **Email Notifications** option and then enter the outgoing mail server (the mail server you use in the form of **smpt-mail.isp.com**). You will also need to enter the email address to which you want to send the alerts. Some routers can also send automatic alerts to this address when someone attempts to access a blocked site or service.

95

96   About Command-Line Tools

✔ **BEFORE YOU BEGIN**

39 Name the Computer and Join a Workgroup

40 Open Connection Properties and Enable Clients, Protocols, and Services

41 Add a Network Client or Service

42 Configure TCP/IP Settings

✔ **SEE ALSO**

97 Use Command-Line Tools

96

It is essential that computers on the WiFi network be properly configured for the *TCP/IP protocol*. Because most WiFi *routers* can also act as *DHCP* servers, you should definitely configure all the computers on the WiFi network to receive their TCP/IP configuration from the router (this includes *IP addresses* and *subnet masks*). There are three TCP/IP-related command-line tools you can use to quickly check the TCP/IP configuration of a computer, check the connection between two devices (such as between two computers or between a computer and your WiFi router), and trace the route that packets take when sent from a computer to a particular destination (meaning a particular IP address). These commands are

- **Ipconfig**: A command-line tool that can be used to quickly check the IP configuration. The **ipconfig** command can be used with different switches to show additional IP configuration information. The command can also be used to release and renew the current IP settings. Some of the different switches you can use with the **ipconfig** command are as follows:

Command	Description
ipconfig	By itself, the **ipconfig** command shows the DNS suffix (the domain), IP address, subnet mask, and default gateway from the computer.
Ipconfig/all	Shows the information provided by the **ipconfig** command (without the switch), the MAC address of the Ethernet adapter, whether the adapter is configured for DHCP and autoconfiguration, the DHCP server for the computer, the DNS servers for the computer, when the IP lease was obtained, and when the IP lease expires.
Ipconfig/release	Releases (meaning removes) all the IP settings for the adapter.
Ipconfig/renew	Causes the adapter to send out a request to the DHCP server for a renewal of the IP settings.

- **Ping**: An excellent way to check the connection between two computers or other devices on an IP network is to use the **ping** command. *Ping* stands for Packet InterNet Gopher and uses echo packets to test the connection. The command syntax is **ping** *ip address*, where *ip address* is the IP address of the target device. The **ping** command can also be used with the DNS name (the Fully Qualified Domain Name—FQDN) of a device such as **mycomputer.localdomain.com**.

- **Tracert**: The traceroute command (**tracert** on a Windows XP computer) sends data packets to a specified IP address or DNS name. The command is useful in that it shows you how many hops it takes for the data to move from source to destination. Because you have only one WiFi router as the central connecting point on the internal network, **tracert** should show only one hop from source to destination. The **tracert** command can also be used to determine how many hops (or routers) are involved when you attempt to connect to a remote network destination such as an IP address on the Internet.

So, in a nutshell, **ipconfig** allows you to view (and renew, if necessary) the current IP configuration for a network adapter (including WiFi network adapters). The **ping** command allows you to see whether you can connect to a device on the network; for example, you could ping your router's LAN interface if you are having a connection issue. The **tracert** command allows you to view the actual path the data takes; you can use that information to determine whether there is a connectivity issue on the network.

▶ **NOTE**

You will find that **ipconfig** and **ping** are useful on small networks to help you troubleshoot connectivity problems. The **tracert** command is also useful, however, although because you have only a single router on your network, it doesn't necessarily provide you with a look at how data is being routed or rerouted on a network. **Tracert** is actually more useful on larger networks that have multiple routers. The command can then be used to determine whether a particular router is down and how data is being redirected to bypass the malfunctioning router.

---

97 | **Use Command-Line Tools**

✔ **BEFORE YOU BEGIN**	→ **SEE ALSO**
91 About Network Connection Problems	**43** Check WiFi Adapter Status
96 About Command-Line Tools	

Command-line tools such as **ipconfig** and **ping** are executed at the Windows command line. The easiest way to access the command line on a Windows XP computer is to open the **Run** dialog box (click the **Start** button and select **Run**), type **command**, and then press **Enter**. A command window opens (yes, it looks like a DOS window) that you can use to execute the various command line tools.

Remember that the whole point of using these commands is to try to figure out why a particular computer can't connect to the local network or is having problems connecting to the Internet. Take a close look at the results of each command when you run it to glean information that will allow you to rectify a particular connection issue.

1 Open Command Window

Click the **Start** button and then choose **Run**. In the **Run** dialog box, type **command** and click **OK**. The command window opens.

2 Run ipconfig Command

At the command prompt, type **ipconfig** (or **ipconfig** with a switch such as **ipconfig/all**) and press **Enter**. The results of the command appear in the command window. If you do not see a default *gateway*, there might be a problem with the IP configuration on the computer or a problem with the *router*'s *DHCP* server (because the router serves as the default gateway).

▶ **NOTE**

97

The default gateway for the computer should be the *IP address* of the WiFi router's LAN interface. You can check this using the router's configuration page.

3 Run ping Command

To ping a computer or another device such as the router's LAN interface, you will need to know that device's IP address. You can find the router's LAN IP address using the router's configuration page. Type **ping** followed by the IP address of the computer or device you want to connect to. Then press **Enter**.

The results of the **ping** command show the milliseconds that it takes for the destination device to respond to your **ping** packet. When you use **ping** on a WiFi network (a local network), the response to your **ping** command from the destination computer should be almost instantaneous. However, the response time will vary depending on the amount of network traffic. If everyone on the network is downloading huge files from the Internet, all that activity will slow the response to the **ping** "challenge." The actual speed of the **ping** (in milliseconds) isn't as important as a consistent speed. If a ping goes from 18ms for a response to 60ms the next time you do it, traffic is either through the roof on the network or there may be a problem with the computer's WiFi adapter or the router (which is responsible for routing the traffic on the network).

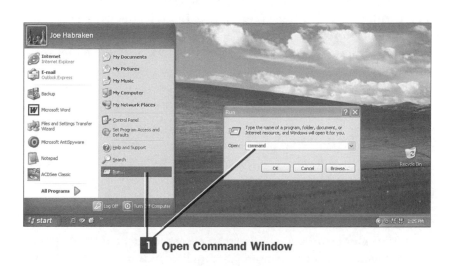

1 Open Command Window

3 Run ping Command   **2** Run ipconfig Command

97

5 Exit Command Window   **4** Run tracert Command

97 Use Command-Line Tools

If you don't get a response at all (the **ping** times out), there is probably a connection problem. Either the target device is not on the network or the router is having trouble routing your request. Check the router's status screen to see what computers are connected to the network. If you don't see the computer you tried to ping, that computer is having a problem connecting to the network. See **93 Check Router Status** for more about viewing a list of computers connected to the WiFi router.

4 Run tracert Command

The **tracert** command will show you the number of hops (routers) it takes for your packet to move from your computer to the destination address. Type **tracert** and then the IP address of the destination computer or device.

The results of the **tracert** command show the number of hops to the destination and the number of milliseconds the packet took to go to the destination; then the command shows the number of milliseconds it took for a response from the destination device (meaning computer).

5 Exit Command Window

97

To exit the command window, type **exit** at the command prompt and press **Enter**. The command window will close and return you to the Windows Desktop.

---

98 About Upgrading Router Firmware and Adapter Drivers

✔ BEFORE YOU BEGIN	→ SEE ALSO
21 About Configuring the Wireless Router	**91** About Network Connection Problems
32 About Configuring the Wireless Adapter	
36 About Updating an Adapter Driver	

If you have ruled out most hardware and software issues when troubleshooting a WiFi network problem, you might want to explore the possibility of upgrading your WiFi router's firmware or a driver for a WiFi adapter. Your WiFi router works because of a set of basic operating instructions (software code) that is burned onto a rewritable chip on the device. This set of code is known as the router's *firmware*. The overall operability of the router is determined by this firmware, so having the ability to update the firmware can not only keep your router running properly, but it can also potentially increase the overall functionality of the router, particularly in cases where security protocols and other features have been upgraded for the router's firmware by the manufacturer.

▶ **KEY TERM**

Firmware—The basic operating system for a device such as a WiFi router.

It is incumbent on you to occasionally check the website of your WiFi router's manufacturer for firmware updates. Most WiFi routers (and other hardware such as adapters) have a registration card you should fill out and mail in, or you can register the device with the manufacturer online. Registering (including information such as a valid email address) can mean that you will get periodic emails related to any upgrade possibilities for the device, such as a new version of the firmware.

Most WiFi networking equipment manufacturers provide support and download pages for the various products they manufacture. This makes it easy for you to view the various versions of firmware available for a device. Locate the page for your WiFi router and download the firmware as needed.

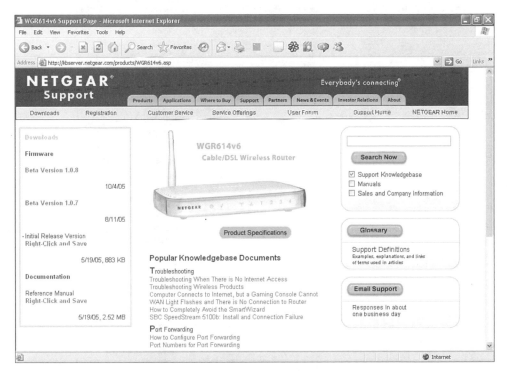

Check the product page for your router to see whether any firmware upgrades are available.

▶ **NOTE**

Some manufacturers release beta firmware versions for their products. It is up to you whether or not you want to install beta firmware. It might be better to wait until a "final" version of a firmware upgrade is available before you upgrade the router. The label *beta* typically means that the software is not ready for prime-time, and you might make a router problem even worse if you use beta firmware.

After you have download the new firmware, use the downloaded file to upgrade the router. This process varies from router to router, but most routers have a configuration page that allows you to browse for the new firmware file and then upgrade the router. You should follow the specifics for upgrading your router provided in your router's documentation.

98

Upgrade the router firmware using the upgrade configuration page for your router.

In terms of WiFi adapters (and any other hardware peripherals you add to your computer), it is important to keep the driver for the adapter up to date. Manufacturers upgrade drivers for devices such as WiFi adapters to resolve problems and issues that were experienced with the device and the driver that it shipped with.

You can download driver updates (and drivers for other versions of Windows if you are not running Windows XP) from the download page for your adapter. After the driver is downloaded, you can install the driver using the **Device** tab on the **Properties** dialog box for the WiFi adapter.

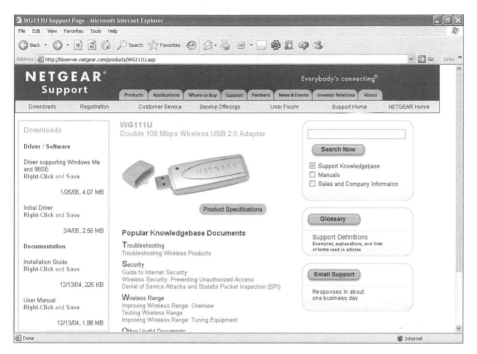

Check the download page for your WiFi adapter to see whether any driver upgrades are available.

The properties for any device on your computer can be opened using the Windows XP **Device Manager**. See **36** **About Updating an Adapter Driver** for more information on updating the driver for a WiFi adapter.

▶ **NOTE**

Updating a driver can actually make a device that is running properly malfunction. Remember that you can also roll back drivers to a previous version if a driver upgrade is causing problems. See **30** **Install Adapter Software Utility** and **36** **About Updating an Adapter Driver** for more about WiFi adapter drivers.

A final word related to firmware and driver upgrades: To a certain extent, you should follow the old adage, "if it isn't broken, don't fix it." If your WiFi router is functioning well and you aren't having any adapter problems, don't bother doing an upgrade to the router's firmware or adapter's driver just for sake of upgrading. Although upgrading a WiFi router can enhance security and operability, if you are happy with your security settings and the router's performance in terms of security, why risk making the router unstable by upgrading to new firmware, particularly beta firmware?

Index

C

F

G – H

M

N

O – P

Q – R

U

X – Y – Z

Windows XP All in One

Greg Perry
ISBN: 0-672-32728-7
$34.99 US / $49.99 CAN

eBay in a Snap

Preston Gralla
ISBN: 0-672-32837-2
$19.99 US / $27.99 CAN

Blogging in a Snap

Julie C. Meloni
ISBN: 0-672-32843-7
$24.99 US / $34.99 CAN

Roxio Easy Media Creator 8 in a Snap

Lisa DaNae Dayley
ISBN: 0-672-32865-8
$19.99 US / $27.99 CAN

Adobe Premiere Elements 2 in a Snap

Steve Grisetti and Chuck Engels
ISBN: 0-672-32853-4
$24.99 US / $34.99 CAN

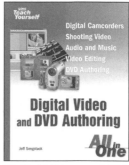

Digital Video and DVD Authoring All in One

Jeff Sengstack
ISBN: 0-672-32689-2
$34.99 US / $48.99 CAN

Adobe Photoshop Elements 4 in a Snap

Jennifer Fulton and Scott Fulton
ISBN: 0-672-32850-X
$24.99 US / $34.99 CAN

Macromedia Flash 8 in 24 Hours

Phillip Kerman
ISBN: 0-672-32754-6
$29.99 US / $41.99 CAN

iPod & iTunes for Windows and Mac in a Snap

Brian Tiemann
ISBN: 0-672-32811-9
$19.99 US / $27.99 CAN

Key Terms

Don't let unfamiliar terms discourage you from learning all you can about wireless home networking. If you don't completely understand what one of these words means, flip to the indicated page, read the full definition there, and find techniques related to that term.

Access point   *A hardware device that acts as the central connecting point for wireless-enabled devices.*
Page 4

Ad Hoc mode   *A computer-to-computer wireless connection mode that allows WiFi-enabled computers to connect directly without communicating through an intermediary device such as a WiFi access point.*
109

Adapter   *A device that allows a computer to participate in the network. The adapter takes the data from the computer and prepares it for transmission over a network medium such as network cabling or WiFi radio signals.*
10

Authentication key   *A hexadecimal character string used to validate a user or device as the intended connection point or recipient of a data stream.*
284

DHCP client   *A computer that has been configured for the TCP/IP protocol so that the IP address (and subnet mask) is automatically assigned to the computer by a device that can act as a DHCP server such as your WiFi router.*
145

Driver   *Software for a device such as a WiFi network adapter that allows the operating system and the device to communicate correctly.*
103

Dynamic Host Configuration Protocol (DHCP)
A protocol used by DHCP servers and clients to negotiate the dynamic assignment of IP addresses over a network. The DHCP server (such as a WiFi router) provides the DHCP client with the IP address.
145

Encryption   *The translation of a message into a secret code. After a message is encrypted, a key or other identification method (such as a password) is needed to decipher the message.*
285

Firewall   *Software, hardware, or both software and hardware designed to prevent unauthorized access to a private network. A firewall can be used to block both incoming and outgoing data traffic.*
269

Flash drive   *A portable flash memory drive that can be attached to a computer through a USB port. They provide an excellent way to transfer limited amounts of data between computers.*
232

Gateway   *A device that serves as an intermediary between two different types of networks. In the case of wireless networks, the WiFi router is the gateway.*
150

Hotspot   *A connection point to the Internet provided by a business or other establishment. The connection point is typically a WiFi router or access point provided by a particular business such as a coffee shop or hotel.*
Page 212

Hub   *A connectivity device that provides multiple LAN ports. Computers can be connected to these LAN ports using network cabling.*
68

IP address   *A dotted-decimal representation of a binary address that is uniquely assigned to each computer and device running on an IP network.*
126

Limited user   *A user account without administrative abilities. This user can change desktop settings and change the password and user account picture.*
43

MAC (Media Access Control) hardware address
A 48-bit hexadecimal number burned onto a ROM chip on a network adapter (for a computer on the network) or network interface card (for a router).
295

Malware   *Malicious software such as viruses, worms, and spyware.*
306

Mapped drive   *A shared folder or drive that is given a drive letter on your computer. Mapping a remote shared folder to a drive letter makes the shared folder accessible from My Computer.*
170

.NET Passport   *A user account that provides access to personalized and special Microsoft web content.*
55

Network adapter   *A device that allows a computer to participate in the network. The network adapter takes the data from the computer and prepares it for transmission over a network medium such as network cabling or WiFi radio signals.*
10

Normal backup   *A backup method that backs up all selected files to the backup archive file and flags the files as having been backed up.*
240

Passphrase   *A text string similar to a password used to configure a WiFi device for WEP or WPA security. Because the passphrase is generated by the WiFi router, the passphrase is used in the WiFi adapters' settings to configure the device with the correct encryption key.*
288

Phishing   *The process of trying to fool people into giving up personal information ,including credit card numbers, by directing them to a website using an official-looking email that purports to be from a egitimate website or web service.*
328